Extending Rights' Reach

Extending Rights' Reach

Constitutions, Private Law, and Judicial Power

Jud Mathews

OXFORD
UNIVERSITY PRESS

OXFORD
UNIVERSITY PRESS

Oxford University Press is a department of the University of Oxford. It furthers the University's objective of excellence in research, scholarship, and education by publishing worldwide. Oxford is a registered trademark of Oxford University Press in the UK and certain other countries.

Published in the United States of America by Oxford University Press
198 Madison Avenue, New York, NY 10016, United States of America.

Library of Congress Cataloging-in-Publication Data

Names: Mathews, Jud, author.
Title: Extending rights' reach : constitutions, private law, and judicial power / Jud Mathews.
Description: New York : Oxford University Press, 2018. | Based on author's thesis (doctoral— Yale University, Dept. of Political Sciences, 2015) issued under title: Constitutional rights, private law, and judicial power. | Includes bibliographical references and index.
Identifiers: LCCN 2017044121 | ISBN 9780190682910 (hardback : alk. paper)
Subjects: LCSH: Civil rights—United States. | Civil rights—Germany. | Civil rights—Canada. | Civil law—United States. | Civil law—Germany. | Civil law—Canada. | Political questions and judicial power—United States. | Political questions and judicial power—Germany. | Political questions and judicial power—Canada.
Classification: LCC K3240 .M3778 2018 | DDC 342.08/5—dc23
LC record available at https://lccn.loc.gov/2017044121

Dedicated to my parents,

Betty and George Mathews

CONTENTS

ACKNOWLEDGMENTS

In a past life, this book was a dissertation, written for Yale's political science department. Earlier still, it was the merest wisp of an idea, which I first shared, somewhat tentatively, with Alec Stone Sweet at a noodle restaurant in New Haven, Connecticut. These two transformations—from wispy idea to dissertation, and from dissertation to book—took a lot of time. But I had a lot of help.

No one helped more than Alec Stone Sweet. With his laser-sharp feedback on multiple drafts, he helped me to think through what questions I wanted to ask and how to go about seeking answers. I'm fortunate to have had the chance to work with Alec not only on my dissertation, which he supervised, but also on a number of writing projects on which we have collaborated. What I've learned from Alec could fill a book. I'm tempted to say it already has.

I also owe a great debt of thanks to Susan Rose-Ackerman and Stephen Skowronek, who also helped see this project along from start to finish. Susan's wise counsel was a constant throughout my time in both law school and graduate school. And in a political science department chock-a-block with extraordinary scholars and thinkers, Steve's teaching has had the greatest impact on my own thinking. I hope some of his influence shows through in this work.

I'm also grateful to the friends and colleagues who offered helpful comments, in discussion or writing, often after reading part or all of the manuscript. These include Justin Collings, Erin Delaney, Mauricio Guim, Vicky Jackson, Noura Karazivan, Hélène Landemore, Jason Mazzone, Adam Muchmore, Steve Ross, Wojciech Sadurski, Johannes Saurer, Raphael Schäfer, David Schraub, and Takis Tridimas. I also appreciate the opportunity to present portions of the manuscript at the Big Ten unTENured Conference, organized by Indiana University's Maurer School of Law, and twice at the Constitutional History: Comparative Perspectives Conference, organized jointly by the University of Illinois College of Law, the University of Bologna School of Law, and the Center for Constitutional Studies and Democratic Development. I had valuable help from five extraordinary law student research assistants, Thomas Bettge, Naiyi Cao, Ylli Dautaj, Koah Doud, and Martin Souto-Diaz. Penn State Law student and all-around awesome person Hojae Chung has earned a special mention in these Acknowledgments through his support of Penn State's THON charity. I'm also very grateful to Jamie Berezin for all he did to help this project find a home at Oxford University Press, and to Alden Domizio and Mary Rosewood for their work on the production of the book.

I could not have written this book without the support of my family. My wife, Kim Mowery, has helped me along through this extended academic odyssey with wisdom, kindness, patience, and a fantastic sense of humor. In other words, it's been par for the course for Kim. This project was first a gleam in the eye around the time our sons, Elliott and Henry, first came onto the scene. It's really not a fair comparison, but I'm much prouder of how they have turned out.

Lastly, I want to thank my parents, Betty and George Mathews, for their steadfast love and support. This book is dedicated to them.

1

Introduction

RIGHTS IN TWO DIMENSIONS

What does it mean to have a constitutional right? For that matter, what is a constitution?

There are no questions more basic than these for modern public law. The global spread of written constitutions with judicially enforceable rights is the defining feature of public law in the decades since World War II. Constitutions regularize the use of government power, and constitutional rights protect citizens against government overreaching.

But rights can—and do—go further. In different ways and to varying degrees, constitutional rights also regulate legal relations among private parties in most legal systems. When they do so, we can speak of rights having *horizontal effect*, in contradistinction to the *vertical effect* they have within the hierarchical relationship between citizen and state.[1] In other words, rights can operate in two dimensions, although their vertical effect typically receives far more attention.

In every constitutional system with judicially enforceable constitutional rights, courts must make choices about whether, when, and how to give those

1. Two quick notes about terminology. First, "citizen" here is a shorthand. Noncitizens and organizations may also have rights that can be asserted against the government.

Second, I use the term "horizontal effect of constitutional rights," and sometimes simply "horizontal rights," but different legal systems have developed different vocabularies to describe whether, how, and when constitutional rights impact the legal relationships of private parties. For instance, the United States has the "state action doctrine," and German jurists refer to the third-party effect (*Drittwirkung*) of rights. The terminological differences are not irrelevant; indeed, the language used in a legal system reflects how the issue is conceptualized. But for simplicity's sake I will refer to horizontal effect or horizontal rights when discussing the issue in general.

rights horizontal effect. Few courts take the position that constitutional rights can *never* affect the legal obligations private parties owe to one another in any way. At the same time, no court handles constitutional rights claims against private parties and government actors exactly the same across the board. Courts must develop special doctrines to define and manage the horizontal effect of constitutional rights. And these doctrines speak to the nature of rights and the character of constitutionalism more broadly. They challenge the classical liberal position—that constitutional rights are defensive rights against the state, and that constitutions are charters of government—as incomplete. What is more, they have tremendous implications for how legal and political decisions get made in a system of governance.

This book is about how different courts manage the horizontal effect of constitutional rights and about the consequences that their choices have. I argue that the choices courts make in this area are as consequential as any that courts ever make, and that they profoundly shape the course of constitutional development in a legal system. In support, I present three case studies, of Germany, the United States, and Canada. For each, I offer a detailed account of the horizontal rights jurisprudence of its apex court—not in isolation, but as a central feature of a broader account of that country's constitutional development. In so doing, I also seek to make the courts' choices intelligible and to untangle the complex skein of normative and strategic factors that bear on judicial activity in this area.

WHY HORIZONTAL RIGHTS MATTER

Before going further, it's a good idea to be more specific about what it means for constitutional rights to have horizontal effect. To this end, I borrow a framework for analyzing legal relationships that Wesley Newcomb Hohfeld developed more than a century ago (1913). As we shall see, there are ways to talk and think about rights besides Hohfeld's. But Hohfeld's set of concepts is a useful place to start for getting a handle on horizontal effect.

Hohfeld had two key insights. One was that the term "right" is used indiscriminately in reference to four distinct legal concepts, which he called claim-rights, privileges, powers, and immunities. The other is that rights are best understood as legal relations: my having a right as against you that you stay off my property implies, and is equivalent to, your having a duty with respect to me that you stay off my property. A claim-right is thus correlative to a duty. A privilege is correlative to what Hohfeld calls a "no-right": if I have the privilege as against you to walk in the park, that means that you have no right to bar me from walking in the park. A power is the capacity to change a legal relation, and its correlative is a liability: your having the power to accept my offer of $5,000 for your car means I am at your mercy to determine whether I will be legal owner of the cash or the car. Lastly, an immunity is correlative to a disability, which is the negation of a power: if I have an immunity, you lack the power to change an aspect of my legal status.

Real-world rights are often complex, and represent a bundle of different jural relations.[2] An individual's legal position vis-à-vis some other legal subject is defined by the set of jural relations that link them (Alexy and Rivers 2010, 114). We can also distinguish between abstract and concrete legal positions, where a concrete position is what an abstract position entails in a particular factual context. (So, if I have an abstract right to the freedom of expression, this may entail a concrete right to run an advertisement stating the prices of alcoholic beverages sold at my liquor store.[3]) Finally, we can say that it *improves* someone's legal position to add claim-rights, privileges, powers, or immunities (or to subtract duties, no-rights, liabilities, or disabilities, which is the same thing), and it *impairs* someone's legal position to add duties, no-rights, liabilities, or disabilities (or to subtract claim-rights, privileges, powers, or immunities, which is the same thing).

These concepts are the building blocks of a working definition of horizontal effect for purposes of the present project. A legal system recognizes the horizontal effect of constitutional rights to the extent that one private party can invoke a constitutional right to impair another private party's concrete legal position. The test boils down to this: may a private party be unable to do something that it otherwise could do, or be required to do something that it otherwise could choose not to do, because of another private party's constitutional rights? If so, rights are having horizontal effect. It matters, of course, whether a given claim succeeds, but it matters at least as much whether a court will even entertain constitutional claims that impair private parties' concrete legal positions. To the extent a court does, it recognizes the horizontal effect of constitutional rights.

Again, a given court may not discuss rights in Hohfeldian terms. But regardless of the particulars of the system-specific rights discourse, at least some constitutional rights will have some horizontal effects, as defined above, in many legal systems. Legal systems will also vary considerably in when and how rights have horizontal effect, as the case studies to come will show.

There is another important distinction to be drawn—between direct and indirect horizontal effect—and Hohfeld's categories can help explain it as well.

2. For an illustration, see Kar (2013, 112).

3. See 44 Liquormart, Inc. v. Rhode Island, 517 U.S. 484 (1996).

Constitutional rights have direct effect when their correlatives vest in private parties. In other words: if your right to equality is understood to mean that I, as another private party, have a constitutional duty not to discriminate against you, the right has direct effect.

But rights also can—and more often do—have indirect effect. The horizontal effect of rights is indirect when it is mediated through the state. In other words, rather than imposing obligations on private parties themselves, rights obligate public authorities to regulate private-party relations in ways that constrain private parties' freedom of action. Suppose, instead, that the right to equality imposes a duty *on the government* to legislate against private discrimination. The ultimate effect may be much the same: a private party's legal position is impaired because of a constitutional right. But the distinction between direct and indirect effect may be important in a legal system, for legal, procedural, and rhetorical reasons.

Two Big Questions

As noted above, in most legal systems with well-developed bodies of constitutional law, courts give horizontal effect to at least some constitutional rights, at least some of the time.[4] Two big questions follow. The first is, why are courts drawn to give horizontal effect to rights, at least to some extent? The second is, why, as I claim above, are the choices that courts make about the horizontal effect of rights so important and revealing?

There are both normative and strategic answers to the question of why, in general, courts in developed systems of constitutional justice give some horizontal effect to rights. One normative answer, which applies more to the indirect effect of rights, is that the most basic role of the state is precisely to protect individuals from other individuals. Social contract thinkers dating back to Hobbes and Locke agreed that the state must defend persons against the predations of their fellows. If constitutional rights express the state's most fundamental commitments to its citizens, it makes sense that they could oblige the state to limit the harms that citizens can cause one another. The question becomes just how far the state is required to go in regulating interactions among citizens.[5]

Relatedly, the behaviors that are protected against government suppression by constitutional rights can often be threatened by private power as well (Chemerinsky 1985, 511). A person's freedom of expression means less as a

4. For a broad survey of approaches in different countries, see Oliver and Fedtke (2007).

5. For a discussion of Hobbes's and Locke's views on what the sovereign owes its subjects, see Eskridge and Ferejohn (2010, 43–48).

practical matter if a letter to the editor on a political issue can cost her job. Some rights in particular—notably social and economic rights—would have very little real-world purchase if they could have no effect at all on the private behavior of others. A right to shelter or to a healthy environment makes little sense if it only guarantees government noninterference.

Third, since the state makes the laws and maintains the legal system, "state action" is at play in every legal transaction, at some remove: the state ultimately controls what is and is not allowed (Hale 1923). Law both allocates individuals' initial legal entitlements and sets the rules by which they can be transferred. The choices of private parties, of course, matter too: what terms a contract has, or who may enter onto a piece of property, depends also on private volition. But the law decides whose volition counts, and which acts of private volition can be legally effective. If ostensibly private legal choices are really shot through with the coercive power of the state, it is natural to ask why they should be immune to constitutional scrutiny.

Of course, this is also a strategic dimension to judicial behavior, and this is true when it comes to choices about horizontal rights. Naturally, what counts as a sound strategy for a court will depend on a host of system-specific institutional structures and political realities. In general, though, as norms of constitutional stature, rights have a special status and potency that can make them attractive to courts. Rights represent powerful normative resources that courts may use to displace the judgments of others. Depending on the particulars of their jurisdiction, apex courts may also unlock new streams of cases by entertaining constitutional claims in private-party litigation. The differences across systems matter a great deal, but it is a rare apex court that can never benefit from bringing rights into play in a dispute between private parties.

The next question is why the choices that courts make about when and how to give horizontal effect to rights matter. There are a number of answers to this question as well. How rights apply to private-party legal relations is substantively important for its own sake, as an aspect of rights doctrines more broadly. But what is more, the positions that courts take on this issue imply positions on other, fundamental questions that go to the heart of the character of constitutionalism in a legal system. In an important sense, horizontal effect doctrines suggest answers to questions about the nature of the constitutional project itself, marking off the boundaries between what is and is not a part of it.

First, in making horizontal rights doctrine, courts are taking a position on what the state owes its citizens. Of course, traditional liberal rights also encode obligations that a state has to its citizens, but these are obligations of a limited kind. Traditional liberal rights just restrict what a government can do to people. But when a constitutional right is pleaded in litigation between private parties, the court is asked to take rights further. As noted above, constitutional rights are more often given indirect horizontal effect than direct horizontal effect. In other words, the claim typically takes the form that the right requires the state to constrain one private party in the interests of another. So in ruling on such claims, courts decide how deeply, if at all, the state is required to reach into society and regulate the interaction of citizens. This amounts to a fundamental, and fundamentally political, question about the proper scope of government intervention, transposed to a constitutional key. And allowing rights to have horizontal effect draws courts straight into the middle of it.

Second, in ruling on the horizontal effect of rights, courts also define the border between ordinary law and constitutional law. When courts find constitutional rights relevant to private-party relationships, they constitutionalize matters conventionally in the province of "ordinary" statutory or common law. Like every redrawing of borders, this one creates winners and losers, although the particulars will depend on the legal system. Horizontal rights bring the institutions that produce ordinary law—legislatures, civil courts, and so on—further under the tutelage of a constitutional court. But at the same time, the more that ordinary law acquires a constitutional dimension, the more the institutions producing it become front-line makers of constitutional meaning. Confronting questions of horizontal effect means making choices about how bodies of law and institutions interact to give effect to the constitution in a legal system.

Third, horizontal effect also forces choices about the nature of constitutional rights more generally. It's conventional to think of rights as entitlements, as against some legal person or persons, to some specific performance or forbearance. This is a categorical conception of rights—either a right is satisfied, or it is not—and it is not well suited to the practical problems of horizontal rights. It would frequently produce intolerable results if we supposed that having a right entitled the holder to the same performance or forbearance regardless of whether the conduct of the government or a private party was at issue. And owing to their constitutional stature, rights as entitlements would run roughshod over the norms and structures of private law wherever they applied. If rights are to apply horizontally, what's needed is a way that rights can be taken seriously while still leaving space for other norms. Horizontal effect encourages innovation in how courts conceptualize rights.

In all of these ways, the choices courts make about whether and how to give horizontal effect to rights speak to the nature of constitutional rights and of the constitutional project more broadly. The development of horizontal effect doctrine is thus central to the broader process of constitutional development in a legal system. The story of how it happens is an aspect of, and should be told as part of, that bigger story.

And the story is not only a legal one, but a political one. Courts' choices about horizontal effect have profound practical consequences—which will vary by legal system—for how power is allocated in that system. Bringing the constitution into play affects which institutions get to decide which issues, and how they have to go about it. Courts *explain* their decisions with reference to legal norms. But in *making* decisions, courts are alert to how their choices allocate power across institutions and to the political realities that govern how their choices will be received by other actors. I work from the starting assumption that courts operate in environments with both normative and strategic dimensions, and that judicial choices are therefore properly regarded as products of both normative and strategic logics—which may sometimes pull in different directions. The choices courts make reflect existing political realities and, over time, can create new ones.

HORIZONTAL RIGHTS AT WORK

Horizontal rights claims are crucibles in which the most important normative commitments and strategic realities in a legal system come together to forge doctrine. These doctrines tell us about what constitutionalism really means in the legal systems that produce them. Significantly, they figure as both effects and causes in processes of constitutional development. Horizontal rights doctrines simultaneously reflect features of the legal systems that produce them, and also shape the further development of those systems. They are deeply embedded in the constitutional history and politics of their legal systems, and understanding the roles they play means engaging in some historical reconstruction.

That is what this book undertakes. This book explores how horizontal rights doctrines have contributed to constitutional development in three legal systems: Germany, the United States, and Canada.

Of course, there are limits to what we can learn about a phenomenon by looking at only three cases. What is more, these three cases are all Western democracies with established legal systems, and count among the "usual suspects" that are most often studied in comparative constitutional law. There are exciting and important developments in other jurisdictions that fall outside the scope of this project.[6] This book depicts only a small sliver of the global engagement with horizontal rights.

6. For instance, the country with the most expansive horizontal rights jurisprudence in the world today may be Colombia, where constitutional rights are currently disrupting processes of private litigation, in ways that some legal experts find difficult to keep up with. See Estrada (2000, 2007).

Still, there are advantages to this research design. The development of horizontal rights doctrines, and their interaction with other features of a legal system, are complex phenomena that play out over time. It makes sense to tackle an object of study such as this through an in-depth, historical approach, which necessarily limits the number of cases. And these three cases are, in many respects, suitable companions for comparative analysis. If the objects of comparison vary in too many respects, it can be impossible to discern any patterns. These cases allow us to "hold constant" many basic regime features, including stable democratic government and advanced capitalist economies, and focus on other factors.

At the same time, these three systems are also rich in variation, both with respect to features of their law and with respect to the roles horizontal rights doctrines have played in their development. Among them, they represent some of the most globally influential families of legal systems (Law and Versteeg 2011). Germany is a continental civil law system, Canada belongs to the Commonwealth, and the United States' legal system, while built on a foundation of English law, has evolved into a distinctive type all its own.

In each, constitutional law developed against the backdrop of another body of law with quasi-constitutional character. This was the venerable civil law in Germany, and in Canada and the United States, the prestigiously pedigreed common law, acquired second-hand from England. These bodies of law influenced the development of constitutional law. They did so both positively, by providing normative resources for the development of constitutional law, and negatively, in that they furnished an established alternative against which constitutional law could be defined.

These legal family differences are also related to relevant institutional differences. Typical of continental legal systems, Germany has opted for a model of centralized review, in which a single, specialized constitutional court decides all constitutional claims, and only constitutional claims. Nonconstitutional claims are handled by a number of subject-specific court systems, each culminating in a supreme court for that area of law. The apex courts in Canada and the United States are supreme courts that hear both constitutional and nonconstitutional cases. However, there is an important difference in the jurisdiction of the supreme courts in Canada and the United States. While the Supreme Court of Canada is the final authority on issues of provincial and federal law, in the United States, state supreme courts have final authority on issues of state law. These jurisdictional differences mean that the choice to give horizontal effect to rights has different institutional consequences across the cases.

The systems also differ with respect to the content and character of constitutional rights enshrined in their respective charters. By international standards, the U.S. Constitution protects a fairly bare-bones roster of rights. Canada's Charter of Rights and Freedoms is somewhat more extensive, and also contains some innovations characteristic of newer charters, including a limitations clause (which expressly contemplates the possibility that rights may sometimes appropriately yield to other interests) and a notwithstanding clause (which permits the legislature to enact a law notwithstanding a prior finding of unconstitutionality). The set of rights in Germany's Basic Law is more expansive still, containing a number of social and economic rights as well as classic liberal rights, and also expressly contemplating that rights may be balanced against other interests. These differences speak to the normative resources available to courts as they resolve disputes before them.

And crucially, the countries vary considerably with respect to outcomes. Horizontal rights doctrines play very different roles in the three systems. Germany's Federal Constitutional Court (GFCC) has taken an expansive approach to horizontal effect, declaring that constitutional rights, as values, are relevant to the whole body of law. The Court has further devised doctrines that require courts, and legislatures, to take rights seriously, even when regulating private-party interactions, under pain of constitutional review. The GFCC's early rulings touched off a constitutional cascade, in which rights reasoning spread outward from the Court, changing how lower courts and legislatures go about their work, and turning the GFCC into a kind of supreme superintendent over all legal decision making in the country. On this view, the Basic Law functions less like a charter of government and more like a blueprint for the whole of society. The responsibility for figuring out how to implement it is shared widely, under the supervision of the GFCC.

The situation is very different in the United States. Under the banner of the "state action" requirement, the Supreme Court has pursued a policy of constitutional containment, sharply limiting the horizontal effect of constitutional rights. While the Supreme Court's refusal to give broad horizontal effect to rights might seem, on its face, to limit judicial power, the Court's approach in fact underwrites a form of judicial supremacy, albeit a very different form than in Germany. The Supreme Court has built itself an effective monopoly on constitutional interpretation, and limiting the contexts in which rights apply helps to maintain its control over the Constitution's meaning. And its state action jurisprudence is famously riddled with inconsistencies, as the Supreme Court has on many occasions reached out to give rights horizontal effect. But the exceptions in the doctrine, which cluster around civil rights and civil liberties in the mid-twentieth century, only underscore the Supreme Court's controlling position over constitutional meaning. In the United States, the Constitution still mostly maps out the boundaries of government power, and the Court jealously guards its supreme authority to say what crosses the line.

The Supreme Court of Canada (SCC) has charted a middle course of sorts. The Court adopted a position, in its first major case on the subject, that seemed to narrow the scope for horizontal effect dramatically: the Charter does not apply in litigation between private parties under the common law. But almost as an aside, the Court noted that judges should develop the common law in accordance with Charter values. On that basis, the SCC went on in future cases to introduce Charter rights into common law decision making. The Court's approach in this area has been of a piece with a practice more generally of treating the Charter as a source of values that should inform Canadian law, including insofar as it regulates private-party interactions. But the SCC has been far less aggressive than Germany's Federal Constitutional Court in constitutionalizing the private law. The SCC's overall approach is a form of caboose constitutionalism, in which the Court generally engages in rights reasoning in an area only once the legislature has begun acting to advance constitutional values.

Germany, the United States, and Canada are much-studied legal systems in part because they have pioneered constitutional innovations that have had worldwide influence. This is true also in the area of horizontal rights: the doctrines developed in these countries have shaped how other jurisdictions approach the issue. For this reason as well, these systems are well-suited for an in-depth comparison. The conclusion to the book also extends the focus beyond these three systems. The conclusion does not attempt a systematic survey of horizontal rights globally, but it does highlight a few developments in other parts of the world, in both national legal systems and the European Union.[7]

Each case study is divided into two chapters and follows a parallel structure. The first chapter lays out the relevant legal, institutional, and political background for each jurisdiction, and the second focuses on the development of horizontal rights jurisprudence and its consequences. The analysis in each first chapter touches on three main subjects: the constitution, the configuration of courts and other government branches, and the broader historical context.

7. This book is not, of course, the only work to address the horizontal effect of constitutional rights from a comparative perspective. Notably, a number of edited volumes relay different jurisdictions' experiences with horizontal rights (Friedmann and Barak-Erez 2001; Sajo and Uitz 2005; Oliver and Fedtke 2007). Several articles or chapters, including ones by Mark Tushnet (2003; 2002; 2005) and Mattias Kumm and Victor Ferreres Comella (2005), seek to explain some of the cross-national variation we see in the horizontal application of rights. Stephen Gardbaum has offered an analytic framework for better understanding the doctrinal differences across systems (2003). This book differs from these other works, among other ways, in its approach, which is to take a deep plunge into the history and politics of a small set of legal systems.

It makes sense that each case study will pay close attention to the constitution itself, with a particular focus on the content and structure of rights. Attention to the text of the constitution sheds light on the normative resources available to the apex court and other actors. Relevant questions include: Does the constitution protect primarily first-generation (i.e., civil and political) rights, or does it also protect second- or third-generation rights (to social, economic, cultural, or environmental goods, for instance)?[8] Are the rights expressly framed as negative rights only (i.e., rights against interference), or as positive rights, entitling rights bearers to something more than being left alone? Are the rights expressly made subject to some limitations, or are they phrased in absolute terms? Does the rights charter specify who is bound by rights, or the procedures through which they are to be adjudicated?

The first chapter of each case study also analyzes the institutional configuration of the legal and political system, with particular interest in how judicial power is organized. Is the institutional environment in which the apex court finds itself a highly competitive one, with multiple institutions occupying a common policy space and open questions about their respective roles in governance? How is judicial authority structured? Does the system practice centralized constitutional review, with a specialized constitutional court, or decentralized review with regular courts hearing constitutional claims, or some combination? Does the court with final authority to resolve constitutional questions have final authority to decide all legal issues, or if not, how is the power of the last word apportioned among courts across different subject areas? Is abstract constitutional review available, or concrete review, or both? What are the procedures for bringing a constitutional complaint, and who can bring them? Are the rulings of the constitutional court binding on all other courts? Was one court established before the others, such that it benefits from first mover advantages? All of these issues are relevant to understanding both the strategic position of the apex court and the extent to which it is equipped with tools to advance its interests.

Each first chapter also widens out the lens to take in relevant features of the historical and political context. What issues loom largest on the political landscape during the relevant period: sectionalism, economic development, postwar recovery, cultural conflict? Any brief distillation of a profoundly complex national political environment will necessarily be selective and contestable. Even so, attention to this context matters, because the broader political context informs the interests of the institutions and actors involved, as well as the resonance that different normative claims have at different points in time.

8. French jurist Karel Vasak popularized the distinction among first-, second-, and third generation rights (1977).

The second chapter of each case study turns to the horizontal effect of rights within the jurisdiction. The first focus is on the critical early moves in the development of a court's horizontal effect jurisprudence, and I subject the apex court's early important cases addressing horizontal effect to sustained analysis. Because of the path dependence of precedent, early cases have an outsized importance: they establish the doctrinal structures that courts must subsequently work within, or else work around.

The case studies then explore the development of horizontal effect doctrine over time and its broader effect on lawmaking processes, including the behavior of legislatures, litigants, and others. For each, I focus on the same three subject areas: the freedom of expression, family law, and antidiscrimination law.[9] Looking at the same areas of law in each country facilitates comparison, and these are good candidates for study, for a few reasons.

These are all areas of law where we should expect to see courts having to confront issues of horizontal effect. First, each of these is an area in which private actors pose significant threats to constitutional values. For instance, libel law permits individuals to penalize others' expression, and private employers could potentially hire and fire on discriminatory grounds. Second, these are all areas in which relevant social norms have evolved considerably over time in each of the jurisdiction, opening a normative space in which constitutional rights might do some work.[10] In other words, for both reasons, these are areas in which we can anticipate courts making moves on the horizontal effect front and witness the different forms judicial action takes. Together, these areas of law afford a prime opportunity to observe how different approaches to the horizontal effect of rights play out in practice.

The case studies showcase the varied, but central, roles that horizontal rights doctrines can play in constitutional development. The case studies retell important chapters in the constitutional history of each country with attention to the development of horizontal rights doctrine, and an emphasis on three issues

9. I define these areas broadly, sometimes more broadly than the legal systems in question. I take a capacious approach because I am interested in looking at similar sets of substantive issues across the three countries and care less about what doctrinal categories they are sorted into.

10. This latter point holds less for Canada, where the Charter of Rights and Freedoms was only adopted in 1982, after the normative convulsions starting in the mid-twentieth century had quieted. As the study of Canada argues, much of that normative space had already been occupied by legislation by the time the Charter took effect, which had an effect on how horizontal effect jurisprudence developed in Canada. In some respects, this difference in timing is actually fortuitous, as it allows us to compare how horizontal rights doctrines develop differently when much of the demand for norms protecting against private-party behavior have already been satisfied by statutes.

in particular. They are (1) the circumstances under which courts start applying rights horizontally, (2) the structure of the horizontal rights doctrines that emerge, and (3) how these doctrines come to impact processes of legal decision making in the system more broadly. It is worth previewing the general findings before proceeding to the case studies.

Initiating Horizontal Effect

First, in order for courts to start applying rights horizontally, there needs to be a normative gap in the ordinary law that can plausibly be filled by a constitutional norm. A normative gap exists when there is a substantial demand for the protection of an interest that is not being met by ordinary law. For example: antidiscrimination statutes may fail to ban discrimination on the basis of sexual orientation at a time when such discrimination takes on an increasing public salience. A court empowered to interpret the constitution may be able to fill this gap by applying a constitutional equality norm. Whether such a move is normatively plausible or not depends: on the text of the constitution, on the court's existing doctrines, and on the particulars of the case. The less plausible the move, the more it taxes the court's legitimacy to make it—so, all else equal, the less likely it is to happen.

The case studies suggest that this kind of normative gap is a necessary condition for the initiation of horizontal effect, not a sufficient one. Courts will not start applying rights horizontally, even when they can plausibly fill a gap in the ordinary law, if it is not in their interests to do so. Different courts have different interests, and every court can have interests of different kinds: institutional, issue-based, and ideological. So, a court could be motivated to secure its own standing vis-à-vis other branches or bodies (institutional), to achieve certain preferred substantive policy outcomes (issue-based), or to advance a particular vision of the law, the polity, or itself (ideological). In deciding whether making rights horizontal advances its interests, we can suppose that a court considers the likely consequences of its actions, which depend on how its moves are received by other institutions. This will depend on institutional arrangements and political realities in a particular system at a particular time.

Conditions certainly favored the turn to horizontal rights by Germany's Federal Constitutional Court, in the late 1950s. In the *Lüth* decision from 1958, the GFCC answered the call to protect the liberal free speech rights encoded in Germany's postwar constitution, the Basic Law, at a time when the ordinary civil courts were failing to do so.[11] This move by the still-new GFCC was one of several to assert the relevance of the Basic Law—and hence, the Court—during

11. Bundesverfassungsgericht [BVerfG] [Federal Constitutional Court], 7 Entscheidungen des Bundesverfassungsgerichts [BVerfGE] 198 (Jan. 15, 1958).

a period when its position was under assault from both the executive branch and other courts. The wide availability of constitutional review meant that other courts had an incentive to follow the GFCC's lead and take rights seriously.

A critical early juncture for the United States Supreme Court came in the *Civil Rights Cases* of 1883.[12] The Court was asked to decide whether Congress's power to enforce constitutional rights authorized legislation banning discrimination by private parties. The idea that constitutional rights could impose a duty on the state to protect against certain private abuses was not alien to contemporary thinking. But in the context of post-Reconstruction America, as the political will flagged to protect African Americans against a rising tide of discrimination in the South, the Court opted instead for a narrower conception of rights. The Court's decision established the foundation for the state action doctrine.

Canada's Charter of Rights and Freedoms was only a few years old when the Supreme Court of Canada was first asked whether it applied to private-party common law disputes, in the 1986 *Dolphin Delivery* case.[13] Officially, the Court answered no. Institutionally, the SCC had little to gain from the horizontal application of Charter rights: as a court of general jurisdiction, the SCC was already the court of last resort for every case in the country, whether a right was pleaded or not. However, the SCC noted almost in passing that courts should develop the common law to comport with Charter values, and in years to come, the SCC did so repeatedly.

Doctrine

Of course, courts don't simply decide that rights categorically apply horizontally or not: they develop doctrines that explain when and how rights have horizontal effect. Moving from a position of exclusive vertical effect to allow horizontal effect means permitting rights to cross some conceptual boundary that had contained them, and there are different ways to characterize it. Courts might, for instance, frame doctrine in terms of the body of law to which rights apply (for instance, private versus public, or statutory versus common law), or the actors to whom they apply (for instance, state versus nonstate actors). Horizontal effect doctrine, then, generally does two things: it identifies a framing dichotomy in the law, and explains when and how rights apply across it.

With respect to the "when" question, a court's doctrine can treat horizontal rights as more or less routine. Horizontal application can be the rule or the

12. 109 US 3 (1883).

13. RWDSU v. Dolphin Delivery Ltd. [1986] 2 S.C.R. 573.

exception. Of course, a coherent doctrine will explain *why* rights have horizontal effect when they do, and not otherwise. Perhaps the most fundamental question to ask of any horizontal rights doctrine is, what is the trigger for the horizontal application of rights? Courts will vary not only in how they answer that question, but in how clearly and consistently they do.

With respect to the "how" question, we can contrast two ideal-type conceptions of rights: rights as entitlements, and rights as values. Rights as entitlements are defined by the correlative responsibilities that they impose on other actors or institutions. They tend to have an all-or-nothing character: a right is either satisfied or not, with no middle ground. The "rights-as-values" perspective treats rights as embodying fundamental normative commitments that courts must ensure are adequately reflected in law. On this view, rights can be relevant to a legal dispute without necessarily being outcome-dispositive. Rights as values are more flexible than rights as entitlements. They can function more like substantive canons of construction that guide judicial decision making than as guarantees of a given outcome.

The choices courts make about how to frame horizontal effect will affect how widely constitutional claims arise in private-party disputes and how these claims will be argued. To fully understand these choices, we need to reconstruct the environments in which they make those choices, as the chapters that follow do. But we can also highlight some common dynamics.

First, there is a connection between when and how rights have horizontal effect. If courts routinely apply rights horizontally, they will tend to apply them more as values than as entitlements. Values can inform outcomes, but entitlements dictate them. For this reason, the former are easier to harmonize with existing bodies of ordinary law.

Second, crafting doctrine is a way of choosing what kinds of claims parties will argue in the future and how they will argue them. A court will frame its horizontal rights doctrine in a way that focuses parties' efforts on the sorts of arguments the court is comfortable handling.

Third, the construction of doctrine is not a static act under the exclusive control of the court, but a dynamic and interactive process. Doctrine evolves, and not only because courts' interests change. Because doctrine provides a template for argumentation that is activated not by the court, but by parties, litigation may push the development of the law in directions not anticipated by courts. At the same time, the duty to respect precedent acts as a constraint, if not an ironclad one, on the arguments that parties can make and courts can accept. Changes in the strategic and normative contexts in which courts operate can generate tension with existing doctrine, and courts' responses can introduce incoherence and inconsistency.

The doctrines that the three legal systems devise to manage horizontal rights are strikingly different. According to the GFCC, the constitutional rights of the Basic Law have a double existence. In addition to being subjective rights applicable against the state, they form an objective order of values that permeates the entire corpus of law, including the private law. Accordingly, all legal decision making takes places in the shadow of constitutional rights. The GFCC has emphasized that rights inform private law decision making without displacing it, and the Court has also crafted deference doctrines that encourage both judicial and legislative actors to take rights seriously in their own decision making.

The United States Supreme Court formally hews to a simple rule: an individual's constitutional rights can only be violated by actions of the state.[14] By foreclosing ex ante any claims based on the state's *inaction*, this framing quietly relieves the court of having to entertain potentially difficult questions about how far the state's obligations to protect its citizens run. What counts as "state action" has been a shifting target, reflecting the variable intensity of the Court's interest in reaching the conduct at issue in a given case at a given time. The Court took a flexible approach to state action when necessary to advance its postwar civil rights and civil liberties agenda, and has since retrenched.

In contrast to the United States, Canadian horizontal rights doctrine is conspicuously plastic. Charter rights apply to the common law as values, and how to develop the common law to reflect Charter values was essentially a matter of judicial discretion. The SCC sought to cabin that discretion somewhat, declaring, for instance, that Charter values only can underwrite incremental changes in the common law, but the Court has not consistently shown such restraint. Over the years, some of the differences between judicial development of the common law to reflect Charter values and true Charter review have narrowed.

Downstream Impacts

Ultimately, horizontal rights doctrines make a broader contribution to the character of legal decision making in a system of governance. These doctrines are key elements in processes of constitutional development that play out over time. Eventually, they reach some equilibrium with respect to the roles the constitution and constitutional rights play in the life of the country. When horizontal rights are involved, these processes can be truly transformative.

Horizontal rights have more potential to transform a legal system the more frequently they apply, but procedural and remedial rules also affect how deeply

14. An exception is made for the Thirteenth Amendment, which bans slavery, and is generally understood to apply against private individuals as well.

constitutional rights penetrate through a legal system. For instance: Can rights only influence the *interpretation* of the law governing private-party relations, or can rights require results *contra legem*: that is, can they require that the law be rewritten? Can rights generate new causes of action of one private party against another, or are they dependent on an existing cause of action? Are rights effectuated in private-party relations only by enjoining certain conduct, or are other remedies possible, including damages or specific performance?

Also relevant are the rules and practices that give other institutions incentives to go along with rights innovations. A single apex court cannot transform a legal system by itself. If lower courts and legislatures can ignore new doctrines with impunity, they will have little effect. It's relevant, therefore, how available judicial review is and how the process for obtaining it works. Courts can also build incentives to engage in rights reasoning into doctrine, by promising deference to lower courts and legislatures that take rights seriously.

Germany illustrates what happens when constitutional rights are really unleashed in a legal system. The result is what Mattias Kumm has termed the "total constitution," in which rights become the jurisgenerative core of the entire legal order (2006). When rights penetrate the whole of law, all legal relations are potentially of constitutional moment. There is no longer a category of "ordinary" legislation defined in sharp opposition to constitutional law. Instead, statutes are the front-line instantiation of the constitution, the stalking horses for constitutional values. And when all forms of lawmaking become different means of elaborating constitutional commitments, the conceptual vocabularies and institutional roles of legislators and constitutional judges come to overlap substantially. Legislatures become constitutional decision makers, deliberating over how constitutional values are best given effect in different policy domains. Owing to their power of review, constitutional courts gain what amounts to a seat at the table of legislative politics. The distinction erodes between the Large "C" Constitution—the formal basic law—and the small "c" constitution—the "working constitution," in Bill Eskridge and John Ferejohn's phrase: the normative commitments that define the public life of a polity as a practical matter (Eskridge and Ferejohn 2010, 9).

The outcome is very different in the United States. It's not that rights never have horizontal effect—they do, and in some very important contexts—but the state action doctrine heavily emphasizes rights' vertical dimension. The doctrine helps the courts maintain a sharp bifurcation between constitutional and ordinary law. This bifurcation supports a sharp division of labor between legislator and judge: the legislature has free rein to regulate as it cares within its proper domain, which is bounded by a set of constitutional strictures enforced by courts. This state of affairs animates that most American of constitutional problems, the countermajoritarian difficulty: once triggered, the constitutional discourse shuts down and supplants the processes of ordinary democratic politics.

Canada shows that there are possibilities beyond those found in Germany and the United States. Canada rejects both Germany's total constitution and the hermetic separation between constitutional and ordinary law practiced in the United States. Charter rights serve as values that inform the production of law in Canada, including as it regulates private-party relations, but not as a blueprint for the whole legal order. The Supreme Court of Canada is selective about enforcing Charter values, and in many cases takes its cues from the legislature.

All these developments are traced in greater detail in the six chapters that follow. The concluding chapter widens the lens somewhat, to consider how these experiences compare with those in other legal systems in certain respects and to explore the connections between horizontal rights and other contemporary developments in constitutional law.

2

Germany's Postwar Constitution

INTRODUCTION

During the annual conference of the Union of German Public Law Professors in October 1950, eminent constitutional scholar Erich Kaufmann gave a presentation on "The Limits of Judicial Review" in the Federal Republic of Germany. The topic was timely, and novel: the constitution establishing the Federal Republic, the Basic Law, had been ratified in May of the previous year. Kaufmann was confident that the new German Federal Constitutional Court (*Bundesverfassungsgericht*), which had not yet begun operations, would do nothing to redraw the boundary between law and politics. "I am convinced," said Kaufmann, "that, when we take into account the viewpoints and limits I have sketched, there is no danger of a juridification of politics or a politicization of justice" (1952, 11).

Kaufmann's remark, like Alexander Hamilton's reference in the Federalist Papers to the judiciary as the "least dangerous branch," underestimated the capacity of courts to upend established norms about how and where consequential decisions are reached in a democracy (Hamilton et al. 2013, 466). In the past six and a half decades, the German Federal Constitutional Court (GFCC) has defined for itself a unique and prominent role in the national politics of Germany. Germany's Constitutional Court is among the world's most powerful, possessing "very probably . . . the furthest-reaching competencies a constitutional court can have" (Häberle 2006a, 70). Also, the Court has elaborated in detail a doctrine of the horizontal effect of rights, pursuant to which "rights penetrate deep into the established structures of private law" and are reference points for legal decision making by other actors (Ruffert 2001, 1). But even as constitutional rights have reshaped ordinary law in Germany, the Constitutional Court's horizontal effect jurisprudence has been faulted by specialists, both in public law and private law, for ambiguities, inconsistencies, and unpredictability (Ruffert 2001, 16; Diederichsen 1998, 180–81; Fedtke 2007, 131).

What happened? Why was Kaufmann so far off in his expectations about the development of constitutional law? A large part of the answer is that the Court's horizontal rights jurisprudence touched off a constitutional cascade, in which the introduction of rights reasoning by the Court enabled and encouraged the further use of rights reasoning in successively more contexts and by successively more institutions. Germany demonstrates what a fulsome embrace of horizontal rights can produce under favorable circumstances: a "total constitution," in Mattias Kumm's phrase, in which the constitution provides the normative blueprint for the entirety of law. In an effort to understand the conditions under which rights can realize their full transformative potential, Germany is a logical place to look.

The GFCC famously initiated its doctrine of *Drittwirkung*—literally, "third-party effect"—in the *Lüth* decision of 1958. The doctrine is a species of indirect horizontal effect, in which rights do not impose obligations directly on private parties, but instead influence the content of the private law, and hence, the rights and duties that private law confers on private parties. The Court's constitutional turn made sense strategically: the Court had much to gain institutionally from finding rights implicated by private law disputes, and the rising cultural and political relevance of liberal values created an opportunity.

In the beginning, the Court was an untested institution that lacked a firm foothold in the unsettled political order of the postwar German republic, and an interloper in Germany's legal establishment, where private law predominated, owing in large part to the prestige of the German Civil Code. In this competitive environment, the Court faced challenges from better-established institutions that sought to amplify their own prerogatives at the Court's expense. These challenges came both from outside the judiciary (from the Chancellor and Ministry of Justice), and from within (from Germany's other supreme courts and the private law establishment).

The scope of the Constitutional Court's authority was hemmed in by its specialized jurisdiction: the Court had the power to hear only cases raising constitutional questions, and so its influence over the law was confined to those cases raising constitutional issues. At the same time, the Court had at its disposal many tools and procedural mechanisms for reviewing constitutional questions. With powers of both abstract and concrete review, the Court could entertain challenges to legislation before it took effect, and also as they arose in concrete disputes. What is more, access to review was broadly available. In particular, the Basic Law permitted individual claimants to raise constitutional complaints, and in a crucial early move, the Court decided that these complaints could be brought against the decisions of nonconstitutional courts. The Court's specialized jurisdiction and the broad availability of review for questions within that jurisdiction in combination meant that expanding the domain of constitutional rights would expand the sphere of the Court's own authority.

At the same time, the Court found itself in a normative environment that was favorable to a broad view of the scope of rights. The Court was tasked with the interpretation of a new constitution that fairly bristled with rights, many written in expansive terms, and some readily lending themselves to horizontal application. Further, as Germany gradually emerged from the "collective amnesia" of the immediate postwar period (Clark 2006, 62), public demand for protection of liberal rights, notably free expression rights, was on the rise, and the authoritative constructions of the civil law by the civil law courts lagged in meeting that demand. At the same time, the GFCC faced competition from the Labor Court, which was beginning to poach on its turf by applying rights horizontally to resolve labor disputes. If the Court was to maintain its primacy as the guardian of the constitution, it needed to place its own stamp on the horizontal application of rights.

The manner in which the Court expressed the horizontal effect of rights in doctrine also reflected the political realities it confronted. Constitutional rights apply to private-party relations only indirectly, as values that shape the interpretation and application of private law norms. This doctrine of indirect effect lets the Court recognize the nominal autonomy of the private sphere and the private law and acknowledge nominal limits on the reach of the constitution (Sommeregger 2005, 42). As a rhetorical gambit, the language of indirect effect offers the GFCC some cover against the claim of overreaching vis-à-vis the private law courts and lawmakers. Scholars have argued that, as a practical matter, direct effect versus indirect effect is a distinction without a difference: that courts can reach the same substantive results whether rights apply directly or indirectly (Kumm 2006). This critique may be correct as a matter of doctrine but does not engage with the context in which the difference has its salience. The direct effect/indirect effect distinction does most of its work not on the plane of legal substance, but of interbranch and intrabranch politics.

Over time, the Court pushed constitutional rights reasoning progressively deeper into the legal order. Successive decisions announced that constitutional rights could: compel the creation of a cause of action; rewrite substantive provisions of the private law code (rather than merely shaping their interpretation); require a damage remedy when foreclosed by statute; and impose on the state an affirmative obligation to legislate to protect rights. No single decision appeared revolutionary in isolation; each built on a foundation laid by the previous case. Taken together, however, the Court's horizontal effects decisions gave parties the tools to demand that a vast universe of legal actions and arrangements be justified as conforming with rights-based constitutional values. And the Court's doctrinal moves were justifiable in terms of a broader normative narrative in which constitutional rights represent values that radiate through the whole of law.

The Court's caselaw initiated a constitutional cascade that made rights discourse part of the legal lingua franca of nonconstitutional courts, legislators, and litigants. Placing the business of legislatures and courts—the production and application of legal norms—in the shadow of constitutional rights, subject to the tutelage of the GFCC, has changed the process and character of this work in subtle but important ways. These bodies are engaged in an ongoing, institutionalized dialogue with the Court in which the relationship between constitutional values and other legal norms is debated and negotiated. The process looks different in different areas of the law. In some, such as the freedom of expression, the Court clearly takes the lead, and in others, such as family law, the GFCC, lower courts, and legislatures all take initiative at different points. The development of Germany's antidiscrimination law also reflects the extraordinary influence of European Union (EU) law and adds still more complexity to the process. The Court of Justice of the European Union has extended the reach of EU norms by applying them horizontally, introducing new dynamics into Germany's lawmaking in this domain (and many others).

This chapter and the one which follows analyze these developments. In some respects, the story they tell is familiar, and in other respects, it is not. The features of Germany's horizontal effect doctrine, and the seminal *Lüth* case that announced it, are important subjects in German constitutional law,[1] but most scholarly treatments of the Constitutional Court's jurisprudence give little attention to the political context or consequences of judicial choices, which are important elements of this narrative. The gap is due at least in part to the conjunction of linguistic barriers and cross-national differences in the sociology of knowledge. The inaccessibility of German legal materials to non-German speakers ensures that relatively few scholars working in English will produce in-depth scholarship on the Constitutional Court.[2] And the fairly sharp division of labor in German universities between the study of politics (handled in political science departments) and the study of law (handled in law schools) means that most German studies of the Court will be heavily doctrinal. Of course there are exceptions: works in both German[3] and

1. The scholarship in German is extensive; in English, less so. For one excellent and detailed account in English, focusing on free expression cases, see Quint (1989).

2. There are, of course, exceptions. Donald Kommers and Russell Miller (2012) and David Currie (1994) have written magisterial books on German constitutional law, which have been joined by an excellent new history of the GFCC from Justin Collings (2015).

3. See, for instance, Landfried (1984), Henne and Riedlinger (2005), and Ooyen and Möllers (2006).

English[4] that offer sophisticated views of the politics of decision making on the Constitutional Court. But none of these have devoted sustained attention to the horizontal effect of constitutional rights.

The rest of this chapter and the following one are organized as follows. The next three sections of this chapter describe in some depth the creation of Germany's postwar constitution, the structure of its judiciary, and the challenges facing the GFCC, as a prelude to the next chapter's discussion of that court's horizontal effect jurisprudence. Chapter Three begins with an in-depth exploration of the GFCC's foundational decision in *Lüth*. The next three sections analyze the further development of doctrine, and the responses of other institutions, in the context of the freedom of expression, family law, and antidiscrimination law, respectively. A final section concludes that chapter.

BUILDING THE BASIC LAW

May 8, 1945, when the remnants of the Nazi regime surrendered to the Allied forces, was *Stunde Null* for Germany—the Zero Hour, when a thoroughly devastated country turned to face the daunting prospect of rebuilding. Over the next decade, Germany would reconstruct not only its shattered economy but also its political and legal institutions. One of the most significant and enduring accomplishments of the early postwar period was Germany's establishment of a new constitutional order defined by the *Grundgesetz*, the Basic Law, which took effect in 1949. The Basic Law provided for the creation of a new tribunal, the Constitutional Court, with the authority to resolve constitutional disputes.[5]

The war's end was *Stunde Null* for public law too, because the collapse of the Third Reich left Germany without a constitutional basis for establishing a new government.[6] The Weimar Constitution had not been formally abrogated, but it had been thoroughly ignored since Hitler's rise to power in 1933. Moreover, the Weimar Constitution was deeply suspect, since it had permitted the Nazi government to come to power (Lindseth 2004). Germany's postwar constitution

4. See, for instance, Kommers and Miller (2012), Kommers (1976), and Vanberg (2009). Georg Vanberg's book is the most prominent recent monograph on the GFCC that explicitly addresses the strategic and political dimensions of judicial decision making.

5. Grundgesetz für die Bundesrepublik Deutschland [Grundgesetz] [GG] [Basic Law], May 23, 1949, BGBl. I, art. 93.

6. Formally, the Allies' June 5, 1945, declaration did not dissolve the German state but empowered the occupying powers to exercise its authority on behalf of the defeated Germany (Fenske 1994, 79). The Potsdam Accords of August 1945 declared the shared goals of the Germany occupation: demilitarization, denazification, democratization, and decentralization of Germany's economy (Kröger 1993, 12).

would be written from scratch, hopefully incorporating lessons learned from the errors of the past.

But importantly, not all of German law was destroyed by the war. Germany's private law establishment, consisting of the Civil Code, the courts that apply it, and a rich scholarly tradition built around the whole enterprise, survived the war largely intact.[7] A bias in favor of private law is said to be "a characteristic feature of the civilian tradition," and certainly it is hard to overestimate the role the Code has played in the German legal imagination (Ebke and Finkin 1996, 8). In its fundamentality to the German legal order and the esteem in which it is held, the Code itself has a quasi-constitutional character. Germany's Basic Law drafters worked against the backdrop of this private law world revolving around the Code, and it deserves some attention at the outset.

When Germany unified in 1871, the production of a national civil code became a top priority, an exercise in legal reform and nation-building simultaneously. Leading legal scholars worked for more than twenty-five years to hammer together a code that distilled the principles of the Roman *ius commune* into a comprehensive logical structure. The intellectual work that went into the codification was immense: the eminent English legal historian Frederick Maitland commented that "[n]ever, I should think, has so much first-rate brain power been put into an act of legislation" (Zimmermann 2006, 29). The imperial Parliament approved the German Civil Code (*Bürgerliches Gesetzbuch*) (BGB) in 1896, and it took effect on January 1, 1900.

The Code consisted of 2,385 sections divided among five books: the general part, the law of obligations, rights in rem, family law, and succession. The general part laid out universalistic legal principles at a high level of abstraction, with specific provisions in each of the other books offering norms to govern successively narrower legal issues. In its specific provisions, the Code did not scruple to regulate intrusively, specifying, for instance, the conditions under which gifts are to be returned in the case of a broken engagement.[8] The Code's insistence on extracting general rules wherever possible means that answering a given legal question requires consulting the rules found in several different sections of the Code, with their application governed by the principle *lex specialis derogat legi generali* (the more specific rule controls the more general one) (Ebke and Finkin 1996, 9–10). The civilian method for resolving concrete disputes by reference to the German Civil Code, then, turns out to be a fairly

7. Civil law "largely retained its normative core" during the Third Reich, although Nazi commentators urged that the general clauses should be used as "entry points" for Nazi ideology (Stolleis 1998, 17). As Michael Stolleis notes, Nazi authorities considered breaking the Civil Code into separate statutes and eliminating its general part, but never accomplished this.

8. Bürgerliches Gesetzbuch Aug. 18, 1896, Reichsgesetzblatt [RGBl.] 195, § 1301.

demanding and technical enterprise requiring real facility with the structure of the Code.

The codification movement also unleashed a torrent of doctrinal scholarship to help guide judges on the application of individual provisions. One bibliography published in 1899—that is, *before the Code even went into effect*—contained roughly 4,000 works (Zimmermann 2006, 15). Although the Code applied to private law, the sheer expansiveness of its scope and its role as a focal point both for the German nation-building project and a generation's scholarly efforts conferred on the Code a certain constitutional quality of its own.

The elaboration of the Civil Code was entrusted to a network of civil law courts. These operated through war, defeat, and reconstruction with only limited interruption.[9] Until the end of the war, the court of final appeal for civil and criminal law matters was the Imperial High Court or *Reichsgericht*. After the war, the *Reichsgericht* was reincarnated as the Federal Court of Justice (*Bundesgerichtshof*), Germany's supreme court for civil and criminal matters. The Court of Justice, which was up and running nearly a year before the Constitutional Court, regarded itself as Germany's supreme judicial authority. The Court of Justice self-consciously cultivated its links to its prestigious predecessor the Imperial High Court, even celebrating its seventy-fifth anniversary in 1954—never mind that the Court of Justice itself began operation in 1950 (Henne 2006b, 16). Moreover, as the final interpretive authority on the Civil Code, the Court shared in the reflected glory of that celebrated centerpiece of the German legal establishment.

By contrast, the fate of Germany's public law was caught up in Great Power politics for years after the end of the war.[10] Early expectations that Germany might be reassembled into a single state were derailed by the deepening of Cold War divisions, as the United States committed to a policy of containment, and the Soviet Union, to the global struggle of socialism against capitalism (Fenske 1994, 92). By the fall of 1947, when the foreign ministers of the occupying powers failed to reach agreement about the future of Germany, it was clear that the eastern and western portions of Germany would be going separate ways. More than three years had passed since war's end when the military governors of the

9. As Supreme Commander of the Allied Forces, Dwight D. Eisenhower declared all courts in Germany closed in March 1945, and courts began reopening as early as May 1945 (Stolleis 1998, 171–72).

10. In Hans Fenske's phrase, "German constitutional politics would be made in Washington, Moscow, London, and Paris" (Fenske 1994, 81). Politics, constitutional and otherwise, resumed at the state (*Land*) level in comparatively short order: occupying powers administered elections for state and local governments starting in January 1946 and presided over the enactment of state constitutions (Fenske 1994, 84).

three Western occupying powers instructed the premiers of the German states (*Länder*) to convene a constitutional convention, to draw up a constitution for a new government for the territories under Western control (Kröger 1993, 18–19).

Work on West Germany's new constitution began in August 1948, with a committee of constitutional experts convened by the *Länder* at the Herrenchiemsee palace in Bavaria to develop a discussion draft (Kröger 1993, 20).[11] The Herrenchiemsee draft served as a starting point for the deliberations of the constitutional convention, which convened in Bonn, the new capital, the following month. The group meeting in Bonn was called the Parliamentary Council and consisted of sixty-five delegates from the *Länder*, plus five nonvoting delegates from Berlin (Kröger 1993, 19, 21). Most members of the Council, who were selected to the position from the legislatures of the *Länder*, had political experience, although many were academics, particularly law professors.[12] The Basic Law that the Council produced was ratified by all the *Länder* except Bavaria in May 1949. There are two features of the Basic Law that are of particular importance for our purposes: its charter of rights and its provisions for the judiciary (and in particular, the Constitutional Court).

Breaking decisively with the atrocities of the Third Reich, the Basic Law's drafters agreed on the importance of entrenching human rights in the constitution (Kröger 1993, 111). Signaling the primacy of rights to the new order, the Basic Law opens with a robust roster of constitutional rights. Articles 1 and 2 in particular underscore the centrality of rights protection to the German constitutional project. Section 1 of Article 1 states that "[h]uman dignity shall be inviolable. To respect and protect it shall be the duty of all state authority."[13] Section 2 declares that "the German people therefore acknowledge inviolable and inalienable rights as the basis of every community, of peace and of justice in the world," and Section 3 declares that "the following basic rights shall bind the legislature, the executive, and the judiciary as directly applicable law."

Taken as a whole, Article 1 establishes the indefeasibility of one particular norm, the guarantee of human dignity; declares more broadly the fundamentality of human rights; and commits the German state to recognize those rights. Notably, Article 1 does not suggest that these rights might be binding on parties

11. The conferees believed themselves to be drafting a temporary document, a constitutional stopgap: Herman Brill's comment that the legal order they were outlining would last "hopefully for only two or three years" reflected the general sentiment (Fenske 1994, 103).

12. The occupying powers intervened in the Council's work occasionally, usually to encourage greater financial federalism (Heun 2011, 11).

13. Technically, the human dignity protection is not a right, but a guarantee, and the highest value of the Constitution. Bundesverfassungsgericht [BVerfG] [Federal Constitutional Court], 109 Entscheidungen des Bundesverfassungsgerichts [BVerfGE] 279, 311 (Mar. 3, 2004).

other than public officials: it is "the legislature, the executive, and the judiciary" who are bound by these rights. However, by obligating "all state authority" to "respect *and protect*" human dignity,[14] Section 1 suggests the possibility that the state may have an affirmative duty to act so as to secure human dignity against threats posed from sources outside the state.

Article 2 likewise signals the ambitious scope of Germany's new human rights agenda. Article 2, Section 1 declares that "[e]very person shall have the right to free development of his personality insofar as he does not violate the rights of others or offend against the constitutional order or the moral law." As discussed below, the GFCC would interpret the scope of this right expansively in the early landmark *Elfes* case.

The Basic Law's rights catalog continues with a roster of familiar liberal rights, including rights to life and physical integrity (Article 2, Section 2); equality before the law (Article 3, Section 1); freedom of faith and conscience (Article 4, Section 1); freedom of religious practice (Article 4, Section 2); conscientious objection from military service (Article 4, Section 3); and the freedom of expression (Article 5, Section 5). Rights to assembly (Article 8); free association (Article 9); freedom of movement (Article 11); freedom to choose an occupation (Article 12); the inviolability of the home (Article 13); and property (Article 14) are also guaranteed. Some of these other rights are expressly qualified as well: for instance, free expression rights "shall find their limits in the provisions of general laws, in provisions for the protection of young persons, and in the right to personal honour" (Article 5, Section 2). The enumeration of rights concluded with a provision that set conditions on any limitations of rights. Article 19 provides that any allowable restrictions on rights must be of general applicability (Section 1) and not affect the essence (*Wesensgehalt*) of the right (Section 2).

A broad consensus in the Parliamentary Council supported the inclusion of these classic liberal rights (Kröger 1993, 26). However, the Council divided sharply over the constitutional recognition of rights relating to the family, with delegates from the conservative Christian Democratic Union (CDU) and Christian Social Union (CSU) parties pushing for them and those from the Social Democratic Party (SPD) opposed.[15] The CDU and CSU prevailed, and the Basic Law recognized "special protection from the public order" for marriage and the family (Article 6, Section 1); the right—and duty—of parents to raise their children (Article 6, Section 2), mothers' claim to "the protection and care of the community (*Gemeinschaft*)" (Article 6, Section 3), and parents' rights to provide their children religious education (Article 7, Section 2).

14. Emphasis added.

15. The CSU is the CDU's regional affiliate in Bavaria.

Notably, the sections of the Basic Law pertaining to family and marriage seem to presuppose that constitutional rights can be more than classic defensive rights against the state. The "special protection" for marriage and the family recognized in Article 6, Section 1 suggests that the state is obligated to take some affirmative step to secure marriage and the family against outside threats. The other provisions in Article 6 seem to impose obligations on the community vis-à-vis mothers and obligations on parents to care for their children. In time, the Constitutional Court would hold that Article 6 did not by itself create directly justiciable rights against the parents.[16] But what is significant for present purposes is that there are rights provisions in the Basic Law that seem to require for their fulfillment certain behaviors from nonstate actors, whether mediated by state action or not.

The Basic Law makes clear that the rights it recognizes are not merely "programmatic" in nature, as were the rights of the Weimar Constitution: generic considerations to be borne in mind in the ordinary course of government (Murkens 2013, 148). Rather, the rights are justiciable legal entitlements: they "bind the legislature, the executive, and the judiciary as directly applicable law" (Article 1, Section 3). The true import of these rights depends on the institutions and routines the Basic Law establishes for enforcing rights and, in particular, on the Constitutional Court.

A CONSTITUTIONAL COURT IN A PLURAL JUDICIARY

The debate in Germany over the organization and competencies of the GFCC, and the relationship of that Court to other institutions, was contentious. It was also long-running, playing out not all at once, but over the course of three crucial junctures involving three different groups of participants, all of which resulted in important decisions about the Court. The issue of designing the Court was first joined at the Herrenchiemsee conference among the assembly of constitutional experts, continued in the Parliamentary Council, and was only finally settled two years after the Basic Law took effect, with the passage of the statute establishing the Court. Two factors in particular informed the design choices ultimately made: the existence of other court systems and the history of judicial review in Germany.

In addition to the *Reichsgericht*, prewar Germany had an administrative court system, a labor court system, and a financial court. The Basic Law established successors for all of these courts in the Federal Republic of Germany, as well as the GFCC and a court for social security and related matters. All

16. 121 BVerfGE 69, 94 (Apr. 1, 2008).

told, there were six apex courts: besides the GFCC, a Federal Court of Justice (*Bundesgerichtshof*, the successor to the *Reichsgericht*); the Federal Administrative Court (*Bundesverwaltungsgericht*); the Federal Financial Court (*Bundesfinanzhof*); the Federal Labor Court (*Bundesarbeitsgericht*); and the Federal Social Court (*Bundessozialgericht*).[17] The courts other than the GFCC are known as the *Fachgerichte*, courts responsible for a specific (nonconstitutional) field (*Fach*) of law. The Basic Law declared that each would be the supreme court for its respective field of law.

The drafters' choice to maintain and expand Germany's system of specialized courts meant the GFCC would take its place in a crowded landscape of multiple court systems operating in parallel. Precisely how the GFCC would relate to these other apex courts was an important issue that the Parliamentary Council largely sidestepped. Except for the GFCC, each apex court sat at the pinnacle of a hierarchically organized pyramid of lower courts over which its rulings were binding. Among the apex courts, however, no hierarchy was stipulated. Nor does the Basic Law specify whether the GFCC would have the power to review other courts' rulings on constitutional issues, or indeed, how cases would come before the Court.[18]

The designers of the GFCC also had to grapple with the complicated history of judicial review in Germany. German legal scholars traditionally distinguished between the power of constitutional review (*Verfassungsstreitigkeit*)—namely, the power to decide constitutional disputes between different branches or organs of government—and the power of judicial review (*richterliches Prüfungsrecht*)—the power of courts to invalidate legislation, or other forms of state action, for inconsistency with the constitution, including violations of individual constitutional rights (Kommers and Miller 2012, 4–6). Constitutional review was a familiar institution in German legal history; judicial review, less so. The idea that there should be a neutral forum for settling constitutional disputes among governmental institutions makes sense in a political federation where the component states retain many of the incidents of sovereignty, and this characterizes not only the Holy Roman Empire but also the German Confederation that

17. GG art. 95.

18. The Council did, however, establish that the GFCC would have an important power over all other judges: the power of removal. Delegates of the SPD pushed for a wide-ranging removal power for the GFCC, "to protect the people from an abuse of [judicial] independence" (Niclauß 2006, 125). SPD delegates worried that ordinary judges could undermine the new regime in the manner of the reactionary Weimar judges and wanted a mechanism to ensure that their decisions measured up to core democratic values (Niclauß 2006, 125). In the end, the Council reached a compromise wherein the GFCC could remove lower court judges, but only by a two-thirds majority vote, and only for offenses against the constitution or the constitutional order (GG art. 98(2)).

succeeded it in the early nineteenth century.[19] Constitutional review had deep roots in the German conception of constitutional monarchy, and it survived Germany's transition to republicanism after World War I, as the 1919 Weimar Constitution vested the power of constitutional review in a new body, the *Staatsgerichtshof* (State High Court) (Kommers and Miller 2012, 5).

Judicial review—the power of courts to overturn laws on constitutional grounds—had a shorter and more controversial history. Although the Weimar Constitution did not grant any courts the power of judicial review, the *Reichsgericht* and other federal high courts asserted the power of judicial review in the 1920s and used it to strike down important pieces of legislation (Kommers and Miller 2012, 6). In the views of many, the courts exploited the power of judicial review to advance a reactionary agenda, reasserting the norms of the old regime as embedded in natural law to roll back the liberalization favored by parliamentary majorities (Stolleis 2004). From the first, then, the antidemocratic potentialities of judicial review were on full display in Germany.

Germany's new regime, however, would have to feature both judicial review and constitutional review: the Allies' military governors made their wishes on the subject clear.[20] But quite apart from the Allies' views, the commitment to a justiciable roster of constitutional rights was widely shared among the Basic Law's framers (Henne 2005, 199). But because judicial review and constitutional review were considered fundamentally different activities in Germany, some had grave concerns about combining the two functions in a single body. Constitutional review was understood to be, at some level, an irreducibly political activity, drawing a tribunal inexorably into the thicket of interbranch politics. By contrast, judicial review incident to ordinary litigation was widely (if somewhat simplistically) regarded as an activity more within the conventional core competence of courts, of applying law by the lights of traditional judicial methods (Kommers 1976, 74). Combining the two functions in a single body raised a risk of cross-contamination: of judicializing politics, politicizing the administration of justice, and undermining the legitimacy of the tribunal. At the same time, splitting the authority to interpret the constitution

19. Already in 1495, the Holy Roman Emperor Maximilian I established the *Reichskammergericht* for settling disputes among the many monarchs who were part of the empire (Kommers and Miller 2012, 4; Stern 1980, 7).

20. An aide-memoire to the Parliamentary Rat indicated that "the constitution should provide for an independent judiciary to review federal legislation, to review the exercise of federal executive power, and to adjudicate conflicts between federal and land authorities as well as between land authorities, and to protect the civil rights and freedom of the individual" (Kommers 1976, 70).

authoritatively among multiple bodies raised concerns about consistency and administrability.

The Parliamentary Council handled the controversial issue in part by compromising and in part by kicking the can down the road. The Basic Law did vest the GFCC with powers of both constitutional review and judicial review. In the end, the delegates agreed to vest jurisdiction over all constitutional disputes in the GFCC, but also to provide for the creation of a Supreme Court (*Oberstes Bundesgericht*), responsible for maintaining the uniformity of federal law.[21] By confining the powers of constitutional review and judicial review to the GFCC, the framers hoped at least to preserve the "absolute purity of the legal domain" of the Supreme Court (Kröger 1993, 27). (Ultimately, however, the Supreme Court was never established, and the Basic Law was amended in 1968 to remove mention of it.) But the Council left the internal organization of the Court almost totally undefined, so that it was not clear from the Basic Law whether, for instance, the same Justices would handle constitutional review and judicial review (Laufer 1968, 62).

This was one of a number of contentious issues on which the delegates punted, by adopting vague formulations that would need to be sharpened in the implementing legislation (Kommers 1976, 77). As originally enacted, the Basic Law gave no indication whether the Court would have the power of abstract review—that is, review of legislation prior to enactment—or concrete review—review incident to the application of legislation—or both. The qualifications of Justices was another contentious issue left largely unresolved by the Council.[22] With respect to the Court's composition, the Basic Law provided only that the Court would be staffed by a mix of judges from the ordinary judiciary and "other members." Half were to be chosen by each of the two houses of Germany's Parliament, the *Bundestag* and *Bundesrat*. Delegates also divided on the question of whether the Court's rulings should have the force of general law,

21. Of the twelve kinds of disputes over which the Court had jurisdiction, the four most important were: constitutional disputes arising between the *Länder* (Article 93, Sections 1.3, 1.4), constitutional disputes between organs of government at the national level (Article 93, Section 1.1), review of both *Land* and national legislation for conformity with the constitution (Article 93, Section 1.2), and determinations whether political parties were opposed to the free and democratic order in Germany, and hence, unconstitutional (Article 21, Section 2) (Kröger 1993, 27). Article 93, Section 2 provided an avenue for subsequent expansions of the Court's jurisdiction, declaring that the Court "shall also rule on such other matters as shall be assigned to it by a federal law."

22. While some favored requiring all to meet the qualifications for professional judges, Carlo Schmid of the SPD warned that the "*déformation professionelle*" of traditional judicial training might impede Justices' performance of their distinctive duties as members of a constitutional court (Niclauß 2006, 120).

as opposed to having binding legal effect only for the parties before the Court.[23] Again, they left the final decision to the legislature: Article 94 provides that the legal effect of Court rulings would be decided by statute.

It took almost two years after ratification of the Basic Law in May 1949 for the Parliament to produce a statute that settled these matters. But for advocates of a strong court, the Constitutional Court Act (*Bundesverfassungsgerichtsgesetz*) was probably worth the wait. The statute established the Court as an "autonomous and independent" constitutional organ and created many paths of access to the court, which were open to a broad set of stakeholders. The government, the *Bundestag*, the *Bundesrat*, and the *Länder* were all authorized to bring challenges to the constitutionality of legislation when their interests were affected. Lower courts could certify constitutional questions of law to the GFCC for decision: directly, in the case of the apex courts, or by way of their respective apex court, in the case of the lower courts. The Court was authorized to issue advisory opinions, when requested by the agreement of *Bundestag, Bundesrat*, and government. Further, the statute makes clear that the Court's power extends not only to overturning legislative acts on constitutional grounds, but executive and judicial acts as well (Section 95). And notably, the statute further provides that the decisions of the court "bind all constitutional organs of the Federation and the States as well as all courts and authorities." This itself represents a significant grant of authority to the court, which distinguishes it not only from other courts in Germany (Heun 2011, 7) but also from the Austrian Constitutional Court, whose rulings were not binding on all other courts (Jestaedt 2011, 112).

The statute established two Senates, each with twelve members (lowered by subsequent amendment first to ten and then eight). As a palliative for concerns about combining constitutional review and judicial review in a single body, the statute largely divided the tasks among the two Senates, with the first taking responsibility mostly for constitutional challenges to legislation, and the second mostly for mediating interbranch disputes. This division of labor was compromised, however, within a few years. The first Senate's workload vastly outstripped the second's, and hobbled it in the performance of its duties (Kommers and Miller 2012, 18-19). The Court sought relief from the legislature and received it in the form of a 1956 statute that transferred part of the first Senate's docket—including some constitutional rights claims—to the second Senate (Kommers 1976, 101; Lembcke 2006, 158). Subsequently, the Plenum itself adjusted the allocation between the two Senates, shifting still more categories of cases to the second Senate (Kommers 1976, 101). These changes blurred the

23. The SPD faction proposed that decisions invalidating statutes have the force of general law and be published in the federal legal gazette, just like statutes passed by the Parliament (Kommers 1976, 76). The conservatives opposed the proposal.

neat institutional division between judicial review and constitutional review, which many of the Basic Law's framers had regarded as an important safeguard against the judicialization of politics and the politicization of judging.

Crucially, the statute did provide for an individual constitutional complaint. Section 90(1) established that "any person who claims that one of his basic rights or one of his rights under Articles 33, 38, 101, 103 and 104 under the Basic Law has been violated by public authority can raise a constitutional complaint to the GFCC."[24] Section 90(2) stipulated that claimants are required to exhaust available remedies before pursuing a constitutional claim, but then noted that this requirement may be waived in cases of serious hardship or when the issue at stake is of general importance. The Constitutional Court Act afforded the right of constitutional complaints not only to individuals, but in some cases to local governments as well (Section 91). From the start, the constitutional complaint was conceived of as a device for expanding individuals' opportunities to participate in governance (Gusy 2006, 211).

INSTITUTIONAL CONTEXT AND CONFLICTS

In many respects, Germany's Constitutional Court was born under auspicious conditions. The Court was created as an "autonomous and independent" constitutional organ, equipped with fairly wide-ranging powers of both abstract and concrete review. Its rulings were to be regarded as binding law. It was given authority to interpret a constitution that guaranteed a large number of rights, some of which seemed written to promise more than a right against infringing action from the state.

But however powerful the Court might appear on paper, as a practical matter, its position in the new German state was far from secure. The Court faced some obstacles to its effectiveness just by virtue of being a court. As forums for dispute resolution, courts are fundamentally reactive institutions. The Constitutional Court could act only when activated by outside parties, and lacking power over the sword and the purse (to borrow Alexander Hamilton's vivid metaphor), could provide "merely judgment" (Hamilton et al. 2013, 466).

But the Constitutional Court faced some additional challenges particular to its own circumstances. While the Constitutional Court Act had resolved many contentious questions about the Court's powers and role, some important questions remained open. For instance, it was not clear whether and to what extent the Court was to be organizationally subordinate to the Ministry of Justice.

24. The rights in the listed articles concern political participation and due process. The right to resist efforts to overthrow the constitutional order was later added to the list.

Questions of the relative authority of rulings of the Constitutional Court and Germany's other apex courts were also unresolved.

Especially in the context of a newly established state, competition among institutions for position and authority can take on a zero-sum quality, since the patterns set early on structure future interactions. And the Constitutional Court faced competition not only from other branches but also from within the judicial branch, owing to the proliferation of apex courts. To the extent that matters might fall within the shared competence of the GFCC and other bodies, any reductions in the Court's authority would redound to the benefit of its rivals (Laufer 1968, 140–41). And specifically with respect to any jockeying for position that would occur within the judicial branch, the Court faced the further disadvantage of being a latecomer to its own legal system. The Federal Court of Justice was up and running for more than a year before the GFCC and thus positioned to accrue first-mover advantages (Garlicki 2007, 50; Jestaedt 2011, 79–80).

The Court's responses to these institutional challenges in the first decade of its existence would prove decisive for its role in the state and for the shape of constitutional law. This section describes with more specificity the challenges the Court faced to its authority from executive and judicial institutions. This background helps to illuminate the strategic logic of the Court's horizontal effect doctrine, as introduced in the *Lüth* decision, which is described at the start of the next chapter. The Court's aggressive and canny articulation of the doctrine of horizontal effect was a crucial element of its campaign to make the Basic Law indispensable to the German legal system, and itself indispensable to the stewardship of the Basic Law.

The story of Germany's experience harbors a more general lesson about the political logic of rights in systems of centralized constitutional review. Stated to a first approximation, the lesson is this: specialized constitutional courts have an incentive to apply constitutional rights expansively, including horizontally, because when a court's only job is to interpret the constitution, the court is only as relevant as it makes the constitution. But the lesson is indeed only true to a first approximation. In order for its strategic logic to hold, a court will need both an opportunity to apply rights horizontally and access to tools for policing compliance among lower courts. The GFCC had both.

Interbranch Conflicts: The Constitutional Court Versus the Adenauer Regime

From the first months of its operation, the GFCC found itself locked in a series of battles with the new nation's executive branch over the Court's proper place in the constitutional hierarchy. The conflict played out in the context of a number of discrete disputes that stretched over the better part of a decade. The government of Germany's first postwar Chancellor, Konrad Adenauer, was determined to limit the independence of the GFCC and to subordinate it to a measure of political control.[25]

It was in response to the government's efforts to subordinate it that the Court first began to narrate its own ambitious conception of its role in the state. In all of these conflicts, the Court found opportunities to tell a consistent story about itself. On this telling, what distinguished the Court from every other public institution was its role as "guardian of the constitution": its unique fiduciary relationship to the country's highest law. This privileged relationship to the Basic Law meant that the Court was simultaneously relevant to the world of ordinary politics, since political outcomes must conform to the constitution, and above it—which also meant being above political criticism.

The question of how much independence the GFCC should have from the Ministry of Justice had been a controversial one from the first, and drafters of both the Basic Law and the Constitutional Court Act had left the issue unresolved. Adenauer's Justice Minister, Thomas Dehlers, took steps early on to integrate the Court into the administrative apparatus of the executive branch, asserting authority over all questions of court administration, including the budget and the appointment of staff.[26] For the Justices of the new Court, this kind of subordination to the executive was intolerable.

And the Court let Dehlers know its views, in a remarkable and remarkably public way. On June 27, 1952, President of the Court Hermann Höpker-Aschoff presented to the Federal President, the Presidents of the *Bundestag* and *Bundesrat*, and the Chancellor a so-called *Statusdenkschrift* (Status Memorandum) in response to Dehlers's moves.[27] The memo argued that, as "Supreme Defender of the Constitution," the GFCC was "vested with the highest authority." In practical terms, what this meant was that the Court needed to control its own budget, make its own personnel decisions, and manage its own administration (Lembcke 2006, 152; Baldus 2005, 239–40; Vorländer 2006, 190). The memorandum demanded that the government and the *Bundestag* correct these constitutional deficiencies legislatively.

25. Under the Basic Law, Germany has both a Federal Chancellor, who leads the government in power, and a Federal President, who acts as head of state.

26. Dehlers's assertion of administrative control meant that, for instance, if the Court wanted to take up contact with the *Bundestag*, the *Bundesrat*, or the Federal President, it needed to route this communication through the Ministry of Justice (Baldus 2005, 239).

27. The document, originally drafted by Justice Gerhard Leibholz, was delivered to the Chancellor personally by Höpker-Aschoff and the Court's Vice President, Rudolf Katz (Baldus 2005, 239).

The dispute continued for a year, but ultimately, the stand-off was resolved through outside intervention. Adenauer and Dehlers cannily engaged the services of an eminent constitutional law professor, Richard Thoma, to offer a second opinion to the Court's constitutional analysis. But the Court rejected Thoma's critique out of hand: the Court was not offering an academic theory; in its capacity as an organ of government, it was demanding a correction to constitutional problems (Lembcke 2006, 154). By mid-1953, a majority in the *Bundestag* was no longer willing to stand with Adenauer in his opposition to the Court's demands. Increasingly, the opposition and the *Länder* largely supported judicial review, seeing it as a means by which they could attain policy aims currently out of reach (Vorländer 2006, 194). The *Bundestag* passed legislation to provide the organizational independence the Court sought. And Höpker-Aschoff hastened the end of Dehlers's career as Justice Minister, insisting to Adenauer in 1953 that he would step down from the Court if Dehlers were reappointed (Baldus 2005, 242).

The conflict over the *Statusdenkschrift* strengthened the Court's hand (Lembcke 2006, 151). And at root, the contending arguments of Höpker-Aschoff and Thoma reflected fundamentally different views of the deeper meaning of judicial review, with the Court's victory amounting to a vindication of its position. The government and Thoma regarded judicial review as just another species of specialized jurisdiction: the GFCC specialized in constitutional claims in the same way that the Labor Court specialized in labor issues and the Administrative Court specialized in administrative issues. But for Höpker-Aschoff, the Court was fundamentally different, because the law it interpreted authoritatively was the supreme law. The "dignity" of the Basic Law, in Carlo Schmid's phrase, extends to encompass its supreme interpreter, the GFCC (Lembcke 2006, 153–54).

The Court also became a central player in a high-profile, protracted dispute over a key foreign policy objective of the Adenauer government: the establishment of a European Defense Community.[28] Members of the SPD opposition in Parliament sought a declaration that German legislation ratifying the treaty was unconstitutional, as it involved German rearmament. As a petition for abstract review of legislation, the matter was addressed to the First Senate of the Court, known colloquially as the "Red" Senate for its supposed left-leaning tendencies. Seeking to head off a ruling, the Adenauer government convinced Federal President Theodor Heuss to request an advisory opinion on the constitutionality of the legislation (Lembcke 2006, 155). This move reflected political calculations of its own: advisory opinions were issued by the Plenum—both

28. For a fuller discussion, see Collings (2015, 14–28).

Senates sitting together—and so the Second Senate, also known as the "Black Senate" on account of its believed Christian Democratic tendencies, could be expected to neutralize the First.

The GFCC declined the invitation to play partisan politics—or perhaps, it chose to play institutional politics instead. The Court chose to take up the opposition's abstract review request first, but ruled it inadmissible. Before the Court had ruled on the advisory opinion request, Adenauer announced yet another challenge in the Court, seeking to preempt what it now feared would be an adverse ruling from the plenum. The new proceeding, brought by the Christian Democratic majority in the *Bundestag* at the end of 1952, was styled as a conflict between organs within Parliament, an *Organstreit*, which would be handled by the (presumptively sympathetic) Second Senate rather that the First.[29] The Court's own rules indicated that it would handle conflicts between government organs ahead of advisory opinion requests, and so the challenge amounted to a canny effort to leverage the Court's own procedures and political divisions in the service of partisan objectives (Collings 2015, 20).

The Justices, however, put institutional solidarity over short-term political preference satisfaction. In a remarkable statement that Höpker-Aschoff read in advance of oral arguments just days after Adenauer's announcement, the Court decried both efforts to manipulate its procedures to political ends and suggestions that nonlegal factors influenced the Court's decisions. The Court went on to rule that it would consider the advisory opinion request before the *Organstreit*, and moreover, that an individual Senate cannot deviate from a ruling issued by the Plenum—rendering the *Organstreit* proceeding irrelevant (Lembcke 2006, 156).[30] Thoroughly routed, the government withdrew its request for an advisory ruling (Lembcke 2006, 157).

The Court and the Adenauer government clashed over several other issues,[31] but the conflict over the regulation of television deserves special mention because it presented the Court with an opportunity to define the proper bounds of interbranch discourse *about* the Court. In late 1959, Adenauer's cabinet proposed a statute that would create a new broadcasting corporation under national control. Several of the *Länder* challenged the constitutionality of the statute, on both federalism and freedom of expression grounds. In a ruling issued in February 1961, the Second Senate of the GFCC upheld the

29. The Court would later clarify that different factions within a chamber of Parliament do not count as distinct organs of the state for purposes of the *Organstreit* procedure.

30. BVerfGE 2, 143 (March 7, 1953).

31. See Lembcke (2006).

constitutional complaint and dissolved the broadcasting corporation, drawing a bright line rule that the national government could provide broadcasting technology but not control the content or organization of broadcasting. The ruling was naturally popular with the *Länder*, confirmed now in their belief that a strong Constitutional Court could be a powerful ally for the cause of federalism.

Just as predictably, it found no favor with the national government, and Adenauer went so far as to publicly criticize the ruling as "wrong" (*falsch*), prompting a remarkable rebuke from the Court. In a public statement, the President of the Court, Gebhard Müller, declared that other constitutional organs were not to publicly declare that rulings of the Court were not in keeping with the law (Lembcke 2006, 157–58). This rebuke also echoed an earlier one: in 1953, President Höpker-Aschoff went on the radio to complain that Justice Minister Dehlers's public critiques of the Court's jurisprudence amounted to inappropriate political interference in the administration of justice (Baldus 2005, 242). By policing how political officials could talk about the Court, its leaders reinforced the message that the GFCC was not of the world of politics and that evaluating its decisions on the plane of politics represented both a category error and a constitutional delinquency. After Müller's statement, the Adenauer government never publicly criticized a decision of the Court as wrong again.[32]

Intrajudicial Conflicts

If the early Constitutional Court fought, and prevailed in, conflicts with the Adenauer government, it also faced hostility and opposition from elsewhere *within* the judicial branch. As one court within a complex ecology of different courts, the GFCC faced challenges to its monopoly over constitutional construction. The challenges played out in several episodes over a period of years, with particularly pointed challenges coming from two courts in particular: the

32. Another attempt to make the Court more responsive to the government also redounded to the Court's autonomy. In the mid-1950s, the Adenauer government proposed reducing the number of Justices to nine but increasing the proportion who came up through the ordinary judiciary and requiring only a simple majority of votes in the *Bundestag* to confirm Justices (Lembcke 2006, 159). The latter proposal in particular raised concern among the Justices about the Court's independence. The legislative compromise that emerged, however, resulted in a reduction to ten judges in each Senate (with a future reduction to eight), a two-thirds supermajority requirement for judicial confirmation, and the creation of an advisory council to propose candidates for the Court. The council ended up enhancing the Court's role in the selection of its own members, since it tended to propose candidates who met with the sitting Justices' approval (Lembcke 2006, 159).

Federal Court of Justice and the Federal Labor Court. Seen in this broader context, the GFCC's choice to make rights horizontal appears as an important—indeed, essential—element within a larger, long-running campaign to secure the Court's position relative to these other courts.

Improving and Controlling Access to Constitutional Review

A court that does not control its docket does not control its fate (Fontana 2013). In order to have national relevance and impact on its own terms, an apex court needs both a large pool of potential cases and some discretionary power to deny review (or at least full review) when it chooses. As described above, the Constitutional Court Act granted wide-ranging powers of review to the GFCC. And 1956 amendments to the statute enhanced the Court's discretion by permitting the establishment of three-judge chambers within the Senates (Kommers and Miller 2012, 20). The chambers perform an initial review of cases, and they may dispose of claims that present no realistic prospect of success.[33] But the Court took important steps in the first years of its operation to further expand its reach and consolidate its control over constitutional review.

The GFCC's early recognition of the *Urteilsverfassungsbeschwerde*—a constitutional complaint (*Verfassungsbeschwerde*) arising out of a judicial decision (*Urteil*)—was an essential prerequisite for its coming confrontations with other apex courts. The Constitutional Court Act granted individuals the right to bring a constitutional complaint to the Court when their rights were violated. In one of its first decisions, the Court recognized that a judicial decision can itself be the source of a constitutional injury that is remediable through a constitutional complaint.[34] In other words, the *Urteilsverfassungsbeschwerde* creates the rough equivalent of a right to appeal the rulings of ordinary courts to the GFCC when they raise constitutional questions.

This procedural device would prove important because litigants have no other means of breaking out of the silos of Germany's coordinate court systems. The general rule in Germany is that appeal is not possible from one branch of the judiciary to another, and courts have a *Kompetenz-Kompetenz*: the power to decide questions of their own jurisdiction. As a consequence, "if the court first approached in one branch holds that it does or does not have jurisdiction with

33. Later statutory changes also permitted the three-judge chambers to resolve cases on the merits, without referring them to the full Senate, when all three Justices agree on the result and the case can be resolved under existing Senate precedent. The chambers dispose of 95 percent of all complaints, vastly amplifying the Court's capacity to process cases (Kommers and Miller 2012, 21).

34. Bundesverfassungsgericht [BVerfG] [Federal Constitutional Court], 1 Entscheidungen des Bundesverfassungsgerichts [BVerfGE] 4 (Sept. 28, 1951).

respect to a dispute, the courts in all other branches are bound by such decision" (Singh 2010, 186). The *Urteilsverfassungsbeschwerde* constitutes an escape hatch that litigants could use to access the GFCC from a legal proceeding in a different court.

If the *Urteilsverfassungsbeschwerde* permitted the GFCC to sit in judgment of ordinary courts' rulings, the so-called advisory opinion dispute (*Gutachten-Streit*) effectively blocked the other apex courts from weighing in on disputes before the GFCC. As originally drafted, the Constitutional Court Act required that trial courts relay any references through the apex court at the top of their hierarchy, rather that approaching the GFCC directly with constitutional questions (Baldus 2005, 243). When they received these referrals, many of the apex courts adopted the practice early on of taking a crack at the constitutional issue themselves and appending their advisory opinion to the referral for the GFCC's consideration. The Court of Justice in particular seemed to delight in offering its own constitutional opinions, setting up a special senate for constitutional questions with up to sixty judges, and publishing some of its constitutional opinions in its court reporter or academic journals (Baldus 2005, 243).

At the beginning, the GFCC seemed to welcome the input of the other courts, and the Court signaled its approval of the practice first in a circular and later in one of its own opinions (Baldus 2005, 243). But by the middle of the 1950s, the Court had soured on other courts' participation in constitutional decision making. The opportunity to express its new position came in 1955, when the Finance Court of Rheinland-Pfalz directly certified a constitutional question to the GFCC, bypassing the Federal Finance Court, in violation of Section 80 of the Constitutional Court Act.[35]

In its response,[36] the Court turned away the request for a ruling, in accordance with the procedures set down in the Constitutional Court Act. But its order of dismissal also included a bombshell: referring courts are not permitted to offer their own opinions when passing on constitutional references. The Court's order touched off an open conflict between the GFCC and the other courts, which played out in court reporters and legal journals.[37] Ultimately,

35. The question concerned when precisely an old imperial statute was effectively readopted as federal law under the new regime.

36. 4 BVerfGE 358 (Nov. 30, 1955).

37. The presidents of the nonconstitutional apex courts took the unprecedented step of composing a joint statement in opposition to the GFCC's ruling and publishing it in leading legal journals. According to the statement, the GFCC is fixing a problem that does not exist: there is no potential for conflict between the decision of the Court and the advisory opinions, because advisory opinions by definition lack the force of law. The Court's new policy of muzzling all other courts' consideration of constitutional issues reduces those courts to "mere couriers

the *Bundestag* stepped in to resolve the conflict, in a manner favorable to the GFCC. The 1956 amendments to the Constitutional Court Act eliminated the apex courts' roles in the referral process altogether, providing that lower courts can apply immediately to the GFCC for a ruling on a constitutional question.[38] With an assist from the Parliament, the GFCC had successfully consolidated its monopoly over constitutional review. A side effect of the legislative fix was to strengthen the alignment of interests between the lower courts and GFCC, at the expense of the apex courts. When a *Land*-level finance court elects to bypass the Federal Finance Court to seek a constitutional reference from the GFCC, for instance, it enhances both its own role in structuring and deciding disputes and the GFCC's, at the expense of the Federal Finance Court's.

The Federal Supreme Court

The GFCC faced a formidable judicial rival in the Federal Court of Justice, Germany's supreme court for civil and criminal matters. The Court of Justice regarded itself as Germany's supreme judicial authority, and as noted above, it boasted several natural advantages, including a year's head start in establishing its authority in the new republic and the borrowed prestige of the old *Reichsgericht* and the Civil Code itself. What is more, the Court of Justice had an extraordinary norm-generative capacity: with scores of judges apportioned among twelve senates, the Court was well positioned to control the production of law in Germany.

As noted above, the Court was especially ardent to offer its own opinions about constitutional law, until the GFCC put an end to the practice in 1955. But the Court also called upon a different source of norms that threatened to trump the authority of the constitution, and thus the GFCC. Led by President Hermann Weinkauff, the Court of Justice advanced a renaissance of natural rights thinking in civil law. Heavily influenced by Catholic, and specifically Thomist, teachings, the Court under Weinkauff articulated a jurisprudence in which positive law was undergirded and animated by a system of universal, divinely inspired values (Henne 2006b, 15). The Court's universalism had a

between the lower courts and the Federal Constitutional Court" and "works an injustice to the development of our own judicial authority."

The GFCC did not take the criticism lying down. In a response published in the most prominent journal, the *JuristenZeitung*, Justice Franz Wessel accused the judges of making a number of errors, and emphatically rejected the idea that Section 80 of the Constitutional Court Act offered an opportunity for the nonconstitutional courts to help carry the burden of constitutional interpretation (Wessel 1956, 94).

38. Gesetz zur Änderung des Gesetzes über das Bundesverfassungsgericht [Law to Amend the Constitutional Court Statute], June 21, 1956, Bundesgesetzblatt [BGBl.] I at 662–66.

distinctly conservative cast in that the set of values was largely drawn from the traditional teachings of the church. Notably, the Court used its natural rights reasoning to reaffirm many traditional gender roles in law, even as the Court remedied some gender disparities, as required by Article 117 of the Basic Law (according to which laws inconsistent with the equality of men and women were invalid after the end of March 1953).[39]

Natural law reasoning poses an implicit challenge to constitutional supremacy, since by their own terms, natural law values occupy a still higher place in the hierarchy of norms than constitutions. The GFCC met this challenge by developing its own doctrine in a way that simultaneously explained why the Federal Republic need not have recourse to natural law and amplified the reach of constitutional values. The opportunity presented itself in the *Elfes* case of 1957.

Wilhelm Elfes, a prominent politician expelled from the ranks of the CDU over foreign policy, contested the constitutionality of the denial of his passport renewal, which he sought in order to attend a foreign conference. In its decision,[40] the GFCC found against Elfes's claim that the denial violated his rights under Basic Law Article 11, which guarantees free movement "within the federal area." But on the way to reaching that result, the Court articulated a robust conception of the scope of constitutional values.

Article 11 does not protect a right to travel abroad, held the Court. "However, the freedom to travel abroad does not evade some measure of constitutional rights protection, as an exercise of the basic right to general freedom of action." Specifically, traveling abroad is part of the freedom protected by Article 2, Section 1, which guarantees to each person the right to the free development of personality, so long as doing so does not infringe the rights of others or offend against "the constitutional order" or good morals. Decisions that infringe upon that liberty are therefore subject to judicial scrutiny, to test conformity with the constitution.

In opting for a construction of the Article 2, Section 1 right in "the broadest sense," the Court effectively rendered the protections of the Basic Law gapless: freedoms not named within its text are nonetheless encompassed by the right to free development of personality. The Court sharply rejected a purely procedural reading of Article 2, Section 1—that it protects only against procedurally deficient infringements on freedom of action—and in so doing,

39. For instance, the Court upheld the provision of the criminal law making it a crime for unmarried persons to share a hotel room, on the grounds that such conduct is "unchaste." Bundesgerichtshof [BGH] [Federal Court of Justice], 6 Entscheidungen des Bundesgerichtshofs in Strafsachen [BGHSt] [Decisions of the Federal Court of Justice in Criminal Matters] 44 (Feb. 17, 1954).

40. 6 BVerfGE 32 (Jan. 16, 1957).

outlined a conception of constitutional rights that rendered natural rights reasoning superfluous:

> The Basic Law has erected a value-oriented order that limits public power. This order secures the independence, self-responsibility, and dignity of persons in the state community. Laws are not necessarily constitutional merely because they are produced by formally constitutional procedures. They must also be substantively in accord with the highest fundamental values of the free democratic order, the constitutional order of values. . . . Above all, the laws may not violate human dignity, which is the highest value in the Basic Law, but they also may not infringe on the spiritual, political, and economic freedom of individuals so much so that would undercut their essence. It follows that the constitution preserves for each individual citizen a sphere of private life definition, that is, each individual possesses a last frontier of untouchable human freedom, from which the operation of the whole of public power is withdrawn. A law that reaches into that sphere cannot be considered a part of the legitimate constitutional order, and must be held as void by the Federal Constitutional Court.[41]

Elfes's strong endorsement of the conception of rights as values (as opposed to entitlements) was extraordinarily consequential across multiple dimensions. First, it decisively closed the door to the fraught, Weimar-era debates between strict positivism and natural law by offering a new way forward. Natural law recommended itself in part as a corrective to the value-neutral jurisprudence of Weimar-era liberalism, under which the constitution possessed no defenses against Nazism. Like natural law thinking, *Elfes* offers the prospect of a committed, value-oriented jurisprudence, but one in which the values are drawn from the Basic Law itself. And when the constitution is read to enthrone an order of values in the law, there is no need to look beyond the law, as the Court of Justice had been doing. The older court's natural law turn suddenly becomes irrelevant, if not downright silly.

Second, *Elfes* paved the way for future developments in the Court's rights doctrine, including the adoption of horizontal effect. Treating rights as values implies a jurisprudence with certain features, including balancing, and facilitates an expansive conception of the scope of rights, since values can have relevance without necessarily trumping other norms.[42] The breadth of

41. 6 BVerfGE 39, 40.

42. Textual support for a balancing approach comes from Article 2's limitation clause, which permits the free development of personality to be limited when use of the right "violate[s] the rights of others or offend[s] against the constitutional order or the moral law."

the value of self-determination identified in *Elfes* implies that a significant portion of government action will implicate a constitutional question, in that many restrictions on individuals' residual liberty will impinge, to some degree, on their free development of personality. Strategically, *Elfes*'s conception of rights made sense for a Constitutional Court seeking to define a robust role for constitutional rights, and hence itself, in the face of efforts by the Court of Justice to become the supreme judicial authority in Germany. It also provided a firm foundation for the GFCC's coming expansion of the domain of rights in *Lüth*.

The Court of Justice's dalliance with natural law had run its course by the end of the 1950s. The most important cause behind its turn from natural law was the retirement of President Weinkauff in 1960. Weinkauff's successor, Bruno Heusinger, had little interest in carrying forward the natural rights project, and the "renaissance" drew to a close (Henne 2006b, 16). But certainly a contributing factor to the demise of natural rights thinking in German law was the work the GFCC had done to obviate natural law reasoning. In the face of a challenge from the emerging natural rights jurisprudence, the GFCC had articulated an account of constitutional rights that offered an alternative to strict positivism without the confessional metaphysics of the natural rights movement.

The Federal Labor Court

The GFCC faced competition of a different sort from the Federal Labor Court. Rather than drawing on a rival set of peremptory norms that implicitly challenged the supremacy of constitutional rights, as the Court of Justice had done, the Labor Court advanced a novel and expansive view of the scope of constitutional rights, effectively branding itself as an alternative source of constitutional adjudication. Starting in the mid-1950s, the Labor Court began applying constitutional norms *directly to private parties* to resolve labor disputes. In other words, the Labor Court advanced the doctrine of direct horizontal effect.

This effort was spearheaded by the President of the Court, Hans Carl Nipperdey, the leading labor law scholar of the day.[43] Nipperdey's freedom to pursue such a significant doctrinal innovation was afforded by his own elevated stature in German legal circles and the fact that labor law doctrine at the time was, compared to civil law, "unsystematic and lacking internal unity" (Henne 2006b, 20). Nipperdey believed that to achieve the social order the Basic Law erected, private parties as well as public entities must

43. For a detailed discussion of Nipperdey's jurisprudence, see Hollstein (2007).

respect certain constitutional rights. As he explained in the *Zölibat* (Celibacy) decision:

> Originally, fundamental rights were intended to protect the freedom of the individual against incursions by the power of the state. Since that time, however, their meaning has changed and expanded. . . . A number of constitutional rights do not merely guarantee individual freedom against the power of the state, but rather are ordering principles for society, which have immediate significance even for the private legal dealings of citizens amongst one another. The Senate [of the Court] has also previously indicated, that private law agreements, legal transactions and undertakings may not be set in opposition to that which one may call the ordering structure, the *ordre public* of the actual political and legal regime.[44]

And so, in that case, the Labor Court invalidated on constitutional grounds employment contracts that provided a woman's employment would terminate upon her marriage.[45] The Court explicitly declined to strike down such termination clauses more conventionally, using the public policy or good morals general clauses.[46] Instead, the Court held that such a contract conflicted with the constitutional protections given to the right to marry, under Article 6, Section 1. Moreover, the Court held that the contract conditions also infringed the residual freedom protected by Article 2, Section 1.

Although the Labor Court's doctrine that some Basic Law rights directly imposed duties on private parties sometimes yielded enhanced rights protection for some litigants, the constitutional theory that underwrote those outcomes was in some respects anti-individualistic and antiliberal. As the passage above reflects, in Nipperdey's view, the value of constitutional rights lay in the contribution they made to maintaining the legal and social order more broadly. Individuals were bound to observe constitutional norms when such strictures served to uphold the public order and the common good. Some have argued that this orientation toward the priority of collective interests over individual interests reflects a holdover from the labor law doctrines of the Third Reich, which were not expunged so thoroughly as in other areas of law (Henne 2006b, 21). Whether or not the hypothesized linkage to Nazi jurisprudence is really

44. Bundesarbeitsgericht. [BAG]. [Federal Labor Court], Neue Juristische Wochenschriftt [NJW] 1957, 1688, 1689 (May 10, 1957).

45. *Id.*

46. Bürgerliches Gesetzbuch [BGB] [Civil Code], Aug. 18, 1896, Reichsgesetzblatt [RGBl] 195, as amended, § 826.

fair, at the very least it is clear that for the Labor Court, rights' importance lay largely in how they underwrote social goods and not individual freedom.

The idea that constitutional rights imposed duties directly on private parties reflected the Labor Court's statist orientation to the project of constitutionalism. However, it did not necessarily dictate different outcomes in concrete cases than the indirect method the GFCC would adopt in *Lüth*. But the doctrine of direct effect did have strategic and symbolic value for the Labor Court. Holding that the Basic Law rights directly apply in labor law "dissolves the hierarchy of constitutional and other law" (Henne 2006b, 24). The Labor Court's ruling is a constitutional ruling: the Court is claiming that the result reached is constitutionally compelled. By contrast, if the Court were instead to take the position that the Constitution applies indirectly, exerting some influence on how labor law is interpreted, then its holding is demoted to judge-made ordinary case-law, made in consideration of constitutional values. If that is the approach, "the court that has the core responsibility for interpreting the constitution stands at the peak of the pyramid, has a higher priority, and the power of the last word on the matter" (*Letztentscheidungskompetenz*) (Henne 2006b, 24). As described in the next chapter, the GFCC would soon retake that high ground.

3

Constitutional Cascades in the Federal Republic

MAKING RIGHTS HORIZONTAL

By the late 1950s, the German Federal Constitutional Court (GFCC) had taken important first steps to establish its place in Germany's postwar regime, vis-à-vis other branches of government and other courts alike. But the other institutions of government did not cede ground willingly. In particular, the Labor Court was horning in on the Constitutional Court's turf, by deciding labor law disputes on constitutional grounds.[1] The *Lüth* case became a vehicle by which the Constitutional Court cemented both its own status as a constitution organ *primus inter pares* and the status of the Basic Law as the cornerstone of German society, by adopting a new doctrine that gave horizontal effect to constitutional rights.[2]

1. The Court of Justice also did so to a more limited extent, finding support in the Basic Law's protection of personality for damages actions for serious nonpecuniary harms to personality interests, notwithstanding the Code's limitation of actions to pecuniary harms. Significantly, the Court of Justice regarded protection for personality rights not as an imposition of the Basic Law, so much as a constitutional recognition of values immanent in the private law. See Bundesgerichtshof [BGH] [Federal Court of Justice], 13 Entscheidungen des Bundesgerichtshofes in Zivilsachen [BGHZ] [Decisions of the Federal Court of Justice in Civil Matters] 334 (May 25, 1954); see also 20 BGHZ 345 (May 8, 1956). The most famous case was the *Herrenreiter* (Dressage Rider) case, which concerned a professional equestrian whose picture was used, without his permission, on packaging for a pharmaceutical product that promised to increase the user's sexual potency. See Ebke and Finkin (1996, 19); 26 BGHZ 349 (Feb. 14, 1958).

2. Bundesverfassungsgericht [BVerfG] [Federal Constitutional Court], 7 Entscheidungen des Bundesverfassungsgerichts [BVerfGE] 198 (Jan. 15, 1958).

Background

The backstory of the *Lüth* case begins in the Third Reich. Veit Harlan, "the [Nazi] regime's favorite film director," was engaged by Joseph Goebbels to make propaganda films, including notoriously "*Jud Süss*" ("The Jew Süss"), which Goebbels described in his diary as "an anti-Semitic film such as we could only dream of" (Kuhlbrodt 2005, 66). Although Harlan was tried after the war for making "*Jud Süss*," he continued to work as a director and continued to find an audience. In 1950, he released a new film, "*Unsterbliche geliebte*" ("Immortal Beloved") an adaptation of a Theodor Storm novel.

Not everyone welcomed Harlan's postwar comeback. At the opening of German Film Week in September 1950, Erich Lüth, director of the Hamburg press club, called on theater owners and viewers to boycott "*Unsterbliche geliebte*" on account of Harlan's wartime propaganda (Riedlinger 2005, 148–49). Harlan's production company and distributor filed suit in November 1950 against Lüth in Hamburg civil court, seeking to enjoin Lüth from calling for the boycott of the film.

The complaint alleged the boycott threatened to destroy the production company's and distributor's business, as well as Harlan's ability to practice his trade as a director. The complaint alleged that this sort of interference with trade was in violation of German Civil Code (*Bürgerliches Gesetzbuch*) (BGB) provisions, notably Section 826, which proscribes intentionally inflicting damage on a person in violation of public policy,[3] under penalty of liability for restitution (Henne and Riedlinger 2005, 459). Lüth defended himself by arguing, among other things, that his call for the boycott was protected by the constitutional right to free expression and that this outweighed Harlan's right to the free development of his personality, given the substantial public interest in open engagement with this topic of national importance (Henne and Riedlinger 2005, 460–61).

In November 1950, the court issued a preliminary order against Lüth, ordering him to give up the boycott. The court's decision relied heavily on civil law precedent that boycotts intended to prevent others from practicing their trade violate public policy. Lüth appealed the preliminary order to the Higher Regional Court in Hamburg and lost, even as prominent civic figures around Hamburg declared their support for him.[4] The trial court issued its final ruling in November 1951, confirming the substance of its decision from the previous year.

3. The German phrase is *gegen die guten Sitten*, which is more literally translated as "against good morals."

4. Lüth's appeal was heard by the second chamber for civil matters, which happened to be staffed by a number of former Nazi Party members (Riedlinger 2005, 161, 162–63).

In its new ruling, the court waded into the merits of Lüth's condemnation of Harlan. Harlan's acquittal on war crimes charges established as a matter of law that he was not guilty of the charges made against him, but rather, acted as an "unwilling tool" of the regime (Henne and Riedlinger 2005, 284). In the court's view, Lüth's boycott was contrary to good morals because the criminal court's acquittal of Harlan absolved him of moral as well as legal responsibility for "*Jud Süss*" (Henne and Riedlinger 2005, 485).[5]

Represented now by the high-profile Adolf Arndt, the "crown jurist" of the SPD and an architect of the GFCC, in late 1951 Lüth filed a constitutional complaint with the GFCC, which had only just begun operations, as well as a further appeal to the Higher Regional Court (Riedlinger 2005, 176). The complaint alleged that Lüth's Article 5 right to free expression had been violated by the lower courts' rulings ordering him to stop the boycott. Although Lüth had not yet exhausted all legal remedies in the lower courts, the complaint urged the Court to accept review, arguing that Lüth's claim satisfied the exhaustion exception for matters of importance to the broader public.

Arndt's argument for waiving exhaustion was closely related to his argument on the merits: it was important for *Germany* that Lüth be able to communicate his message about Harlan. What was at stake in this case, Arndt argued, was not merely Lüth's freedom of conduct but the freedom of expression in Germany. Arndt articulated for the Court a theory of Article 5 that linked an individual entitlement to collective, public, and democratic ends: "The constitutional right of freedom of expression has a social character, and guarantees a subjective public right to participate in forming public opinion through intellectual activity and to take part in determining the character of the state the people will form" (Riedlinger 2005, 179). Sidelining Lüth from this important debate over Germany's Nazi past inflicts a constitutional injury on him, of course, but the harm is broader.

In April 1952, the Court agreed to accept the case, although it would not hand down its ruling for nearly six years.

The *Lüth* Decision

When a judicial decision stresses its own moderation and modesty, it's usually a sign that something big is afoot. In *Lüth,* the Court denied any intention of settling the "controversial" questions of whether and how constitutional rights

5. Ironically, considering that he was sued for interfering with Harlan's business, Lüth's boycott was probably the best thing to happen to "*Unsterbliche geliebte*." The boycott drew massive publicity to the movie, which ultimately sold an astonishing nine million tickets (Kuhlbrodt 2005, 67).

norms affect the private law. Instead, the Court positioned itself as offering a reasonable, middle-ground approach between the absolutist answers that other judges and scholars had offered to those questions. The Court characterized these other positions—either that constitutional rights apply against the state only, or that at least some constitutional rights apply to every person engaged in private legal conduct—as "extreme views." In particular, the Court singled out the conclusions that the Labor Court's *Celibacy* decision drew as "go[ing] too far."

In constructing a third way, the Court offered a different conception of what constitutional rights are, one that draws on the important distinction in German law between subjective and objective legal norms. Elaborated most famously by fin de siècle legal theorist Georg Jellinek, a subjective public right entitles an individual to some action or omission in his or her interest on the part of the state (1892). Objective norms of public law are also binding on the state, but they are not personal to any individual, and as a result cannot usually be vindicated by an individual suit against the state.[6]

Lüth offers a kind of quantum theory of constitutional rights, in which rights simultaneously exist on the planes of subjective law and objective law. The Court first confirmed the conventional view, that constitutional rights are primarily subjective rights: "Without a doubt, the constitutional rights are in the first instance intended to secure the individual's sphere of freedom against infringements by public authorities: they are defensive rights of the citizen against the state." At the same time, the Court makes clear, the Basic Law does not establish a value-neutral order. Rather, the Basic Law's charter of rights sets up "an objective order of values" (*objektive Wertordnung*) that finds expression in an enhanced role for constitutional rights. At the core of this order of values, according to the Court, lie human dignity (as guaranteed in Article 1) and personality rights (as recognized in Article 2), and this "system of values" must serve "as a foundational constitutional commitment for all spheres of law."

This has profound implications, also for private law disputes. The value system "naturally influences the civil law as well; no provision of the civil law can stand in contradiction to it, and each must be interpreted in its spirit." But even as the Court asserts the relevance of constitutional rights to adjudication under the Code, the Court is careful to circumscribe its own role in the review of civil courts' decisions. A dispute between private parties over rights and duties

6. A terminological difficulty arises because in German, the word *Recht* translates as both "right" and "law." I refer to "subjective public rights" but "objective norms of public law" because in English, it sounds odd to refer to a "right" where there is no rights-holder.

under the civil law "remains materially and procedurally a civil law dispute"; only, the content of the civil law must be interpreted to reflect the influence of constitutional values. The principal "portals" through which constitutional values enter the civil law are the general clauses, such as Section 826 of the Civil Code, which themselves make appeals to values outside of the civil law (such as good morals). The civil judge must interpret and apply these clauses with an eye to the constitutional values embodied in the constitutional rights. This is precisely what it means for civil judges to be bound by the constitutional rights, as provided for under Article 1, Section 3 of the Basic Law.

The Constitutional Court does not sit over the civil courts as a court of revision or "superrevision," to correct errors in the application of law. Rather, the Court's role is only to judge the "radiation effect" (*Ausstrahlungswirkung*) of the constitutional rights on the civil law and to bring to effect the content of the constitutional provision.

At the same time, the Court makes clear that the fact that the Basic Law contains an explicit reservation clause for the free expression right—Article 5, Section 2 permits expression to be limited by general laws—does not mean that *any* limit on expression imposed by a provision of the Civil Code will pass muster. Rather, general laws must themselves be interpreted in light of the constitutional values that they limit. The right and the law limiting the right therefore have a reciprocal effect (*Wechselwirkung*) on each other, in that the law not only limits the right, but the right also sets limits on how much the law can permissibly infringe. In other words, the civil court has to balance the values protected by the constitutional right and the interests advanced by the civil law provision. The decision must be based on a comprehensive consideration of the relevant factors in the case at hand, and "an incorrect weighing can create a constitutional injury and ground a constitutional complaint to the Constitutional Court."

The rest of the Court's opinion carefully considers the legally protected interests at stake on both sides in the dispute between the film companies and Lüth, and their analysis by the lower courts. The Court concludes that the trial court failed to recognize Lüth's constitutionally protected interest in free expression where it came into conflict with the private interests of the plaintiffs.[7] The lower court's ruling therefore violated Lüth's constitutional right and was void.

7. Whereas the Court was receptive to the constitutional interests that Lüth pleaded, it was fairly dismissive of Harlan's. Harlan claimed his own right to the free development of his personality was infringed by a boycott that made it harder for him to work as a director. The Court avoided having to balance this interest against Lüth's by ruling that Harlan's Article 2 rights would be implicated only if he was excluded from his profession entirely.

Making Sense of *Lüth*

The *Lüth* decision received little public attention when it was handed down, but among sophisticated public lawyers, it was acknowledged from the start as a watershed event (Collings 2015, 59). Today, *Lüth* is universally regarded as one of the cornerstones of German constitutional law. In addition to inaugurating Germany's horizontal effect doctrine, *Lüth* laid the groundwork for a second defining feature of German constitutional jurisprudence: the embrace of balancing. If the values encoded in rights radiate through the law, the task of the judge becomes to mediate between these and competing interests. Thanks in substantial part to *Lüth*, starting in the 1960s, constitutional adjudication in Germany increasingly became a matter of balancing the interests and values at stake (Bomhoff 2013, 82).

The *Lüth* decision raises two main questions for present purposes. First, why did the Court grant horizontal effect to constitutional rights? Second, why did it do so in the way it did, by treating rights as creating an objective order of values that radiated through law?

From a strategic perspective, the decision to give horizontal effect to Lüth's expression right makes sense. There was a normative gap in the ordinary law that could plausibly be filled with a constitutional norm, and bringing the constitution into play served the Court's interests.

Extending the reach of constitutional rights was a way for the GFCC to assert and enhance its relevance in the face of efforts by other courts and the executive branch to cabin its influence. Allowing rights to apply in private law disputes meant bringing more cases within the scope of the Court's jurisdiction. The broad access to constitutional review provided by the Court's organic statute, amplified by the Court's early recognition of constitutional complaints against rulings of other courts, meant that such moves would, as a practical matter, expand the Court's docket and influence: specifically, because these procedural features meant that other courts could not act as gatekeepers to the GFCC or hope to ignore its rulings with impunity. Moreover, the GFCC had some natural allies in the lower nonconstitutional courts and the *Länder*, institutions whose interests the Court could champion against the federal government's top judicial and political authorities, which otherwise faced little check. Under these circumstances, it is hardly surprising that the Court had moved to give an expansive reading to the scope of rights already in *Elfes*, the year before *Lüth*.

Furthermore, a liberal political sensibility had begun finding broader favor in West Germany by the late 1950s, making an expansive application of free expression rights seem less anomalous than it would have a few years prior. Ulrich Herbert and other historians have argued that German intellectual and political elites in the immediate postwar period tended to regard the Nazi "catastrophe" not as a specifically German phenomenon but as a consequence of modernization, the rise of mass society, and the decline of religious moorings.[8] For many, it followed that the way out of the abyss lay in a return to the deeper German past, rebuilding society on a foundation of traditional religious and cultural values (Herbert 2003, 20–21).[9] But by the mid-1950s, Germany was enjoying political stability, extraordinary economic growth, and rising prosperity. As modernity and democracy came to look increasingly attractive, the rush to embrace the values of the past diminished in urgency, and the "anesthesia" of the immediate postwar period began to wear off (Herbert 2006, 97, 97–99; Lepsius 1983).[10]

Herbert sees in the mid- to late 1950s the prelude to the high phase of liberalization in Germany, which he dates from 1959 to 1973/1974 (which—not coincidentally—overlaps almost perfectly with the period of the Constitutional Court's most active innovation in horizontal rights doctrine) (Herbert 2003, 14).[11] One way in which this sociopolitical shift registered in the law was in the legal reform effort in the late 1950s to decriminalize deviations from traditional family arrangements and sexual practices (Herbert 2003, 14). Emerging liberal sensibilities were also reflected by the media, as a new generation of TV journalists promoted a critical engagement with topics of public affairs, turned unaccustomed scrutiny on the actions of political elites, and focused "to an increasing degree on the pervasive avoidance of a concrete coming-to-terms with the Nazi past" (Herbert 2003, 28).

The private law, however, lagged behind the emergent demand for protection of free expression rights in the public sphere, as the civil court rulings in

8. The eminent historian (and committed anti-Nazi) Friedrich Meinecke influentially advanced this view in his 1946 book *The German Catastrophe* (Meinecke 1946).

9. Herbert likens the "conservatism modernization" of the immediate postwar period to the tradition-oriented mindset of late Wilhelmine Germany (Herbert 2003, 39).

10. To give one marker of this development: on five occasions between 1949 and 1963, public opinion polls in Germany asked respondents which of four constitutional rights was the most important: freedom of religion, freedom of expression, freedom from fear, or freedom from want. In 1949, freedom from want was the clear leader, with 35 percent of respondents choosing it. Starting in the late 1950s, the number of respondents who listed freedom from want as the most important right started falling, with only 15 percent choosing it in 1963. The number naming freedom of expression as the most important right increased steadily throughout the period, going from 26 percent in 1949 to a remarkable 56 percent in 1963—more than chose the other three rights put together (Eberlein 1968, 102). Similarly, a 1964 poll asked registered voters to rank order a set of values. "Freedom" took first place, ahead of order and prosperity (Eberlein 1968, 106).

11. Similarly, Jürgen Habermas writes of a "fundamental liberalization" that gripped Germany, though he identifies the student movement of 1968 as the catalyst (Herbert 2003, 7).

the *Lüth* case demonstrated. Lüth's complaint served up to the Court a normative gap in the ordinary law that could plausibly be filled with a constitutional norm. The extraordinary six-year delay in the Court's ruling is suggestive that the Court itself appreciated how the timing of its ruling mattered to how it would be received.[12] In 1952, the war was less than a decade in the past. West Germany was still scrambling to escape from postwar privations, and few were in a mood to revisit the transgressions of the Third Reich, as the Adenauer administration's successful lobbying for the abrupt ending of "denazification" in 1951 underlined. Moreover, the Constitutional Court in 1952 was a new and fledgling institution, ill-equipped to take on the civil law establishment and popular sentiment simultaneously. The picture was very different, however, in 1958, when liberal democracy was more mature and self-confident in West Germany, and the Court itself had spent the past six years building its own stature (Collings 2015, 134).

If *Lüth*'s decision to recognize rights' horizontal effect was consequential, the specific doctrinal framework it crafted to regulate their effect was what really shaped the decision's impact. *Lüth*'s recognition of the dual character of rights—that they have both objective and subjective dimensions—is what makes it possible for rights to influence private law (as objective values) without binding private actors (as subjective entitlements). Their horizontal effect on private actors is indirect, as it is mediated through the Civil Code.

The Court did not pull the idea that rights have indirect horizontal effect out of thin air. Even before the Basic Law had taken effect, legal journals were publishing pieces on constitutional rights' possible impact on the private law from prominent legal scholars such as Helmut Coing and Herbert Krüger (Ruffert 2001, 10). The work that most clearly prefigured the Court's approach was offered by a young law professor in Tübingen named Günter Dürig, in a 1956 article (Dürig 1956; Vitzthum 2005, 349–51; Cherednychenko 2007, 71). Dürig endorsed indirect effect over direct effect owing to concern that the latter would result in constitutional law, in effect, swallowing the private law.

Lüth's recognition of rights as values also echoes the integrationist constitutional theory of Rudolf Smend, first propounded during the Weimar Republic and paraphrased in the *Lüth* decision. Smend's approach to constitutional law was heavily indebted to his political theory. Smend rejected the perspective, advocated by the school of state law positivism dominant in the Weimar years, that the state was merely a legal person. Rather, the state was the site where individuals joined together—were integrated—into a shared life

12. It is true that the Court's docket was overloaded in 1952 (Riedlinger 2005, 181, 183), but this does not suffice to explain the delay: most complaints filed in 1952 did not wait six years for decision.

experience (Jacobson and Schlink 2000, 210). As Smend described in his 1928 book *Constitution and Constitutional Law*, the constitution was to serve as a "stimulus and channel" (*Anregung und Schranke*) for this process of integration (195).

Smend's teleological orientation had implications for how courts should interpret the constitution. Constitutional interpretation should be fluid rather than rigid, aimed at minimizing tensions between different provisions, meeting the state's evolving needs, and promoting the unity of the whole (Jacobson and Schlink 2000, 210). Constitutional rights were important, in Smend's view, as sources for the shared values that define life in the state (Jacobson and Schlink 2000, 210). Indeed, Smend is responsible for the insight, which is central to the *Lüth* decision, that the fundamental rights are not only subjective individual rights but values (Forsthoff 1964, 157).[13] On this view, fundamental rights cannot be treated like the personal property of rights-holders, to be asserted or not as they please, but have an objective character that in some sense is independent of the rights-holders.[14] One of Smend's students, Wilhelm Hennis, worked in the chambers of Arnold Arndt, and his contributions to Lüth's filings played an important role in transmitting these ideas into the *Lüth* litigation (Henne

13. As Ernst-Wolfgang Böckenförde noted, "[I]t is no longer generally appreciated that the value theory of the basic rights has its starting-point in Rudolf Smend's integration theory" (Böckenförde 1991, 188). In a recent book, Jacco Bomhoff traces the Constitutional Court's debt to Smend in detail (2013, 94–122).

14. Smend's Weimar-era theory was long on abstractions and short on specifics about constitutional doctrine or method. It also had statist and antiliberal tendencies, owing to its single-minded focus on the use of the constitution to achieve the unity of the state. To some extent, though, what now look like statist and antiliberal elements are best understood as reactions against particular features of Weimar-era legal theory. Smend conceived of his theory as an antidote to state law positivism, which, owing to its value-neutrality, was incapable of raising any defenses against the antidemocratic forces that threatened to tear the Weimar Republic apart. Smend's integration theory, by contrast, was emphatically non-neutral on the question of the Republic's continued existence. A constitutional theory that prizes integration so highly perhaps makes the most sense when the legal order threatens to disintegrate.

After the war, Smend reworked his ideas for the new era and became an influential teacher in Göttingen until his retirement in 1969. After the Basic Law was enacted, Smend became less blasé about disregarding constitutional text in the service of the unity of the state (Günther 2004, 166). Now the constitution itself, not the state, became the focal point of integration for Smend. And this implied a hugely important role for the Constitutional Court, as the institution that could fulfill the Basic Law's promise of integration (Günther 2004, 166–70). As Frieder Günther characterized the view of Smend and his followers, constitutional rights functioned as "individual, freedom-enhancing elements of a comprehensive, objective order of values, which gave its stamp to the entire commonwealth as its ethical basis" (Günther 2004, 171).

2006a, 143).[15] But Hennis was not the only channel for Smend's ideas: Justice Gerhard Leibholz was also influenced by Smend's integration theory (Henne 2005, 213–14; Wiegandt 1995, 201–02).

The idea that rights are not only individual entitlements but also values is in many ways a radical one. As former German Federal Constitutional Court Justice Brun-Otto Bryde has argued, it makes sense that this model of rights would originate during the Weimar era, when constitutional rights were not justiciable. Smend's theory of rights was just that, a theory, and not intended to be operationalized in litigation (Bryde 2007). As the Justices of the Constitutional Court would discover, this way of conceptualizing rights had considerable potential to disrupt existing dispute-resolution practices.

Assessing the Doctrine of Indirect Horizontal Effect

If this helps explain where the Court found the raw materials for its doctrine, it still does not explain why the Court chose to give indirect horizontal effect to constitutional rights, instead of declaring them directly applicable. And even as the doctrine of indirect horizontal effect solves some problems, it creates others of its own. First, there is a problem of justiciability. The Constitutional Court is authorized to hear constitutional complaints in which an individual alleges that one of his or her basic rights have been violated.[16] To the extent that a right is not creating a legal obligation that is owed to an individual, but is instead a person-independent legal norm, whence does a given individual derive the right to bring a constitutional complaint? The Constitutional Court has never given a consistent and satisfactory answer to this question (Ruffert 2001, 67).

More generally, some have argued that the *Lüth* approach amplifies problems of legal uncertainty. At least conventionally, a subjective right has some particular content: as defined by Jellinek, a subjective right has something as its object—some particular thing or act in which the right's holder has an interest (1892, 40).[17] An objective legal norm that radiates through the legal system, by

15. Hennis, who would later gain prominence as one of Germany's leading political scientists, argued that the right to free expression had to be given broad protection in a democracy, as the exchange of views on matters of public interest was the lifeblood of democratic politics (Hennis 2005, 192–93). For Hennis, the operative distinction that should determine when constitutional protection flowed did not concern the identity of the parties, but the expressive content of the communication. In Hennis's view, speech in the public sphere, not the private sphere, merited constitutional protection, no matter the source of the threat (Henne 2006a, 146).

16. GG art. 93, sec. 4a.

17. For a sophisticated discussion of constitutional rights as subjective rights in English, see Alexy (2010, 111–62).

contrast, is arguably something more slippery. Although the Court has subsequently backed away somewhat from the radiation effect language (Jestaedt 2011, 138), the concern persists.

Perhaps most important, although the Court characterizes the doctrine of direct effect as an "extreme view," several scholars have argued that, as a practical matter, indirect and direct effect could amount to the same thing. Mattias Kumm, for instance, has argued that "a doctrine of indirect horizontal effect . . . seems to have much the same consequences, substantively and institutionally, as the embrace of a doctrine of direct horizontal effect" (Kumm 2006, 357). This is so because in either case, the reviewing court is under an obligation to ensure that the challenged legal provision or action comports with the Basic Law. Substantively, of course, it is not immediately obvious what exactly it means for a private law norm or private legal action to comport with the Basic Law. But the key point is that constitutional rights' implications for private action do not, or at least *need* not, turn on the distinction between direct and indirect effect. Even if constitutional rights bind private actors directly, it does not follow that the obligations that they impose are identical to the obligations they impose on state actors. Similarly, the Court could take different positions on how much deference it owes to the legislature's or ordinary court's judgment about what is constitutionally required, but there is no reason why this choice (which relates to institutional competence) should turn on whether rights have direct or indirect effect (Kumm 2006, 357).

Some aspects of the indirect approach to the horizontal effect of rights thus are perplexing or unsatisfying from a jurisprudential perspective. But doctrine does not do all of its work on a jurisprudential plane. In addition to justifying the outcome of the case under review, a court's formulation of doctrine sets the argumentation framework that filters cases prospectively. It organizes how the issues will be presented for resolution and also contributes to a broader metanarrative about the court and its role in governance. Viewed from these perspectives, the GFCC's choices make much sense.

As an argumentation framework, the *Lüth* decision's doctrinal formulation created some potentially useful strategic ambiguity for the Court. If no one could say precisely what it meant for rights, as objective values, to have a radiation effect on the whole of law, that could also work to the advantage of a court working its way carefully through unfamiliar terrain. As Matthias Ruffert has explained, the open-endedness of the Court's formulation meant that a broad range of different substantive outcomes could credibly be characterized as faithful applications of the *Lüth* approach:

> The *Lüth* decision's key statements about the substantive legal relationship between constitutional law and private law are at the same time unequivocal

> [in their rejection of direct effect] and vague. . . . The Court leaves open how this will work concretely, how widely rights will influence the interpretation of private law, and therefore, also what this means substantively for the decision of individual cases where this arises. It makes sense to see in this open-endedness one of the chief reasons for the consistency of the jurisprudence on the horizontal effect issue since the *Lüth* decision. The construction of indirect effect creates a wide range of discretion for the one applying the law, because it does not specify the content for the "modification of the private law" [that it requires], which in individual cases occurs through interpretation of private law in private-party legal relations. This makes it possible to fill the rationes decidendi of the *Lüth* decision at different times with different contents (Ruffert 2001, 16).

Moreover, the doctrine of indirect horizontal effect reinforced and harmonized two, potentially contradictory, elements of the normative narrative that had already begun emerging from the Court's jurisprudence: the centrality of rights to the whole of the legal order and the Court's commitment to appropriate judicial restraint. As objective norms, rights were not confined to intersubjective legal relations, but instead pervaded the entirety of law. And at the same time, declaring that rights only have indirect effect underscored the narrative that the Constitutional Court respects the autonomy of the private law and the role of the civil law judiciary. Rather than explicitly displacing the normative structures of the private law, the Court in effect offered a way to leave them in place, and to let them be animated by constitutional principles. Had the Court given direct effect to constitutional rights, it would be hard pressed to say (as it does in *Lüth*) that:

> From the point of view of substantive and procedural law a dispute between private citizens on the rights and duties that arise from rules of conduct thus influenced by the basic rights remains a dispute of private law. It is private law which is interpreted and applied even if its interpreters must follow the public law of the constitution.[18]

The indirect approach thus paid lip service to the autonomy of the private law even as, as a practical matter, it subordinated it to constitutional rights.

Lüth set the terms for the GFCC's engagement with the horizontal effect of rights. In the years after, in a series of cases, the Court refined and extended the logic of *Lüth* to further amplify the disruptive, transformative effect of

18. Translation from Markesinis and Unberath (2002, 394–95).

constitutional rights. These moves set the stage for a constitutional cascade in which lawmakers, litigants, and other courts increasingly turned to rights reasoning, altering the nature of lawmaking in Germany.

The following sections trace these developments in the context of three substantive areas of law: free expression law, family law, and antidiscrimination law.[19] These are by no means the only areas in which rights have had substantial effects on private-party relationships: horizontal effect has significantly shaped, among other subjects, freedom of contract, property law, the law of remedies, and labor law (Ruffert 2001; Schmidt 1995). But focusing on developments in these areas facilitates comparative analysis with the other case studies.

Moreover, these three areas lend themselves particularly well to highlighting important features in Germany's experience with the horizontal effect of rights. The Constitutional Court's freedom of expression jurisprudence shows how it repeatedly expanded the effects that constitutional rights can have on private law matters, increasing the extent to which private-party relationships were subject to regulation by rights, even as it offered reassurances about the limits of its review over nonconstitutional courts. In the area of family law, the Court's jurisprudence and its reception by civil law courts showcase the disruptive and jurisgenerative effects constitutional rights have had in adjudication under Germany's Civil Code. It is also in that context that the GFCC developed its doctrine that the Basic Law can impose a duty on the legislature to provide statutory protection for the rights-protected interests of private parties against threats from other private parties. The family law and antidiscrimination fields both highlight how the project of giving concrete meaning to constitutional commitments is carried forward by legislatures as well as courts. And the development of antidiscrimination law in Germany also showcases how European norms, themselves given horizontal effect, spur more changes in the law, more interactions among institutions, and more blurring of boundaries between different kinds of law.

FREEDOM OF EXPRESSION

Lüth itself concerned the collision between freedom of expression and other significant legal values, and the Constitutional Court addressed other clashes

19. As mentioned in Chapter One, I define these areas of law broadly, and in some respects differently than the legal systems themselves do. In particular, as a doctrinal matter, the regulation of abortion would not be considered a topic of family law in Germany, but of criminal law. But to facilitate cross-country comparisons, it makes more sense to define the areas functionally. For purposes of this project, I treat family law as encompassing the legal regulation of choices made in the context of intimate or family relations.

with the freedom of expression many times in subsequent years. It makes sense that free speech cases would become a principal site where the Court developed and expanded on the principles of horizontal effect first announced in *Lüth*. This is so because an expanding commitment to the liberal value of free speech necessarily collided with other values that traditionally received strong protection in private law, including not only economic interests (as in *Lüth*) but also reputation.

Through the mid-1970s, the Court's free speech jurisprudence functioned as a kind of laboratory for doctrinal innovation. The Court repeatedly leapfrogged itself in successive cases, establishing and then exceeding high-water marks for how powerfully rights could act on the ordinary law, extending again and again the transformative potential of rights. Though each individual change represented only a minor increase in the disruptive power of rights, the net effect was dramatic.

Upgrading Private Law Interests to Constitutional Stature

The *Mephisto* case from 1971 marked a significant development in doctrine, and like *Lüth*, arose from processes of *Vergangenheitsbewältigung*—coming to terms with the past, and more specifically, the Nazi period—in Germany. In 1936, Klaus Mann (Thomas Mann's son) completed a novel titled *Mephisto*, which told the story of an actor who opportunistically supported the Nazi regime, which rewarded him with fame and professional advancement. The story was a thinly veiled fictionalization of the life of Mann's one-time brother-in-law Gustaf Gründgens, who appears in the book as Hendrik Höfgen.

When a publisher announced plans to release the book in West Germany in 1963, the family of Gründgens sued to enjoin publication, relying on one of the great general clauses of the Civil Code, Section 823(1), which imposes liability for damages on one who injures "the life, the body, the health, the freedom, the property, or another right of another person in a manner contrary to law."[20] Notably, the claim for injunction rested on an amalgamation of ordinary and constitutional law: the "other right" the plaintiffs alleged was threaten by publication of the book was the right to the free development of personality, as guaranteed by Article 2, Section 1.

The publisher fought the injunction on the grounds that blocking publication of the book would violate the right to artistic expression, as guaranteed by

20. Gründgens had died in 1963, and the case was carried forward by his adopted son and heir. Mann himself had died in 1949, having spent the last several months of his life trying in vain to find a West German publisher for *Mephisto* (Quint 1989, 292 n.148).

Article 5, Section 3 of the Basic Law. A lower court and the Federal Court of Justice both ruled against the publisher.

The publisher brought a constitutional complaint before the GFCC's First Senate, but it did not succeed.[21] The GFCC's decision was notable for a number of reasons. First, by its terms, the Article 5, Section 3 right to artistic production was not subject to limitation by general laws, in contrast to the free speech right that the Court had addressed in *Lüth*. Did it then follow that Article 5, Section 3 protected artistic expression absolutely?

No, the Court answered: general laws may not limit artistic freedom, but it does not follow that artistic freedom is limitless. Rather, "the boundaries of artistic freedom are defined only by the constitution itself."[22] In other words, the legal protection for artistic expression must itself comport with the Basic Law. When artistic expression comes into conflict with another constitutional right, the conflict must be resolved, in effect, by balancing the rights, with an eye to the constitutional order of values as a whole. Here, the Court found, the publication of the novel would implicate both the Article 2, Section 1 right to the free development of personality and the Article 1, Section 1 guarantee of human dignity, which is the cornerstone of the whole constitutional order.[23]

Another key issue the Court took up in *Mephisto* concerned the scope of the Court's review. As noted above, the decision comes down to a weighing of the different rights interests present on either side of the case. The members of the First Senate deadlocked on the merits. But significantly, the majority and dissenting Justices all agreed in principle that the weighing should be carried out in the first instance by the ordinary courts and not overturned lightly.

Both the majority decision and the dissent from Justice Rupp-von Brünneck invoke the "Heck Formula" (named after the Justice who introduced it in a different context):[24] the Constitutional Court does not review the assessment of facts, the interpretation of ordinary law, or its application in the concrete case by the court of the first instance.[25] When it comes to the balancing of rights, this means that the GFCC will not overturn a ruling merely because the lower court assessed the balance differently than the GFCC would. Rather, the lower court made a reviewable error only if it failed to balance altogether or rested its

21. The Court actually deadlocked 3–3, with the result that the decision of the Federal Court of Justice was allowed to stand.

22. 30 BVerfGE 173, 193 (Feb. 24, 1971).

23. Ultimately, the novel was published in West Germany in 1981 by a different publisher.

24. 18 BVerfGE 85, 92 (June 10, 1964).

25. There was one more dissenting opinion in the case, authored by Justice Stein.

decision on a fundamentally mistaken perception of one or the other right, or the scope of its application.

Peter Quint sees in *Mephisto* "the re-assertion of private law [in] two forms: first, certain traditional legal values that can limit expression—values long protected in the ordinary law—were accorded very significant weight as an independent constitutional right; and, second, the Constitutional Court sharply limited its scope of review in private law cases" (1989, 291). In my view, this perception is insightful, but incomplete. *Mephisto* has at least a passing resemblance to *Marbury*, in that, notwithstanding its show of judicial modesty, the decision actually amplifies the Court's powers in some respects.

It is true that the Court cuts back on the (textually unlimited) scope of the Article 5, Section 3 right, ruling that it is subject to limits notwithstanding the absence of a reservation clause. And it is also true that reputational interests of the sort classically respected by the private law—and the reputational interests of a dead man, no less—ultimately carry the day against the right to literary expression, a prototypical liberal right. But crucially, the Court *constitutionalizes* the reputational interest, upgrading reputation from a private law value to a constitutional value, encompassed by the rights to human dignity and the development of personality. In other words, the Court is creating something like a constitutional right against reputational harm.

Doing so effectively shrinks the set of matters within the exclusive jurisdiction of the civil courts and brings more within the purview of the Constitutional Court. Instead of treating this as a clash between constitutional and ordinary law values, the Court raises the stakes, making this case and all similar ones a clash *between* constitutional values.[26] As a practical matter, the distinction between limitations imposed by constitutional rights and by general laws would diminish in importance, since the Court's expansive rights jurisprudence renders almost every general law a stalking horse for one or more constitutional values (Quint 1989, 296).

One could argue that the expansiveness of the Court's conception of rights is offset by the deference it shows toward the ordinary courts. As a practical matter, however, the Court's adherence to the Heck Formula (and similar deference standards) would prove to be inconsistent.[27] In the words of leading

26. Recall that in *Lüth*, Harlan had asserted that his Article 2, Section 1 rights were infringed by the boycott, but that the Court had given this claim short shrift.

27. Another formula for deference often cited by the Court is the so-called Schumann Formula, after the scholar who described it in his dissertation. The Schumann Formula instructs that errors that a lower court makes in interpreting ordinary law are irrelevant to the Constitutional Court unless it would have been unconstitutional for the lawmaker to propound the legal norm that the lower court announced (Roth 2014).

scholars Bodo Pieroth and Bernhard Schlink, reviewing the Court's jurisprudence in gross, it is hard to avoid the conclusion that the Court "reviews for itself what it wants to review for itself, and doesn't review for itself what it doesn't want to review for itself" (Pieroth and Schlink 2013, 323). And in any case, the Court would qualify the broad deference announced in *Mephisto* just a few years later, in the *Deutschland-Magazin* case, discussed below.

Rights as Swords as Well as Shields

The Court went still farther in *Blinkfüer* and *Soraya*, employing more coercive means against private parties to give legal protection to the constitutional rights of others. After the Berlin Wall was erected in 1961, the conservative publisher Axel Springer announced it would not sell its magazines to any Hamburg news dealers who also carried any publications that listed East German television programming. The boycott was directed at *Blinkfüer*, a leftist weekly which promptly sued Springer in civil court under German Civil Code Section 823(1). Much as Erich Lüth had, Springer claimed that its boycott was constitutionally protected. Springer won initially and before the Court of Justice, which balanced Springer's freedom of expression against *Blinkfüer*'s commercial interests, in the manner of *Lüth*, and concluded that the former carried the day.

In 1969, however, the Constitutional Court reversed. The Court concluded that Springer's boycott was not protected, because Springer was using its economic power to compel news dealers to adopt its position, rather than making a contribution to public information and debate. The Court went on, however, to conclude that Springer's boycott violated *Blinkfüer*'s right to freedom of the press and that the judicial ruling against *Blinkfüer* perpetuated the rights violation by failing to provide a remedy for the infringement. In other words, not only did the other courts mistakenly find that Springer had constitutional interests that trumped the normal operation of BGB Section 823(1), they failed "to bring the right to press freedom into the balancing on the side of the plaintiff."[28] The decision suggests that courts might be called on to do more to vindicate constitutional rights in private litigation. Not only could rights serve as a basis for a defense, or give content to an interest already protected by the Civil Code, as in *Mephisto*. In addition, rights could serve as the basis for a freestanding constitutional complaint in a dispute between private parties. To borrow the terminology of Walter Dellinger, *Blinkfüer* shows that constitutional rights may function not only as shields but also as swords in litigation among private parties (Dellinger 1972).

28. 25 BVerfGE 256, 263 (Feb. 26, 1969).

Forging New Remedies for Rights

Soraya, from 1973, realized the possibility not only that rights might imply a private cause of action against third parties but that they could imply extrastatutory remedies as well. In 1961, the tabloid daily *Die Welt* published an interview with Princess Soraya, the ex-wife of the Shah of Iran, that turned out to be a complete fabrication. Soraya sued the publisher in civil court for damages. The difficulty for Soraya's claim was that while the German Civil Code provides protection for personality rights, it expressly excludes damages for most intangible and nonpecuniary harms.[29] However, the trial court granted her 15,000 DM damages, and the Court of Justice affirmed. Building on previous decisions finding that Articles 1 and 2(1) together define a general right to personality,[30] the Court of Justice reasoned that courts could adequately protect Soraya's right only by providing a damages remedy against the publisher. In other words, the Basic Law *compels* the creation of a constitutional cause of action with a damages remedy against private parties.

The Constitutional Court affirmed. In principle, the *Soraya* decision expands substantially the disruptive potential that constitutional rights have on ordinary law and the relations of private parties. Constitutional rights can not only limit the legal powers that one private party has vis-à-vis another (for instance, the power to suppress a boycott), they can also subject parties to damages. And *Soraya* laid bare the potential for conflict between the demands of the ordinary law and the Basic Law that *Lüth* had minimized, by pointing to the general clauses as the chief vehicle through which constitutional rights influence the Civil Code. The damages award affirmed in *Soraya* is plainly *contra legem*: it is expressly foreclosed by the Code. Here, the Basic Law is not just animating, but rewriting, private law, and critics of the Court's horizontal effect jurisprudence have pointed to *Soraya* as evidence of the Court overreaching (Diederichsen 1998). The Court's defenders against this charge can point to the fact that the *Soraya* decision was only affirming a move first taken by the Court of Justice.

Rights Overwriting the Civil Code

The *Lebach* case, also decided in 1973, confirmed that constitutional personality rights could effectively rewrite provisions of the Civil Code, even in the face of a countervailing interest in press freedom. In 1969, two armed men stormed a military facility in Lebach, killed four soldiers, and stole munitions.

29. See BGB §§ 253, 847.

30. See the discussion of the *Herrenreiter* case, above.

In 1972, Gernot Wenzel, an accessory to the murders who was nearing release from prison, sued to block the German TV broadcaster ZDF from airing a documentary about the killings. Although Wenzel did not contest the accuracy of the account, he claimed that its broadcast would interfere with his successful reintegration with society following release, in violation of his rights under Articles 1 and 2. The claim failed in the lower courts, but prevailed in the Constitutional Court, which undertook a detailed balancing of the interests at stake on both sides.[31] In blocking the broadcast, the Court went beyond any protections provided by the Civil Code: the Code's protection against defamation extends only to false claims (Quint 1989, 301). As in *Soraya*, the Constitutional Court engaged in a constitutional balancing that overwrote the positive provisions of the private law, but this time, it did so in the face of uniform contrary rulings from the civil courts that heard the case.

Discretionary Deference

Three years later, the Constitutional Court's ruling in the *Deutschland-Magazin* case cut back on the deference offered the civil courts in *Mephisto*. The Court reviewed an order of a civil court upholding an injunction against a labor union that blocked the union from calling a conservative magazine a *rechtsradikales Hetzblatt* (loosely, a "radical right-wing riot rag"), but permitted the union to voice its critique using less incendiary language.[32] In affirming the decision, the Constitutional Court introduced a new sliding scale of deference to the interpretations of civil courts. The Court affirmed that "the Constitutional Court does not review the interpretation and application of ordinary law as such."[33] However, as the impact on an interest within the zone protected by a constitutional right becomes more substantial, the Court's review becomes correspondingly more vigilant. At the far end of the spectrum, deference evaporates entirely: "in cases where the infringement is most intense, the Court is fully entitled to substitute its own judgment for that of the civil courts."[34]

While *Deutschland-Magazin* does not obliterate Constitutional Court deference to the ordinary courts, it conditions deference on the Court's assessment of

31. The Court's conclusion rested largely on its finding that the documentary would seriously reduce the likelihood of Wenzel's successful resocialization, in part because it referred to homosexual relationships between him and the killers.

32. The phrase *rechtsradikales Hetzblatt* carried strong associations with Naziism, as Peter Quint explains (1989, 319 n.222).

33. 42 BVerfGE 143, 148 (May 11, 1976).

34. *Id.* at 149 (citing *Lebach* as a case where the rights infringement is most intense).

the severity of the infringement.[35] The Court will decide what deference is due on a case-by-case basis. The *Deutschland-Magazin* approach shares a feature with all such formulas for variable intensity review: they amplify the discretion of the courts that apply them. As Peter Quint writes,

> The use of an adjustable standard of review—in which the factors triggering a greater or lesser degree of scrutiny are themselves vague in nature—adds another layer of uncertainty to an already complex doctrine. Moreover, the technique opens the possibility that a court could employ the standard as a method of reducing the substantive protection of certain constitutional interests without actually acknowledging that those interests are receiving reduced protection (Quint 1989, 329).

I would add that such a standard amplifies judicial discretion in two directions. It allows a court not only to relax the protection of disfavored interests but to enhance the protection of favored interests.

The Constitutional Court has decided a number of important and high-profile free expression cases in more recent years, but the most important doctrinal innovations belong to the period ending in the mid-1970s.[36] The Court's free speech jurisprudence was important not only in its own right but because it raised the benefits to litigants, courts, and legislators of giving heed to constitutional values, and raised the costs of failing to do so. Rights were not merely values that shaped the application of ordinary law: they could rewrite ordinary law, generate new causes of action, and ground demands for new remedies. The

35. Moreover, the Court's assessment of the severity of the infringement relates to the merits question of whether the constitutional complaint is grounded. As Peter Quint notes, the merits question is broader, but at least as to this important issue, the Constitutional Court necessarily substitutes its judgment for the ordinary court's (1989, 320 n.226).

36. The most significant cases since then include the *Böll* case, in which the Court held that the Court of Justice failed to give adequate constitutional protection to author Heinrich Böll's personality rights when it dismissed his libel suit against the *Bild* magazine, which had accused him of encouraging terrorism (54 BVerfGE 208 (June 3, 1980)); *Wallraff*, in which the Court held that the Court of Justice provided insufficient protection to the *Bild* newspaper's editorial confidentiality, as protected by the guarantee of press freedom, when it declined to grant an injunction against investigative journalist Günther Wallraff's account of editorial meetings, access to which he gained through acts of deception (66 BVerfGE 116 (Jan. 25, 1984)); and the *Parabolantenne* case, in which the Court held that a renter had a constitutional right, grounded in access to a free press, to affix an antenna to the exterior of his apartment in order to receive television broadcasts in his native language, notwithstanding the landlord's property right (90 BVerfGE 27 (Feb. 9, 1994)). In the successive rounds of the *Benetton* litigation, the

Heck Formula and related devices held out the promise to other courts that the Court might reward them with deference for taking constitutional values into account, whereas they could count on reversal if they failed to do so. The following two sections do not shift the focus away from the GFCC entirely, but they begin to explore how other courts and lawmakers engage with rights in dialogue with, and in the shadow of, the Constitutional Court.

FAMILY LAW

The legal regulation of family matters showcases some of the ways in which constitutional rights have changed how the rules governing private-party relationships are made in Germany. First, it is in the context of the law governing abortion that the Constitutional Court developed the idea of a protective duty on the part of the legislature to protect constitutional interests against infringement by private parties. Under this banner, the Court has effectively enlisted legislators as the front line of constitutional construction, elaborating what rights mean for how citizens treat one another. What is more, the *Bundestag* has substantially reconfigured the Civil Code to bring family law (among other subjects) into alignment with constitutional equality norms. Also, we see ordinary civil courts balancing family law norms and constitutional rights under the tutelage of the GFCC.

As noted before, the Basic Law contains a number of rights relevant to family law, not all of which are phrased strictly as defensive rights against the state. For instance: Article 6, Section 1 declares that "[m]arriage and the family shall enjoy the special protection of the state," and Article 6, Section 2 stipulates that the care and upbringing of children is both the right and the duty of parents.

Court wrestled with the free speech implications of Court of Justice rulings banning controversial advertisements (Ipsen 2009, 319). The longest-running chapter in the FCC's efforts to mediate between freedom of the press and the right to personality concerns claims brought by Princess Caroline of Monaco, claims that bounced for years among courts in Germany and Europe. To mention some of the high points: in 1999, the Constitutional Court rejected an injunction by the Court of Justice barring a tabloid from publishing photos of Princess Caroline's children (101 BVerfGE 361 (Dec. 15, 1999)), only to be reversed by the European Court of Human Rights on the grounds that the publication of pictures would violate a provision of the European Convention on Human Rights (Von Hannover v. Germany [2004] [2] (Application no. 59320/00)). In 2008, however, the Constitutional Court rejected a subsequent effort by Princess Caroline to enjoin publication of a different set of pictures of her family, as the different context for these photos justified legitimate public interest in their publication (120 BVerfGE 180 (Feb. 26, 2008)), and the Grand Chamber of the European Court of Human Rights accepted this result in 2012 (Von Hannover v. Germany [2012] [2] (Application nos. 40660/08 and 60641/08)).

Section 3 limits the state's ability to remove children from their parents, Section 4 declares that "[e]very mother shall be entitled to the protection and care of the community," and Section 5 guarantees children born outside of marriage the same treatment as children born to married parents. Moreover, Article 3, Section 2 declares that men and women shall have equal rights. Recognizing that many family law provisions reflected traditional gender norms, however, Article 117, Section 1 gave the *Bundestag* until March 31, 1953, to bring inconsistent provisions into conformity with Article 3, Section 2, after which time they would cease to be in effect.

Family law is also governed by Book 4 of the Civil Code. While the other books of the Civil Code have changed modestly since the enactment of the Basic Law, alterations to the text of the family law section "have left hardly any part of it unchanged" (Zimmermann 2006, 21). Most of the changes have arisen as a result of the collision between the constitutional equality norm and the deep patriarchal assumptions built into the Code (Crosby 2008, 219–20). Changes have come from several sources: a "stupendous" number of Constitutional Court decisions (Ruffert 2001, 421), a large body of decisions from the civil courts (Fedtke 2007, 132–33), and more than thirty important legislative amendments to the Code (Zimmermann 2006, 21). But if the changes have been pervasive, they have also been "unspectacular," in large part because the Constitutional Court has accepted and built on many of the basic private law values already encoded in family law (Ruffert 2001, 421, 422).[37] Much of the work of modernizing family law—in particular, to reflect norms of gender equality—has been undertaken by the legislature, and the Constitutional Court more often than not has accepted these legislative choices as valid efforts to give shape to the constitutional guarantees protecting marriage and the family (Ruffert 2001, 406).

Abortion Law and the Duty to Protect

The Constitutional Court's abortion jurisprudence brought prominence to a conceptual innovation that marked a shift toward legislative constitutionalism, as it recognized the legislature as the Constitutional Court's co-venturer in the project of giving meaning to the Basic Law. This innovation was the idea of the duty to protect, or *Schutzpflicht*.

Prior to 1975, Section 218 of Germany's Criminal Code (*Strafgesetzbuch*) (StGB) provided criminal penalties of up to five years for women who have abortions. In 1975, the *Bundestag* enacted the Abortion Reform Act, which would

37. See also Frank (2000, 406).

eliminate criminal penalties for abortion under a number of circumstances. Members of the *Bundestag* and the governments of several *Länder* brought an abstract review proceeding to challenge the constitutionality of the law.

Significantly, and in contrast to the U.S. Supreme Court, the Constitutional Court found that the right to life, as recognized in Article 2, Section 2, encompasses fetal life.[38] Moreover, the Court concluded that this right contained not only a defensive right but a positive claim to the state's protection. The Court found support for this "duty to protect" in Article 1, Section 1 of the Basic Law, which declares that it is "the responsibility of all state power to respect and protect" human dignity. In other words, the Basic Law imposes on the state not only a responsibility to *respect* human dignity itself but to *protect* it, including from threats that emanate from *outside* of the state—that is, from nonstate actors.

The Court described the state's responsibility in expansive terms:

> The state's duty to protect is comprehensive. Of course it encompasses direct state interference with developing life, but it also requires the state to play a protective and encouraging role vis-a-vis this life, meaning above all, to protect against the unlawful interference on the part of others. All areas of law must orient themselves around this directive, each according to its particular tasks. The state's obligation to protect must be undertaken more seriously the higher the rank of the legal value that is at stake in the constitutional order of values. Human life quite evidently represents a supreme value in the constitutional order: it is the essential basis for human dignity, and the precondition for all other fundamental rights.[39]

These conclusions opened on to still more difficult questions for the Court. What precisely did that duty entail in this context? What steps must be taken to protect the right when the regulation of abortion is at issue?

Given the breadth of the scope of constitutional rights in the Basic Law, the Court recognized that any legislation dealing with abortion would implicate additional rights, which must be taken into account. Most obviously, laws regulating abortion plainly implicated women's autonomy rights under Article 2, Section 1. The Court made clear that the task of choosing how to balance competing rights interests in legislation fell in the first instance to the legislature. But although the Court did not purport to dictate the contents of the legislation, it did mark out some fixed points. While the right to life predominates in

38. BVerfGE 39, 1 (Feb. 25, 1975).

39. BVerfGE 1, 42.

general, according to the Court, the legislature must permit pregnancy terminations when the woman's life or health is at stake and may also permit termination without criminal penalty in other cases where carrying the pregnancy to term would impose extraordinary burdens. But a blanket decriminalization of abortion was unconstitutional, because the state was not fulfilling its affirmative obligation to protect the right to fetal life against a pregnant woman's decision to terminate the pregnancy.

The *Abortion I* decision was a controversial landmark, which had the practical effect of permitting abortions widely in Germany (Levy and Somek 2001, 111 n.4).[40] The Constitutional Court had obliquely recognized that constitutional rights can impose on the state a duty to protect even before *Abortion I*,[41] but this was the first decision to clearly present the concept of the *Schutzpflicht*. And the idea of a duty to protect was significant not least because it provided a template for thinking about constitutional construction as a shared competence of the Court and lawmakers. Understanding how requires a short excursion deeper into the doctrine of the duty to protect.[42]

Although constitutional rights do not apply to the behavior of private law *subjects* (*Privatrechtsubjekte*; that is, private parties), they do apply to the *norms* of private law, such as the provisions of the Civil Code, which are enacted by legislatures. And vis-à-vis the norms of the private law, constitutional rights chiefly serve their traditional function, as negative rights; as defenses against infringement (*Eingriffsverbote*). So for instance, in *Mephisto*, Section 823(1) of the Civil Code infringes on the freedom of artistic expression: this provision provides legal authorization for banning the publication of a novel. Properly posed, the question that is the key to the publisher's constitutional complaint is whether Section 823(1), which is directly and fully subject to the Basic Law, as

40. The decision was followed almost two decades later by *Abortion II*, 88 BVerfGE 203 (May 28, 1993), which relaxed the state's responsibility to penalize abortion criminally.

41. See, for instance, 35 BVerfGE 79 (May 29, 1973) (Higher Education Decision) (ruling that the state of Nordrhein-Westfalen was obligated by the constitutional guarantee of the freedom of research and teaching to regulate university governance to prevent nonacademic staff from having full voting rights in academic appointment decisions). Some of the Court's free expression decisions, including *Blinkfüer* and *Wallraff*, implicitly rely on a protective duty concept of rights (Ruffert 2001, 518–19).

42. As is often the case with German constitutional doctrine, the finer points of the concept of a right as a duty to protect were worked out by legal scholars, including most influentially by Claus-Wilhelm Canaris (1984). In the mid-1980s, Canaris offered an elegant reconstruction of the Court's horizontal effect doctrine that linked together a number of opposing concepts: between direct and indirect effect; legal norm and legal action; infringement ban and duty to protect. Christian Starck's work on this subject has also been influential (Ruffert 2001, 21), but the account I present here is based on Canaris's work.

applied by the civil court, infringes on artistic freedom disproportionately, and hence, unconstitutionally (Canaris 1984, 211–12).

But the defensive function does not exhaust the role of rights, as the Constitutional Court found in *Abortion I*. Constitutional rights also impose on the state a responsibility to protect the interests of private parties against the actions of others, much as a core responsibility of the state has always been to provide citizens basic security against the predations of their fellows (Canaris 1984, 226; Starck 2001, 100). This protection is provided in the first instance by the ordinary law, which regulates the legal interactions of private parties. So, for instance, provisions of the commercial code that limit the use of non-compete agreements give concrete form to the constitutional right to practice one's occupation promised in Article 12.[43] Significantly, when judging whether ordinary law adequately discharges the state's constitutional duties to protect rights, it is essential that the Constitutional Court give "a very wide discretion" to the legislator who crafts the provisions of ordinary law (Canaris 1984, 227). To do otherwise would mean transferring wholesale from the legislature to the Constitutional Court the authority to balance competing considerations in crafting statutes.

Thinking of rights as containing both a defense against infringement and an entitlement to state protection against threats from private parties offers a new way to understand horizontal effect. And this way offers a solution to some of the problems of the radiation thesis, notably, the mystery of how rights composing an *objective* order of values can provide individuals with a *subjective* right to sue. Here instead, rights' subjective character is always front and center: rights are first and foremost individual entitlements against the state, either to be left alone or to be protected against others (Canaris 1984, 227).

But from the perspective of institutional politics, what is most significant about the Constitutional Court's shift is that it marks a more direct acknowledgment of the legislature's role in giving meaning to constitutional rights. As the Court framed the radiation thesis in *Lüth* and other cases, it is principally the task of *courts* to determine what constitutional rights require of ordinary law. This is implied not least by the Court's emphasis on the general clauses as the "portals" through which constitutional values enter ordinary law: the general clauses get their constitutional content through acts of judicial construction.

By contrast, if constitutional rights impose a duty to protect rights through the ordinary law, this duty falls in the first instance to the legislatures that craft the statutes. *Abortion I* put legislatures on the hook not only for giving officials and private parties legal tools that could be used to violate constitutional

43. See Handelsgesetzbuch [HBG] [Commercial Code], May 10, 1897, Reichsgesetzblatt [RGBl] 219, § 74 ff.; Canaris (1984, 228–29).

rights but for failing to enact legislation to defend rights against infringement by private parties. In other words, "the legislature is no longer free to decide whether it wants to solve certain problems or not. If non-action leaves citizens unprotected in their fundamental rights the legislature is constitutionally obligated to act" (Grimm 2006, 278). And this obligation implies that the legislature will be juggling multiple rights: protecting one (here, the right to life) by limiting another (here, the woman's autonomy right). So in *Abortion I*, it is the *Bundestag*'s responsibility to regulate abortion in a way that adequately protects the fetus's right to life.

In introducing the duty to protect, the Constitutional Court thus fully enlists the federal and *Länder* legislatures in the project of constitutional lawmaking and further erodes the distinction between constitutional law and ordinary law.[44] In doing so, the Court was careful to respect legislatures' institutional competence as primary policymakers. The doctrine signaled a broad deference to considered legislative judgments about what measures best balanced competing rights, giving legislatures another incentive to take constitutional rights seriously. (This deference was on display in the *Abortion II* case, in which the Constitutional Court signaled that the legislature would have a fairly free hand in making abortion policy (Fedtke 2007, 149).) As a result, constitutional considerations penetrate into policy deliberations in Germany, with the result that "few political questions today are publicly discussed and resolved, without the answer depending at least in substantial part on the constitution" (Jestaedt 2011, 87). Germany has become a polity in which "thinking proceeds from the constitution outwards" (Jestaedt 2011, 87), as the section that follows illustrates.[45]

Gender Equality and Legislative Constitutionalism

Ordinary courts, the national legislature, and the Constitutional Court have all engaged in the long-running project of restructuring the legal treatment of men and women, including in the context of the family, to bring it into accord with constitutional values. Judicial efforts in this direction date back to the first decade of the Republic. The Adenauer government had failed to correct the unequal treatment of men and women in many provisions of family law (and elsewhere) by the 1953 deadline set in the Basic Law, and the Court of Justice in effect rewrote substantial portions of the Code in the 1950s to remedy gender

44. And although the Court has not always been consistent, the trend in its more recent jurisprudence favors the conceptual vocabulary of the duty to protect over the radiation effect (Ruffert 2001, 146–52; Jestaedt 2011, 137–39).

45. For a discussion of how the Court encourages the legislature to meet its constitutional obligations, see Härtel (2013).

disparities. The Constitutional Court rejected a challenge to the Court of Justice's activity in this area,[46] and the Court of Justice continued to remake the law until the *Bundestag* finally passed an equal treatment law in 1957 (Fedtke 2007, 132–33; Frank 2000, 402).

In some cases, the GFCC concluded that the legislature had not done enough to secure gender equality. For instance, in a case brought by the German League of Women Jurists, the Court invalidated provisions of the Code that gave the father greater power to make decisions for children than the mother.[47] The *Bundestag* followed up by officially striking the offending provisions from the Code.[48] In the early 1990s, the Court also invalidated a provision of the Code that required married couples to have the same last name, and specifically, the husband's name if they could not agree, leaving the legislature to devise a correction.[49] As a general matter, the Court afforded the legislature wide discretion in shaping family law, even preserving space for the legislature to fix constitutional problems the Court had identified (Ruffert 2001, 405–07).

The Constitutional Court, ordinary courts, and legislature also interacted in a number of issues dealing with the rights of children. This is one of the areas of family law most pregnant with possibilities for conflict: the rights of a parent qua parent, to educate and raise the child, potentially interfere with the child's own constitutional rights, including the broad right to personality. The Basic Law requires the equal treatment under the law of children born to married and unmarried parents, but set no deadline for the legislature to eliminate unfavorable treatment of children born out of wedlock, which was rife in the Code (Frank 2000, 402). In a decision in 1969, the Constitutional Court instructed the *Bundestag* to amend the Code to treat children born in and out of wedlock equally. What was perhaps most unusual about the decision was the degree to which the Court inserted itself in the legislative process: the Court demanded that the *Bundestag* act by the end of the legislative period (that is, in the same year), or else have the courts realize the will of the constitution judicially insofar as possible.[50] Faced with the choice between drafting the reform itself or having the Constitutional Court do it, the *Bundestag* hastily passed a statute which

46. 3 BVerfGE 225 (Dec. 18, 1953).

47. 10 BVerfGE 59 (July 29, 1959).

48. Aug. 20, 1959, BGBl. I at 633.

49. 84 BVerfGE 9 (Mar. 5, 1991); Gesetz zur Neuordnung des Familiennamensrechts (Familennamensrechtsgesetz—FamNamRG), Dec. 16, 1993, BGBl. I at 2054.

50. 25 BVerfGE 167, 181 (Jan. 29, 1969). The claim was brought by an orphan who was not entitled under the Code to a share of his dead father's estate because he was born out of wedlock.

eliminated most, but not all, distinctions between children born in and out of wedlock.

With the passage of the 1969 reform law, most observers agreed that the reform law satisfied all constitutional concerns (Frank 2000, 405). But in later years, the Constitutional Court would prod the legislature and civil courts to make further changes to the fabric of family law, largely driven by the rights of children. In the 1980s and 1990s, the Constitutional Court struck down limits in the Code on joint custody arrangements for divorced parents[51] and parental rights for both parents of children born out of wedlock,[52] referring both to the rights of parents and children contained in the Basic Law. Again, the actions of the Court called forth new legislation. In 1997, the *Bundestag* passed a comprehensive reform of the legal status of children, which eliminated different treatment of children born in and out of wedlock with respect to inheritance rights, custody, and other matters (Frank 2000, 403).

In a case from 1989, the Constitutional Court ruled that all children have a right, derived from the right to personality, to know their parentage, and invalidated provisions of the Civil Code that effectively stripped children born to a married woman of the right to have the identity of their biological father judicially determined.[53] In a suit brought by a daughter born out of wedlock against her mother to reveal the identity of her father, the Court concluded that the child's right to learn her parentage must be balanced against her mother's rights and that the constitution does not dictate which right should prevail: rather, the civil courts have broad discretion to conduct the balancing in the context of the general clauses of family law.[54] On remand, the civil court concluded that the daughter's right should prevail.[55]

The Reception of Horizontal Effect Doctrine in the Civil Courts

Family law also offers an opportunity to consider the impact of constitutional norms on the everyday adjudication of civil courts.[56] Reliable generalizations are difficult to come by, however, because the sheer scope of judicial activity in

51. 61 BVerfGE 358 (Nov. 3, 1982).

52. 84 BVerfGE 168 (May 7, 1991).

53. 79 BVerfGE 256 (Jan. 31, 1989).

54. 96 BVerfGE 56 (May 6, 1997).

55. Landgericht [LG] Münster Aug. 26, 1998, NJW 1999, 726, 1 S 414/89.

56. Franzius (2005) offers a good treatment of the subject in German, albeit one focused exclusively on the first few years of the Federal Republic.

the ordinary courts means that a comprehensive empirical analysis is out of the question. Perhaps not surprisingly, scholars' assessments tend to reflect their own perspectives.

Public law scholars such as Matthias Jestaedt argue that the relationship between the Constitutional Court and other courts is, for the most part, a harmonious one (Jestaedt 2011, 94). Private law scholars have generally been more critical of the impact of the Constitutional Court's horizontal effect jurisprudence on private law doctrine (Fedtke 2007, 134). Uwe Diederichsen has faulted the Court's horizontal effect jurisprudence for being insufficiently respectful of the norms and resources of the private law. According to Diederichsen, the Court undervalues private autonomy when it fails to distinguish sharply between mandatory norms of the private law (which should have to comply fully with the Basic Law) and those that emerge from a "private, autonomous creation of law," such as a contract (Diederichsen 1998, 206). The latter, according to Diederichsen, should be afforded more deference from the Court than they often receive, because private autonomy is itself a value of constitutional stature.

Moreover, Diederichsen argues that the piecemeal interpolation of constitutional law throughout the private law threatens the well-functioning civil law with incoherence and unpredictability. Diederichsen notes that the constitutional provisions are themselves too vague to be given determinate meaning, especially in light of the Constitutional Court's predilection for fact-bound rulings based on the balancing of factors in individual cases. Whenever possible, according to Diederichsen, the Constitutional Court should use the normative resources already available in the private law to resolve cases. In particular, the Court should follow *Lüth*'s instruction to use the general clauses of the Code as the channels for introducing constitutional considerations.[57]

Two further family law cases from the Constitutional Court help to illustrate Diederichsen's criticisms of the difficulties that the Court's approach prepares for ordinary courts. The *Guarantee* decision from 1993 garnered widespread attention—much of it critical—for the links it drew between the constitutional status of the family and commercial law (Teubner 2000, 388). The Court voided a Court of Justice decision upholding a surety agreement that made a young woman with dim employment prospects and no assets liable for a very substantial debt her father had incurred. The Constitutional Court faulted the Court of Justice for failing to consider all of the constitutional values at play when

57. Others take the dislocation of private law norms as inevitable under the indirect effect approach. Johannes Hager argues that once constitutional principles have entered the picture, logically they dictate rather than inform the analysis, leaving the private law clauses no real work to do (1994, 10).

it upheld the surety agreement. A contract that does not reflect the autonomous wishes of the parties is inconsistent with the personality right of Article 2, Section 1, and thus violates the good morals clause of the Civil Code. The Constitutional Court remanded so that the civil court could give due consideration to the constitutional values involved.[58] Diederichsen faulted this decision for running roughshod over existing private law doctrine and introducing new structures of argumentation that would be difficult for civil court judges to integrate with their adjudication practices under the Code (1998, 247–48).

The 2001 *Marital Agreement* case appeared after Diederichsen's critique, but arguably fits the pattern he identified. The Constitutional Court overturned the decision by an appeals court in Stuttgart upholding a premarital agreement, on the grounds that the lower court failed to give due regard to the constitutional issues it raised.[59] When the agreement was signed, in 1976, the woman was seven months pregnant, and the unborn child's father required her to sign a premarital agreement as a precondition to marrying. In the agreement, both spouses renounced any claim to spousal support in the event of divorce, and the husband agreed to pay child support in the amount of 150 marks a month. The Constitutional Court found that the lower court's ruling had violated the claimant's constitutional rights, including rights to personal autonomy, equality, and to the protection of marriage, by failing to take due account of them. As in the *Guarantee* case, the Court took the position that the circumstances indicated the kind of gross disparity in bargaining position that impinged on the woman's rights. And as with that decision, this ruling also would complicate the efforts of civil courts to determine what contractual agreements are valid.

Public law scholars might counter that the complaints of private law scholars and judges rest on an idealized and unrealistic description of private law adjudication. Part of the ideology of the Civil Code is that it reduces adjudication to a legal science, in which judges serve as expert technicians operating the intricate machinery of the Code. But civil law judges have always drawn in values and decision-making techniques from outside of the Code, including "the undisguised appeal to general legal intuition or common sense" and result-driven readings of legislative history (Zimmermann 2006, 20). Over the course of the nineteenth century, civil judges gained considerable experience in incrementally modernizing the *ius commune* to meet the changing demands of an industrializing society. They did much the same thing in the twentieth century with the Code. In fact, interpreting and applying the Code gave Germany's civil judges an ample outlet for judicial creativity and independent

58. 89 BVerfGE 214 (Oct. 19, 1993).

59. 2 BvR 571/00 (Feb. 2, 2001).

judgment. Among other things, the courts relied heavily on the Code's famous general clauses, such as the "good morals" clause of Section 138(1) and the good faith requirement of Section 242, to "achieve a balance between doctrinal stability and flexibility" (Zimmermann 2006, 24). The private law critique of the Constitutional Court's horizontal effect jurisprudence appeals to a pure pandectist legal science that has long been part of how civilian judges represent their work, but has never fully corresponded to reality (Merryman 1994, 50–53).

Perhaps it is fairest to say, to borrow a phrase from Gunther Teubner, that constitutional rights have functioned as kind of "legal irritant" in family law doctrine. Teubner coined the term to describe the effect of a foreign legal transplant—the continental principle of good faith—on British contract law. But constitutional law is itself a kind of foreign law to the institutions and doctrines of Germany's private law, and Teubner's characterization is apt:

> [W]hen a foreign rule is imposed on a domestic culture . . . it works as a fundamental irritation which triggers a whole series of new and unexpected events. . . . [I]t irritates law's "binding arrangements." It is an outside noise which creates wild perturbations in the interplay of discourses within these arrangements and forces them to reconstruct internally not only their own rules but to reconstruct from scratch the alien element itself. "Legal irritants" cannot be domesticated; they are not transformed from something alien into something familiar, not adapted to a new cultural context, rather they will unleash an evolutionary dynamic in which the external rule's meaning will be reconstructed and the internal context will undergo fundamental change (Teubner 1998, 12).

Constitutional rights have introduced a permanent tension into private law adjudication, requiring both Constitutional Court Justices and ordinary judges to mediate between competing normative orders and decision-making practices. The *Guarantee* and *Marital Agreement* cases bear out the claim that constitutional rights, as applied by the Constitutional Court, have reshaped the terms on which family law cases are resolved.

EQUALITY

The evolution of antidiscrimination law offers not only a window onto the impact horizontal rights have had on the production of law in Germany but a prime view of how the German and European legal orders interact. For this reason, it is a fitting coda to this chapter.

Germany is one of the twenty-eight member states of the European Union. While this chapter has focused on domestic German law, national and European law intersect in EU states in so many ways that the distinction itself becomes blurred. This legal integration has been driven, in significant part, by the Court of Justice (ECJ), based in Luxembourg, which has used a number of strategies to make member states take EU law—and its own jurisprudence—seriously. Among other things, the ECJ has given horizontal effect to some EU legal norms, amplifying their impact on member states. And in recent years, in the context of antidiscrimination law, the ECJ has expanded this approach further.

This section explores the complex interactions among European and German institutions, focusing in particular on those touched off by European antidiscrimination directives, and how these interactions shaped the development of antidiscrimination law in Germany. A significant driver of change has been the ECJ's choice to make an expanding set of European equality norms horizontally effective, which impacted both legislative and judicial action in Germany. The GFCC's horizontal application of Basic Law rights to constitutionalize ordinary German law finds striking parallels in the ECJ's horizontal application of European norms to Europeanize member state law.

First, some background on lawmaking and judging in the European Union. Like most national legal systems, the law of the European Union is organized hierarchically. At the top, enjoying something like constitutional status, is EU primary law: the treaties that define the powers of the Union, as well as general principles of EU law. Below is secondary legislation, the most important forms of which for present purposes are regulations and directives. Regulations are like statutes: they establish legal norms that are effective in the member states. Directives are instructions to the member states to pass legislation to achieve certain results.

Judgments of the ECJ are a key mechanism for the enforcement of regulations and directives in member states. (The ECJ also gets to decide what counts as a general principle of EU law.)[60] Through the preliminary reference procedure, national courts apply to the ECJ for authoritative interpretations of EU law, as it is relevant to the case before them. Aided and abetted by litigants and member state courts, the ECJ has made use of the preliminary reference procedure to drive legal integration in Europe (Stone Sweet 2004, 66–75).

The ECJ has also adopted a number of judicial doctrines that amplify the effectiveness of EU norms. Back in 1963, the *Van Gend en Loos* decision established that treaty obligations can have direct effect: meaning, in this context,

60. There is a second EU court—the General Court, known until 2009 as the Court of First Instance—which has original jurisdiction over many actions against EU institutions. The General Court's decisions are subject to review by the ECJ. The ECJ and General Court together are known as the Court of Justice of the European Union. The General Court has played an important role in shaping EU law in its own right, including in formulating general principles of law (Tridimas 2006, 9–10).

that they can be enforced in a domestic court.[61] *Van Gend en Loos* was a case of vertical direct effect: a suit brought by a citizen against a member state for failing to meet its obligations. In due course, the question arose: Could treaty obligations give rise to horizontal direct effect: in other words, could one private party sue another on the basis of an EU treaty provision?[62] Yes, answered the ECJ in the 1976 *Defrenne* decision.[63] The ECJ permitted Defrenne, a flight attendant, to sue her employer, a private airline, for disparate treatment of men and women, in reliance on an EU treaty provision—now Article 157 of the Treaty on the Functioning of the European Union—obliging member states to ensure equal pay for equal work for men and women. General principles can also have horizontal direct effect (Cabral and Neves 2011). Directives, on the other hand, lack horizontal direct effect,[64] and often lack direct effect entirely. But, the Court established, they can have indirect effect: if a member state has failed to transpose a directive, or has done so incorrectly, national courts are still obliged to interpret national law, as far as possible, in light of the directive.[65]

Fast-forwarding several years and shifting from Luxembourg to Brussels, two antidiscrimination directives adopted in 2000 prodded further developments in German equality law.[66] Council Directive 2000/43/EC (the Racial Equality Directive) broadly prohibits a narrow band of discrimination, requiring equal treatment without respect to racial or ethnic origin only, but throughout public and private law with very few exceptions. Council Directive 2000/78/EC (the Employment Equality Framework Directive, or Framework Directive) has a broader scope but a narrower field of application: it requires equal treatment without respect to sex, racial or ethnic origin, religion or belief, disability, age, or sexual orientation, but only in matters of employment and occupation (Sommeregger 2005, 36). As directives, these EU norms are not themselves

61. Van Gend en Loos v. Nederlandse Administratie der Belastingen [1963] Case 26/62.

62. When it comes to horizontal effect, the terminology in EU law is slightly but maddeningly different from that employed in the national law context. "Direct" in "horizontal direct effect" only means that the EU right is judicially enforceable as is: that is, does not have to be first transposed into national law through further legislation. The effect could still be "indirect" in the sense used in this book: in other words, the obligation may lie in the first instance with the government, which has a duty to regulate private-party relations a certain way.

63. Defrenne v. SABENA (No 2) [1976] ECJ 43/75 [1976] ECR 455.

64. Marshall v. Southampton and South West Hampshire Area Health Authority [1986] ECJ 152/84.

65. Marleasing SA v. La Comercial Internacional de Alimentacion SA [1990] ECJ C-106/89.

66. The Council is empowered to legislate on matters of discrimination by Article 13 of the Treaty Establishing the European Community.

directly applicable in member states, but must be transposed into national law through national legislation.

In Germany, these EU developments played out against—and played into—normative conflict and institutional competition over the proper scope of equality protections. Article 3 of the Basic Law contains both general equality norms and an affirmative obligation on the part of the state to eliminate gender-based discrimination. Article 3, Section 1 declares that "[a]ll persons shall be equal before the law." Under Section 2, "Men and women shall have equal rights. The state shall promote the actual implementation of equal rights for women and men and take steps to eliminate disadvantages that now exist." And Section 3 names specific prohibited bases for discrimination: "No person shall be favored or disfavored because of sex, parentage, race, language, homeland and origin, faith, or religious or political opinions. No person shall be disfavored because of disability."

Different courts in Germany had taken very different approaches to the constitutional equality guarantees, with the result that they meant quite different things in different areas of law. The GFCC tended to take a fairly conservative, deferential approach to the Article 3 equality guarantees. Over the years, the Court identified a wide variety of circumstances that would trigger a "generous appraisal" (*großzügige Prüfung*) of challenged measures, amounting to arbitrariness review, as opposed to a more intensive proportionality review (Jarass and Pieroth 2012, 115–18). The Court of Justice has also taken a relaxed approach to equality claims in the civil law cases coming before it. For instance, the Court of Justice has given testamentary dispositions something close to a free pass from compliance with antidiscrimination norms. In the 1990s, it upheld an inheritance contract in the Hohenzollern family that conditioned the inheritance of an estate on the heir's marriage to a spouse of noble birth.[67] The Constitutional Court declined to review the decision (Heldrich and Rehm 2001, 121–22).[68]

The German Federal Labor Court, on the other hand, has taken a much more intensive approach to protecting equality rights, in part by employing a device of its own invention, the so-called General Clause of Equality (Stone Sweet 2011, 11–12). The result is that equality protections have been especially robust in cases before the Labor Court, namely, labor relations cases, and especially those involving collective bargaining agreements. For instance, the Labor Court

67. BGH, 140 BGHZ 118 (Dec. 2, 1998). The Hohenzollerns were the ruling family of Prussia and, eventually, of the second German Empire. Notwithstanding Article 3, the Court concluded that the agreement did not violate the "good morals" clause of § 138 of the Civil Code, because it was consistent with accepted values at the time it was entered into, in 1925.

68. BVerfG, NJW 2000, 2495 (Feb. 21, 2000).

has invalidated collective bargaining agreements that disadvantage part-time workers, workers from the former territories of East Germany, and students.[69]

Even prior to the 2000 directives, the ECJ had already tipped one intrajudicial German bout over equality to the Labor Court, thanks to the horizontal application of European norms. In the 1980s, German labor courts sent preliminary references to the ECJ that sought to extend treaty-based protections against workplace gender discrimination to include forms of indirect discrimination (that is, formally neutral workplace policies with a disparate adverse impact on women). In its *Bilka*[70] and *Rinner-Kühn*[71] decisions, the ECJ agreed. Ultimately, the GFCC capitulated to the broader conception of equality pushed by both the Federal Labor Court and the ECJ, at least in certain contexts, updating its own Article 3 jurisprudence to align with the other courts'.[72] Among other things, by getting religion about equality, the GFCC reasserted its own relevance: in the wake of the ECJ's favorable rulings, the Federal Labor Court had begun building a new workplace equality jurisprudence based on Article 157 rather than German constitutional law (Stone Sweet 2011, 99).

The reception of the European Union's Race and Framework directives played out against this backdrop in Germany. If history did not repeat itself, it followed a similar pattern. Once again, German institutions differed on how aggressively they embraced antidiscrimination norms. Once again, the institutions favoring a more aggressive approach (again, labor courts) looked to European law for support. And once again, the ECJ answered the call by expanding the horizontal application of EU legal norms. Action at the EU level engulfed a range of domestic institutions, which were enlisted in the process of upgrading Germany's equality norms.

A first effort to transpose the directives into German law failed. The Anti-Discrimination Act (*Antidiskriminierungsgesetz*) (ADG), introduced as a draft in late 2001, would have gone further than the directives required, prohibiting discrimination on all of the bases specified by the Framework Directive not only in employment law but in most areas of civil law. To this end, the ADG would have amended the Civil Code, adding several new provisions. The ADG was a subject of sustained debate, both in political and legal circles, and ultimately it was defeated, largely owing to concerns that it would go too far in curtailing the principle of private autonomy (Sommeregger 2005, 36–40).

69. BAG, 86 Entschiedungen des Bundesarbeitsgericht [BAGE] [Decisions of the Federal Labor Court] 291, 296 (Sept. 18, 1997); 71 BAGE 68, (July 30, 1992); 109 BAGE 180, 191 (Jan. 20, 2004).

70. Bilka-Kaufhaus GmbH v. Weber von Hartz (1986) C-170/84.

71. Rinner-Kühn v. FWW Spezial-Gebaudereinigung GmbH & Co KG (1989) C-171/88.

72. 97 BVerfGE 35 (Nov. 27, 1997).

The *Bundestag* not only failed to enact the protections called for by the EU directives but actually changed the law to license more age discrimination. Legislation from 2002 reduced some of the protections against dismissal for new hires of older workers, in a bid to make them more attractive to employers. A collusive suit challenging the change was brought in the Munich Labor Court, which made a preliminary reference to the ECJ. The obvious problem with resting the claim on the Framework Directive was that it had not yet been transposed into German law by national legislation—indeed, the deadline for doing so had not yet passed—and, as noted above, directives do not have direct horizontal effect.

In its landmark 2005 *Mangold* decision,[73] the ECJ found a way around the problem. The Court noted, first, that existing caselaw prevents member states from enacting measures during the transposition period for a directive that makes the goals of the directive harder to achieve. Then the Court dropped the bomb. The Court declared that the Framework Directive was not really the source for the ban on age discrimination, but rather, that a ban on age discrimination was a general principle of EU law, which by itself has horizontal effect. Therefore, it did not depend on transposition of the Framework Directive to have effect.

The *Mangold* decision was extremely controversial, as it promised not only to Europeanize but effectively to constitutionalize a big swath of the employer-employee relationship (Stone Sweet 2011, 102). In its wake, though, German institutions carried the logic of *Mangold* forward. The Federal Labor Court was quick to adopt *Mangold*'s approach in its own caselaw, declining in *Honeywell* to apply a provision of German law disfavoring older workers.[74] Honeywell challenged the Labor Court's ruling in the GFCC, claiming that the ECJ's ruling was ultra vires and violated the Basic Law.

Honeywell's challenge offered the GFCC the opportunity to disapprove the ECJ's approach in *Mangold* as inconsistent with German constitutional law. The GFCC could reassert control over equality law in Germany—but at the cost of provoking something like a constitutional crisis and positioning itself as the opponent of robust equality rights (Stone Sweet 2011, 102). The GFCC declined to go down this road, yielding to the ECJ's and Labor Court's broad conception of EU general principles of nondiscrimination.[75] Meanwhile, after some initial waffling, the ECJ doubled down on *Mangold* in the 2010 *Kücükdeveci* case,

73. Mangold v. Helm, [2005] ECJ C-144-04.

74. BAG, 7 Aktenzeichen Recht [AZR] [Legal File Number] 500/04 (Apr. 26, 2006).

75. BVerfGE 126, 286 (July 6, 2010).

finding that German labor law provisions disfavoring younger workers violated both the Framework Directive and general principles of EU law.

But much of the business of charting the way forward on antidiscrimination law fell to German lawmakers and lower courts. Not long after *Mangold* was handed down, the *Bundestag* did manage to transpose the Framework and Racial Equality Directives into law. The 2006 General Equal Treatment Act (*Allgemeines Gleichbehandlungsgesetz*) (AGG) was different, though not radically different, from the stillborn ADG (Hoentzsch 2006, 796). Reflecting the broader conception of discrimination originally propounded by the Federal Labor Court and the ECJ, the AGG covers not only direct discrimination but also indirect discrimination, although (again tracking the Framework Directive's approach) such measures will be upheld if shown to be appropriate and necessary means to achieve legal ends.[76] The AGG established a burden-shifting framework for the proof of claims of discrimination and an independent agency to advise individuals who may been subject to discrimination. As far as remedies go, damages are available under the AGG as well as injunctive relief, although whether courts can order unsuccessful defendants to enter contracts is a subject of debate (Wiemann 2010).

In the years since enactment of the AGG, the contours of equality norms in private law have been defined with increasing precision by courts. Decisional law has imposed new duties of equal treatment on private parties, but without totally obliterating the traditional preserves of private autonomy. Some of the decisions have come from the Constitutional Court: for instance, in 2013, a chamber of the Second Senate ruled that the refusal to enter a patient onto a waiting list for heart transplants because he could not communicate well in German could constitute a violation of Basic Law Article 3 as well as the AGG.[77]

Most of the significant post-AGG antidiscrimination decisions, however, have been issued by the civil courts and labor courts.[78] A number of cases concern indirect discrimination on the basis of language: for example, the state labor court in Nuremberg ruled that a job requirement of "very good knowledge of German" in a job posting for a software specialist could be evidence of discrimination.[79] Cases concerning unequal treatment on the basis of religion have been numerous, and their outcomes have often turned on whether equal treatment would infringe the employers' own confessional rights. A Muslim

76. AGG, Aug. 14, 2006, BGBl. I at 1897, § 3(2).

77. BVerfG, 1 BvR 274/12 (Jan. 28, 2013).

78. For fuller descriptions of the following cases and many others, see the 2012 report of the Federal Antidiscrimination Agency.

79. Landesarbeitsgericht [LAG] [State Labor Court] Nürnberg, Oct. 5, 2011, 2 Sa 171/11.

dental trainee had a right to wear a headscarf at work, according to a labor court in Berlin,[80] but a Protestant hospital could legally forbid a Muslim nurse from wearing a headscarf, according to the state labor court in Hamm.[81] The Federal Labor Court ruled that it could violate the AGG for an employer to fire a Muslim warehouse employee for declining on religious grounds to move alcohol,[82] and a labor court in Stuttgart ruled that a Catholic organization could fire a teacher for entering a same-sex civil union.[83]

Courts have also considered gender discrimination claims in a number of contexts, reaching various results. A labor court in Cologne held that an airline's minimum height requirement for pilots could constitute a form of indirect discrimination,[84] while the state labor court in Mainz held that employers may give women preferential access to parking spaces.[85] A series of cases concerns unequal access to discos and nightclubs, on the basis of gender or race. A man won a 300 euro judgment against a dance club in Berlin that turned him and his friends away because, according to the bouncer, "you guys are too many men."[86] A dark-skinned law student in Bremen won his claim that he was turned away from a disco on account of his race because several witnesses confirmed his account and the defendant could not prove its claim that he was in fact turned away because he was dressed unfashionably.[87]

Of course, Germany's antidiscrimination statute was enacted to transpose the European Union's equal treatment directives, not as a legislative embodiment of Article 3 of the Basic Law. But even if the statute goes beyond what the Basic Law strictly requires, it does make sense to consider it an expression of the constitutional value of equality, a value that German courts, with European prodding, were applying more aggressively even before the AGG was enacted (Sommeregger 2005, 33). The content of the antidiscrimination protections have been heavily shaped by the labor courts and the ECJ, which have used EU norms to spur developments in national law, thanks to an expansive conception of the horizontal effect of European antidiscrimination principles. Ordinary

80. Arbeitsgericht [ArbG] [Labor Court] Berlin, Mar. 28, 2012, 55 Ca 2426/12.

81. LAG Hamm, Feb. 17, 2012, 18 Sa 867/11.

82. BAG, Feb. 24, 2011, 2 AZR 636/09.

83. ArbG Stuttgart, Apr. 28, 2010, 14 Ca 1585/09.

84. ArbG Köln, Nov. 28, 2013, 15 Ca 3879/13.

85. LAG Mainz, Sept. 29, 2011, 10 Sa 314/11.

86. ArbG Berlin, Feb. 24, 2011, 137 BAGE 164.

87. Amtsgericht [AG] [District Court] Bremen, Jan. 20, 2011, 25 C 0278/10.

law becomes a vehicle not only for constitutional norms but European ones. And bringing European norms into the mix expands the set of institutions involved in giving shape to these norms and the scope for their interaction.

ASSESSMENT

Erich Kaufmann was confident in 1950 that constitutional review in the new German republic would do nothing to blur the lines between law and politics. More than half a century later, Mattias Kumm reports that the line has been erased entirely: Germany has become the land of "the total constitution," in which "politics is conceived as the continuation of law by other means" (Kumm 2006, 343). According to Kumm, in Germany today,

> The constitution serves as a guide and imposes substantive constraints on the resolution of any and every political question. The validity of any and every political decision is subject to potential challenge before a constitutional court that, under the guise of adjudicating constitutional rights provisions, will assess whether such an act is supported by good reasons.[88]

The GFCC's choice to recognize the horizontal effect of constitutional rights, and its insistence on the relevance of constitutional values to private law orderings, are central to Germany's turn toward the total constitution.

For the Constitutional Court of the 1950s, beset from all sides with challenges to its authority, pushing for an expansive conception of rights' horizontal effect made sense. Owing to the limits of its subject matter jurisdiction, the GFCC is relevant only to the extent that the constitution is. On this view, the Court's embrace of horizontal effect is of a piece with the other vigorous efforts it made to fight against marginalization by the political branches and the rest of the judiciary in the first decade of its existence. The Court's moves in *Lüth* and later cases were responsive to an emergent demand for the protection of liberal values, including freedom of speech, that were not being met by the ordinary private law establishment, which retained strong ties to Germany's antiliberal past. In championing constitutional rights in private law matters, the Court appropriated and expanded a strategy first pioneered by the Federal Labor Court.

It was significant that the GFCC gave horizontal effect to rights, but just as important was *how* the Court did so. A defining feature of the Constitutional Court's doctrine, of course, was its insistence that constitutional rights apply to private parties only indirectly. Rights were conceptualized as values that

88. See also Ipsen (2009, 322–23).

influence the whole of law. This theory fit neatly with a broader normative narrative in which the Court associated rights with the fundamental normativity of the constitutional order, self-identified as the defender of that order, and at the same time respected the autonomy of the coordinate court systems. As a practical matter, though, the indirect approach did little or nothing to blunt the impact of rights on the private law. Nor did the Court's insistence that it would not sit as a court of revision over nonconstitutional courts translate into a consistent practice of restraint. A series of cases after *Lüth* successively built up rights' capacity to preempt processes of nonconstitutional decision making, by creating causes of actions, justifying new remedies, and demanding results in contravention of the clear text of statutes.

Based on the downstream consequences of the Court's horizontal effect jurisprudence, on both litigation in nonconstitutional courts and the legislative process, it is fair to say that the Court unleashed a constitutional cascade.

The *Lüth* regime gave litigants a strong reason to articulate constitutional rights claims whenever they could plausibly be pleaded (Jestaedt 2011, 119). Constitutional rights claims gave litigants another potential ground for relief, but they did more than that. They also opened up the possibility of access to another forum to hear their claims: the Constitutional Court. In the absence of the *Urteilsverfassungsbeschwerde* (constitutional complaint; see Chapter Two), the German subject-specific court systems were almost hermetically sealed: for a litigant to move her case from whichever had jurisdiction was impossible.

Lüth imposed on all courts a duty of *verfassungskonforme Auslegung*—interpreting the ordinary law to comport with fundamental rights—a task they had every incentive to perform (Jestaedt 2011, 137–39). The Court adopted deference doctrines, such as the Heck Formula, that gave lower courts credit for taking constitutional values into account in their rulings. While other courts were required to consider the Basic Law in their rulings, they were themselves not issuing constitutional holdings but rather interpreting other norms in light of constitutional rights. The approach simultaneously obliged all courts to engage in constitutional reasoning and preserved the Constitutional Court's monopoly position as the ultimate authority on constitutional meaning (Henne 2006b, 24). Even when the GFCC cut back on its pledge of deference in the *Deutschland-Magazin* case, and even if it did sometimes act as a court of revision, nonconstitutional courts certainly improved their chances of escaping complaint to—and reversal by—the GFCC by making good faith efforts to take account of constitutional values in the course of adjudication.

The previous sections give some measures of how constitutional rights have changed adjudication in Germany, but there are other indicators as well. Starting with the GFCC itself, since the late 1950s, the number of constitutional claims filed with the Court continually increased, steadily throughout the 1960s and dramatically starting in the 1970s.[89] The *Urteilsverfassungsbeschwerde*, which was not even contemplated when the Basic Law was drafted, came to make up the overwhelming majority of the Court's docket. By 2006, litigants had filed more than 160,000 *Urteilsverfassungsbeschwerden* with the Constitutional Court, which represents roughly 93 percent of all constitutional complaints filed (Jestaedt 2011, 114). (Naturally, not all of these claims raise horizontal effect issues.)

Of course, only a small fraction of constitutional complaints ultimately prevail (Garlicki 2007, 52). Over roughly the past two decades, only 2.6 percent have succeeded (Jestaedt 2011, 117). In a sense, though, the failure rate of constitutional claims in the GFCC is itself testimony to the thoroughness of the horizontal effect revolution. The Constitutional Court does not hesitate to overturn decisions when lower courts fail to give due regard to the constitutional values at play. The low reversal rate suggests that the ordinary courts have largely internalized the horizontal effect of rights to the Constitutional Court's satisfaction.

Just how often do ordinary courts resolve private law cases with reference to constitutional rights? It is not possible to obtain a comprehensive empirical picture. But the empirical glimpses that are available, as well as the assessments of experts, suggest both that rights have had a substantial impact on private law adjudication and that fears about the full-scale constitutionalization of private law are overblown. One rough measure of the impact of indirect horizontal effect in Germany is the number of references the Court of Justice makes to constitutional rights provisions in its resolution of civil law cases. Between 2000 and 2013, the Court of Justice had explicitly considered constitutional rights in the course of resolving an average of roughly two hundred civil law cases a term, varying between approximately 6 percent and 12 percent of its civil docket in a given year. The figures suggest that the impact of constitutional rights on the way the Court processes cases is significant: no other single source of law, apart from the Civil Code and Criminal Code, is used more often.

But even so, the majority of cases are decided now, as they were before *Lüth*, without explicit reference to the Basic Law. Robert Alexy distinguishes between potential constitutional rights cases, in which constitutional rights arguments can be made, but the constitutionality of the challenged provision is not in doubt, and actual constitutional rights cases, in which "doubts about constitutional protection or non-protection are appropriate, so that constitutional arguments are necessary" (2010, 213). The number of potential constitutional rights cases dwarfs the number of actual constitutional rights cases. Still, to put the point in comparative terms, as Matthias Jestaedt has written: "In probably

89. The Court's docket increased by an average of 4.2 percent annually throughout the 1960s, and 13 percent throughout the 1970s.

no other nation and at probably no other time does the resolution of everyday legal disputes, whether they are play out between private parties, between the state and citizens, or within the state itself, involve consulting the constitution so frequently and intensively [as in Germany]" (Jestaedt 2011, 85–86).

And as illustrated in the previous sections of this chapter, the constitutional cascade has engulfed lawmakers as well as courts and yoked legislatures, ordinary courts, and the Constitutional Court together in interactive and iterative processes of constitutional construction. Lower courts and legislatures, working in the shadow of the GFCC, give substance to constitutional norms. And the way law is constitutionalized in Germany mirrors, in important respects, how it becomes Europeanized. The European Court of Justice drives European norms deeper into national law by insisting that they apply horizontally. And the integration of normative orders that horizontal effect kicks off drives interaction among the multiple institutions responsible for different aspects of lawmaking, whether with a cooperative or competitive dynamic.

In part, legislatures' incentives to take constitutional rights seriously were derivative of courts'. Horizontal effect jurisprudence empowered courts—all courts—to undertake a form of constitutional review of the whole body of ordinary law. *Lüth* and the cases that followed invited the entirety of the judiciary, from the humblest court of first instance to the apex courts, to partake of the supremacy of the constitution and to sit in judgment of legislative and executive choices on that basis. To exaggerate slightly, lawmakers faced a choice between either choosing themselves how to give concrete form to constitutional values legislatively or having courts make those choices. And as described above, in areas of law such as equality law, the *Bundestag* has in recent years worked to inoculate itself against judicial reversal on constitutional grounds, by providing ample legislative protection to equality values.

But in addition, the Constitutional Court has been explicit about recognizing legislatures as having the power and responsibility in the first instance to give concrete form to constitutional guarantees. The Court's *Abortion I* decision created a conceptual space for legislative constitutionalism, by recognizing the state's affirmative obligation to protect constitutional rights against threats from private parties. This obligation would be discharged, in most cases, through legislation, with the particulars to be worked out by the lawmakers. Like the ordinary courts, the legislatures would be rewarded with a measure of deference just for trying to take constitutional rights into account.

The horizontal application of rights in Germany required a rights jurisprudence with certain features. At least in a system where the scope of rights is as broad as it is in Germany, a robust horizontal effect doctrine presupposes, or demands, an openness to balancing in rights adjudication, because when rights are implicated by private legal relationships, competing rights claims will collide. The Constitutional Court's deference to lower court rulings involving rights, however inconsistently practiced, contributes to a culture of rights pluralism: to a degree inconceivable in the United States, the German legal system tolerates different courts reaching different answers to the same constitutional questions (Häberle 2006b, 40; Stone Sweet 2011, 10).

A tolerance of constitutional pluralism may be a prerequisite for a robust horizontal effect doctrine, because it may be that when rights apply so frequently, no single court has the capacity to ensure that they are applied uniformly. An expansive approach to horizontal effect will also have an easier time gaining traction in a legal system that accepts the idea that the constitution may impose positive obligations on the state. Otherwise, individuals could have no legal claim to protection against the actions of others that threaten the values or interests protected by rights.

Germany's constitutional cascade could unfold as it did because none of these features were anathema to Germany's postwar constitutional culture. A balancing approach in rights adjudication was not off the table, in part because Germany had no well-developed prewar tradition of constitutional rights review. Anxiety about "balancing rights away" is liable to be less acute absent a history of treating individual constitutional rights as entitlements with fixed content. The GFCC was in some respects writing on a blank slate as it began elaborating the meaning of constitutional rights, and the business of deciding cases with reference to abstract constitutional values was not altogether different from the work that civil law judges did in deciding cases with reference to the general clauses and undefined legal concepts that littered German civil law. Balancing could take root in German courts, and Jacco Bomhoff reports, for instance, that "it became common [in the 1960s] for the ordinary, that is, criminal and civil, courts to explicitly formulate their own treatment of free speech issues in terms of a balancing of values and interests" (2013, 82).

The idea that constitutional rights could impose positive obligations on the government also provoked little controversy in the context of postwar Germany's expanding welfare state. It is also significant that the GFCC was held in high esteem by the postwar German public, owing to the eminence of its Justices and perhaps also to the halo effect surrounding the Basic Law with which the Court was so closely identified. A less respected court might not have been equally able to introduce such important doctrinal innovations.

All things considered, *Lüth* and what followed meant a constitutional revolution for Germany. But the impact was not registered in vastly different substantive outcomes across the board. The consequence was not that the substance of all private law became radically different—that the set of primary obligations it imposed on German citizens changed their content fundamentally. The change was both widespread and subtle, and involved both the relations of the institutions involved in legal decision making and the nature of reasoning used to justify case outcomes.

Again, this is not to say that the conflict between constitutional law and private law has been eliminated, so much as it has been institutionalized and regularized. Horizontal effect has added a new variable to private law adjudication. And notwithstanding the widespread acceptance of the basic tenets of indirect horizontal effect, some holdouts in the German legal order remain, notably in the Federal Labor Court. The Labor Court avoided some of the practical effects of the *Lüth* ruling by grounding some of its own rulings not in the constitutional rights but in a judge-made doctrine it termed the General Clause of Equality (Stone Sweet 2011). While some judges on the Court accepted the indirect effect approach (Heldrich and Rehm 2001, 124), others persisted in embracing a doctrine of direct horizontal effect of rights, and in recent years, the seventh Senate denied any role for constitutional rights in wage agreements (Singer 2007, 246–47).

Despite the occasional high-profile conflicts, Matthias Jestaedt argues that the relationship between the GFCC and other courts is generally lower in tension than many suppose, with real friction arising mostly when a constitutional case also requires a depth of subject-specific knowledge (Jestaedt 2011, 94).[90] And the German legal academy has largely promoted horizontal effect doctrine as well. In stark contrast with the Weimar era, the dominant strains of public law scholarship of postwar Germany were built on the foundations of constitutional doctrine as articulated by the GFCC, including the doctrine of indirect horizontal effect (Jestaedt 2011, 127). Although the legal academy was not an uncritical echo chamber for the Court, accepting the basic premises of the emergent constitutional order was a prerequisite for having any influence with the Court (Jestaedt 2011, 128). The general receptiveness to horizontal effect among public law scholars is in keeping with the close—some would say too close—relationship between the Constitutional Court and public law scholars.[91]

All of these features together make Germany something of a poster child for the transformative effect that horizontal rights can have on a legal system. The next two chapters turn to the United States, which in some respects is Germany's polar opposite. It is not that rights never have constitutional effect in the United States; sometimes they do. But doctrine aims to block the spread of rights reasoning beyond the confines of public law, so that horizontal rights work not as agents of constitutional transformation, so much as tools of the Supreme Court's control, to be deployed selectively and at the Court's discretion.

90. Certainly other courts have now internalized the *Lüth* revolution much more than they had in 1959, when Adolf Arndt gave a lecture faulting ordinary courts for ignoring constitutional rights (1960).

91. For a discussion of the criticisms, see Sadurski (2007, xiv).

4

The American Constitution: First and Second Foundings

INTRODUCTION

On June 13, 1973, Shirley Brooks, a widow and mother of three working as a nurse's aide, was evicted from her apartment in Mount Vernon, New York. That same day, her belongings were moved into storage owned by Flagg Brothers, Inc. A few months later, she received a letter from Flagg Brothers informing her that she was delinquent in paying her storage charges and demanding payment within ten days to avoid a foreclosure sale. The company was, in fact, authorized by New York state law to sell her belongings in order to pay her bill. Provisions of the Uniform Commercial Code, as enacted into state law by New York's legislature in 1962, grant a warehouseman a lien on stored property for the costs of storage and permit the warehouseman to enforce the lien by selling the property according to procedures specified by the statute.[1]

The following month, Brooks and co-plaintiff Gloria Jones filed a class action lawsuit in federal court, naming Flagg Brothers "and all others similarly situated" as defendants.[2] The lawsuit claimed that the sale of stored property without a prior hearing violated due process rights, as guaranteed by the Fourteenth Amendment.

Following a loss in the trial court and a win in the appeals court, the case duly made its way to the U.S. Supreme Court, where it was argued on January 18, 1978.[3] By a vote of five to three, the Court ruled that the plaintiff class had suffered no deprivation of constitutional rights, because the action they found

1. N.Y. U.C.C. §§ 7-209, 7-210.

2. The plaintiff class consisted of all persons with goods stored in New York state and subject to sale under the statute. Brooks v. Flagg Bros., 404 F. Supp. 1059, 1060 (S.D.N.Y. 1975).

3. Flagg Bros., Inc. v. Brooks, 436 U.S. 149 (1978).

objectionable—the sale of their property without hearing—was undertaken by Flagg Brothers, a private company.[4] Plaintiffs would have a claim, according to Justice Rehnquist's opinion for the majority, only if "Flagg Brothers' action may fairly be attributed to the State of New York."[5] It may not, according to Justice Rehnquist, because the power New York delegated to Flagg Brothers by statute—the power to resolve private disputes—was not a power "traditionally exclusively reserved to the State."[6] To the contrary, the Court countered that the "system of rights and remedies" embodied in New York's statute "recogniz[es] the traditional place of private arrangements in ordering relationships in the commercial world, [and] can hardly be said to have delegated to Flagg Brothers an exclusive prerogative of the sovereign."[7] Nor was the State of New York itself directly involved with or encouraging Flagg Brothers' decision to sell the property: it has "merely announced the circumstances in which its courts will not interfere with a private sale."[8] To hold that the sale of property could be attributed to New York merely because New York has "*refused* to act" (by proscribing or declining to honor a sale of property under the statute) would start us down the slippery slope to the total constitution: "all private deprivations of property would be converted into public acts whenever the State, for whatever reason, denies relief sought by the putative property owner."[9]

Flagg Brothers is a suitable starting point for this chapter not because it is particularly important but because it is unexceptional. The decision points up some of the characteristic pathologies of the Supreme Court's approach to managing the effect of rights. Famously, federal constitutional doctrine in the United States draws a sharp line in the sand: most constitutional rights offer individuals protection only against "state action." As the Supreme Court put the point in *Shelley v. Kraemer*, "[t]he action inhibited by the first section of the Fourteenth Amendment is only such action as may fairly be said to be that of the States," and the same holds for almost all provisions of the U.S. Constitution.[10] The state action doctrine is equally famous for being a mess—a

4. Justice Brennan did not take part in the case.

5. 436 U.S. at 152.

6. *Id.* (quoting Jackson v. Metropolitan Edison Co., 419 U.S. 345, 352 (1974)).

7. *Id.* at 160.

8. *Id.* at 166.

9. *Id.* at 166, 165.

10. 334 U.S. 1, 13 (1948). Notably, the Thirteenth Amendment, which forbids slavery, is understood to bind all persons and not only the state.

"conceptual disaster area," in the memorable phrase of Charles Black (1967, 95).[11] In fact, colorfully heaping abuse on the state action doctrine has long been something of a pastime among constitutional law scholars.[12]

What is wrong with state action doctrine? The *Flagg Brothers* decision suggests some of the problems.[13] At the outset, there is confusion about what exactly the target of the legal challenge is. The parties are bringing a challenge to the constitutionality of New York's statute.[14] But the Court makes the act of the warehouseman the focus on the constitutional analysis. Rather than asking whether *what the state has done*—namely, passing this statute—is consistent with the Constitution, the Court asks whether *what the warehouseman has done* can be treated as an act of the state.

On its own, the Court's conclusion that Flagg Brothers is not acting as the state is eminently reasonable. But the question draws attention away from the inquiry that one might expect to lie at the heart of the Court's analysis: whether the challenged provisions, enacted into law by New York's legislature, are constitutional. Although it is a statute that permits the transfer of title from Brooks to Flagg Brothers, and passing a statute is clearly an action of the state, the state seems to keep slipping out of the frame in the majority's analysis. Why is the state's action so hard for the Court to see?

Justice Stevens picks up on this problem in his dissent. Stevens notes that the power to sell the stored property "derives solely from the State, and specifically from §7-210 of the New York Uniform Commercial Code."[15] Stevens teases

11. A quick note about terminology. I use the phrase "state action rule" to refer to the idea that constitutional rights only offer protection against state action. "State action doctrine" refers to the broader body of law on the state action issue—the rule as elaborated by the courts, including its numerous exceptions, qualifications, and perplexities.

12. See Phillips (1984, 683) (recounting other scholars' characterizations). Of the jibes directed at state action doctrine, my favorite is Paul Brest's. Putting a positive and literary spin on things, Brest describes the doctrine's "Whitmanesque capacity to encompass contradictions" (1982, 1330).

13. State action doctrine has different branches, each with characteristic difficulties. So, for instance, "public function" cases often raise knotty historical questions about whether a given activity now being performed by private actors is traditionally exclusively performed by the state, and "entanglement" cases set before courts the unenviable task of deciding whether a given quantum of state involvement suffices to subject nominally private decisions to constitutional scrutiny. I would argue, though, that state action doctrine is beset by deeper conceptual problems and that the taxonomy of cases into different branches of doctrine is itself often confusing and confused.

14. Brooks v. Flagg Bros., Inc., 404 F. Supp. 1059, 1061 (S.D.N.Y. 1975).

15. 436 U.S. at 169.

out the implications of the majority's position that state action is not at issue because the state merely permits, but does not compel, the sale of property:

> Under this approach . . . [a] state statute could authorize the warehouseman to retain all proceeds of the lien sale, even if they far exceeded the amount of the alleged debt; it could authorize finance companies to enter private homes to repossess merchandise; or indeed, it could authorize any person with sufficient physical power, to acquire and sell the property of his weaker neighbor. An attempt to challenge the validity of any such outrageous statute would be defeated by the reasoning the Court uses today: The Court's rationale would characterize action pursuant to such a statute as purely private action, which the State permits but does not compel, in an area not exclusively reserved to the State.[16]

In a footnote, Justice Rehnquist counters that, while "the validity of property interests . . . depends on New York law, . . . [i]t would intolerably broaden . . . the notion of state action . . . to hold that the mere existence of a body of property law in a State, whether decisional or statutory, itself amounted to 'state action' even though no process or state officials were ever involved in enforcing that body of law."[17]

Justice Rehnquist's rejoinder is not responsive to Justice Stevens's argument, in that it does not provide a basis for distinguishing between the outcome of the instant case and Stevens's parade of horribles.[18] But Justice Rehnquist's reaction is revealing. Why would it be "intolerabl[e]" for every rule of decisional or statutory law to count as state action?

Suppose counterfactually that every rule of decisional or statutory law *did* count as state action. It does not follow that all actions, including those taken by private parties, that derive their legal effect from these rules must be treated as acts of the state. There is a conceptual difference between holding relevant state actors responsible for the *content of the law* and holding them responsible

16. *Id.* at 170 (Stevens, J., dissenting) (internal quotation marks and citations omitted).

17. *Id.* at 160 n.10.

18. One difference between Stevens's hypothetical and the *Flagg Brothers* case is that the former contemplates radical alternations to the common law rules of property law, throwing the state's role in the reordering of things into sharper relief. Although the warehouseman's right to sell stored property was not part of common law, the warehouseman's lien on that property was, and the right to sell represents a fairly modest extension. The examples that Justice Stevens gives represent far greater departures from the common law rules. State action in *Flagg Brothers* is being assessed against a common law baseline that is never directly acknowledged.

for all the *actions of nonstate actors that have legal effect*.[19] Some private choices made under the auspices of law may raise constitutional problems: it might be unconstitutional for state actors to permit or empower persons to use law to do certain things. When and whether this is the case amounts to a *substantive question* about what obligations constitutional rights impose on state actors.

This is the structure of the claim that the plaintiffs mounted in *Flagg Brothers*: Brooks argued that it is inconsistent with the requirements of due process for the legislature to permit warehousemen to take title to bailed property with no form of hearing. Other legal actions authorized by law may not raise meritorious constitutional claims. In every instance, assessing whether a given use of law comports with the Constitution will require a substantive legal judgment as to what, exactly, the implicated right requires of the state. So, for instance, a victory for Brooks would not automatically mean that it is unconstitutional for a homeowner to use the law of trespass to regulate admission to a dinner party at her home on a racially discriminatory basis (Chemerinsky 1985, 538). The cases may come out differently because they involve different rights and different facts.

With this point in mind, it is easier to understand Justice Rehnquist's objection to Justice Stevens's analysis and the work that state action doctrine does more broadly. The majority's approach in *Flagg Brothers* permits the Court to sidestep difficult, substantive questions about how the Fourteenth Amendment constrains states' ability to privatize dispute resolution. More generally, a substantial part of the functional value of American state action doctrine is precisely that it permits courts to avoid entertaining arguments and making judgments about what rights require of the state across a wide set of cases. The state action doctrine works as a constitution containment device that the Supreme Court can use to keep constitutional law within narrow banks, preempting many questions about what the government owes rights-holders and maintaining a sharp division between the domains of constitutional law and nonconstitutional law. The state action doctrine undergirds a particular model of judicial supremacy, in which constitutional rights have fixed content and the Supreme Court is the final authority on what that content is.

This chapter and the next trace how state action doctrine came to play this role in American constitutional law. I argue that modern state action doctrine, with all its peculiarities, was forged in two postwar constitutional settlements, the first after the Civil War, and the second after World War II. Litigation over the constitutional rights brought online by the amendments adopted during Reconstruction gave the Supreme Court its first real opportunity to articulate

19. See Canaris (1998).

a doctrine of horizontal effect. The Court was asked to give meaning to a new roster of rights that were not limited in their application to the national government. The idea that these rights could impact private law relations—more specifically, that the state's failure to protect citizens against others could be legally actionable—had substantial currency at the time and resonated with antebellum ideas about rights and fundamental law. And a gap yawned conspicuously between the grossly inadequate protections the ordinary law provided to African Americans in the South and the principle of equality as embodied in the Fourteenth Amendment.

But the Supreme Court chose another path. As originally adopted in the 1883 *Civil Rights Cases*[20] and refined subsequently, the state action rule committed the Court to something like a position of exclusive vertical effect. Only the acts of state organs that directly and adversely impacted the legal positions of others could trigger constitutional scrutiny. As applied by the Court for three generations, the state action rule meant that litigation between private parties would take place outside the auspices of constitutional law. It also meant that legislation adopted by Congress to enforce constitutional rights could regulate state actors only.

I argue that, in the context of post-Reconstruction politics, there was a strategic logic for the Court's refusal to give horizontal effect to rights. The political compromise that resolved the disputed 1876 election rang down the curtain on Reconstruction for once and for all. The legislature and executive were united in abandoning the national commitment to combat racial inequalities in the political and civic life of the South. And for its part, even twenty years after its disastrous misstep in *Dred Scott*, the Supreme Court was still a weakened institution. The state action rule ensured that neither the Constitution, nor federal statutes to enforce constitutional rights, could reach most matters of state law. It also kept federal *courts* out of the business of supervising state law, since jurisdictional rules largely conditioned access to federal courts on the existence of a question of federal law.

In washing its hands of responsibility to supervise the private law's conformity with equality rights (or with legislation to enforce those rights), the Supreme Court was, in a sense, capitulating to the reality of its own weakness. Lacking support from either Congress or the President, the judiciary was hardly in a position to vindicate broad equality rights in recalcitrant Southern states, even if it had wished to. If the last Reconstruction Congress had written a check it could not cash in the form of the Civil Rights Act of 1875, the Supreme Court voided the check in the *Civil Rights Cases*.

20. 109 U.S. 3 (1883).

The state action rule inaugurated a policy of constitutional containment, erecting a *cordon sanitaire* that kept constitutional rights out of the private law. Strikingly, the policy of constitutional containment, which emerged from the Court's political weakness, in time became a foundation for institutional strength. The state action rule facilitated the Court's construction of a new normative narrative that linked constitutional supremacy and judicial supremacy. The Supreme Court's jurisprudence in the late nineteenth century reinforced the hierarchical relationship between constitutional law and ordinary law and stressed the Court's role as the ultimate arbiter of constitutional meaning. In insisting on its exclusive authority to give content to constitutional rights, and in using that authority to define the scope of rights narrowly, the Supreme Court displaced a less court-centered, less univocal set of ideas in the American legal tradition about the character of legal obligation between government and governed.

The Supreme Court's containment of rights and its assertion of interpretive primacy were mutually reinforcing. It is easier for a court to maintain an effective monopoly over constitutional interpretation when the scope of rights is limited and the border between constitutional and ordinary law is vigorously policed. For the U.S. Supreme Court, building and maintaining a virtual monopoly over constitutional interpretation was a key to its institutional strength, which redounded to the federal judiciary more broadly. The story of the state action doctrine is therefore part of the story of the institution-building of the Supreme Court and federal judiciary, although it has not figured in most accounts of this development.

This first postwar constitutional settlement held for more than sixty years. But in the years after the Second World War, the Supreme Court began to chafe under the limitations of the state action doctrine. As the Court inaugurated a newly activist rights jurisprudence, it permitted rights to be horizontally effective in a number of cases, without ever formally abandoning the idea that the Constitution does not bear on private law relationships, either directly or indirectly. In handing down these rulings, the Court could preserve the state action fiction only by engaging in considerable intellectual acrobatics.

The contrast between the Supreme Court's state action jurisprudence following the Civil War and World War II furnishes material for a within-case comparison: Why did the Court turn to constitutional rights to fill normative gaps in ordinary law following the Second World War but not the Civil War? The difference, I argue, is that owing to a changed political landscape and a new judicial agenda, the Court in the latter period stood to benefit from the selective horizontal application of rights. The Supreme Court had begun to redefine its role substantially in the wake of its New Deal–era conflicts, abandoning an agenda centered around the protection of economic freedom for one emphasizing civil rights and civil liberties. *Carolene Products*' footnote four was the keynote for the Court's new normative narrative, which emphasized its role as the protector of rights, paradigmatically the rights of minority groups vulnerable to abuse by local majorities.[21] Civil rights cases played a huge part in defining the postwar judicial role. And crucially, the Court was not acting alone. Unlike in the 1880s, this time the civil rights agenda was undergirded by vigorous support from social movements and, increasingly, political support in the other branches of the national government. From the 1940s through the 1960s, the politics of civil rights took on an increasingly sectional cast, with the intransigence of the South putting it at odds with an emerging national consensus.

It was against this backdrop that the Supreme Court adopted a new jurisprudence that showcased its role as a rights-promoting court. For the first time, the Supreme Court permitted Congress to legislate against private (as well as public) discrimination under the banner of enforcing constitutional rights. Doing so required the Court to permit a level of interpretive pluralism that the Court had long resisted: to some degree, Congress got to say for itself what constitutional rights meant. But even so, there remained redoubts of private law not reached by the civil rights statutes, where state courts could continue to undercut these constitutional values. And these were the areas of law where the Supreme Court bent the rules of the state action doctrine, deploying constitutional rights horizontally to bring wayward states back into line. In making both of these moves, the Court demonstrated its unique contribution to American government. Without the Court, there could be no national response to racial discrimination under private law in the states. And without turning to constitutional rights, the Court could not address that discrimination. The Court's moves were part of a new postwar constitutional settlement that placed the protection of rights at the heart of American constitutionalism.

It is in the civil rights and civil liberties context, during the postwar years—and the Warren Court years in particular—that the Supreme Court most nearly resembles Germany's Federal Constitutional Court, both with respect to its horizontal application of rights and its tolerance for a measure of legislative constitutionalism. In the Supreme Court's hands, horizontal rights could be potent: applying as entitlements that brooked no consideration of competing values; underwriting new causes of actions against private parties; overriding contrary provisions of law. But unlike in Germany, the Court gave no across-the-board green light for the horizontal application of rights, and there was no constitutional cascade. Instead, the Supreme Court relaxed the strictures of the state action rule on an ad hoc basis. As a matter of rhetoric, the Court's answer

21. United States v. Carolene Products Co., 304 U.S. 144, 152 n.4 (1938).

to the question "when are constitutional rights horizontally effective?" was still "never." But in practice, the answer was, "when we say they are."

If the Supreme Court's state action jurisprudence is confusing on its own terms, it becomes more intelligible when viewed from a strategic perspective. The Supreme Court deviated from the state action rule when doing so furthered the substantive agenda that the Supreme Court had made its own, the agenda of civil rights and civil liberties. The next chapter demonstrates this point comparatively. Constitutionalizing family law, for instance, would not meaningfully advance any normative vision or strategic interest of the Court. And so, the Court did not constitutionalize family law to any significant extent. The Court brought constitutional rights to bear on libel law to the extent that it threatened civil libertarian values: when public figures brought suits that could chill debate on matters of public concern. The Court was less apt to disturb other private law regulations of speech. And the area nearest the heart of the Warren Court's agenda, race discrimination, generated the most deviations from the state action rule. As the 1960s ended and the Court sloughed off its identity as a protector of rights first and foremost, it also retreated from its expansive state action jurisprudence.

The Supreme Court's state action doctrine also needs to be understood in relation to two other bodies of constitutional law: Congress's authority to legislate under the Commerce Clause and Congress's enforcement powers under the Reconstruction Amendments. As disparate as these doctrines are, they overlap functionally insofar as they serve as vehicles for bringing constitutional values into private legal relationships governed by state law. In the 1960s, the Court did expand Congress's enforcement power under the Reconstruction Amendments to uphold antidiscrimination statutes, including legislation addressing discrimination by private parties. In so doing, the Court gave Congress a freer hand to define for itself the practical meaning of constitutional guarantees. But the Court also allowed Congress to pass some of its most far-reaching equality legislation under the banner of regulating commerce, which altogether sidestepped tricky questions about the scope of rights. In the mid-twentieth century, the state action doctrine picked up the slack where there were regional gaps in the protection of favored constitutional values that were unreachable by federal legislation.

The Supreme Court's ad hoc postwar renovations of state action doctrine had both costs and benefits. One cost was paid in coherence and predictability. The state action doctrine became "a conceptual disaster area" precisely because the Court refused to repudiate it even while reaching results incompatible with it. The Court pays some price in legitimacy when its jurisprudence is unintelligible, and perhaps a higher price still when it is intelligible only with reference to "political," as opposed to "legal," considerations.

At the same time, this unpredictability bolstered the Supreme Court's position as the ultimate expositor of the Constitution. By formally insisting on a state action requirement, the Supreme Court discouraged lower courts and other institutions from developing novel rights theories on their own. The Court alone enjoyed the latitude to stretch the Constitution's reach. At other times, the state action doctrine provided the Court with cover, permitting it to avoid reaching difficult substantive questions about what rights required (as in *Flagg Brothers*).

Another consequence of state action doctrine registers in a sharp bifurcation between Big-C and small-c constitutionalism in the United States. When an issue has a Big-C Constitutional dimension, the courts' involvement displaces normal politics entirely. At the same time, the Supreme Court is sidelined from many policy debates that have a small-c constitutional character (in that they speak to core national commitments), with the result that these policy projects are insulated from the language and solemnity of constitutionalism, except in an attenuated way. Certainly the domains of constitutional politics and ordinary politics are not totally self-contained and sealed off from each other in the United States (Ackerman 2007). But the notional divide between the two tends to hamper, rather than promote, meaningful interinstitutional dialogue over important issues of national concern. This sharp bifurcation is not necessarily a net negative, but it is a feature that distinguishes constitutionalism in the United States from its counterparts in other countries.

This chapter and the next are organized as follows. The next section describes the contents of the constitutional rights contained in the antebellum Constitution, in relation to the normative world of the common law. The following section explains the structure of federal court jurisdiction in the context of antebellum legal thought and the Supreme Court's position during the Civil War years. The first section of Chapter Five picks up with the dramatic transformation in constitutional law wrought by the post–Civil War amendments to the Constitution and the Supreme Court's original articulation of the state action doctrine in the wake of those changes. The remainder of the chapter details how the twentieth-century Supreme Court adapted state action doctrine to meet contemporary challenges in the areas of discrimination, freedom of expression, and family law, and considers broader impacts on lawmaking processes in these areas, before concluding.

AMERICAN CONSTITUTIONAL RIGHTS

Americans face a problem in thinking about our own constitutional history. We think that we know the Constitution that the delegates to the Philadelphia Convention signed in 1787 because the Constitution is a part of our civic culture as Americans. Its signing is indelibly memorialized in Howard Chandler Christy's iconic painting, with its tableau of framers arrayed across the canvas.

But our world is not the world of the framers. What the words of the Constitution—and the amendments shortly to be added to it—meant to them is not necessarily what they mean to us. Quentin Skinner warns of the danger "that the historian may conceptualize an argument in such a way that its alien elements are dissolved into an apparent but misleading familiarity" (Skinner 1969, 27). The danger is all the greater when the object of study already seems so familiar to us.

This section analyzes the character of constitutional rights in the antebellum American state, and the following section discusses the constitutional basis for judicial power and the relation of judicial power to federalism. In these sections, I emphasize two too-easily forgotten features of the American constitutional project. First, that it presupposed, and built upon, a robust common law heritage that already supplied important baseline legal norms, including, paradigmatically, for private law. The common law itself had something of a constitutional character, as it was understood to be fundamental law that formed the foundation for the whole legal order. Indeed, the dividing line between constitutional law and common law was not always drawn with precision in the early Republic.

Second, and relatedly, interpreting the Constitution was generally not understood to be the exclusive province of the judicial branch. Most antebellum officials subscribed to the departmentalist view that each branch of government possesses independent authority to interpret the Constitution (Kramer 2004, 201). In other words, if the Constitution was not regarded as the exclusive source of fundamental rights in the early republic, neither were the courts considered the exclusive arbiters of constitutional meaning. While the Supreme Court reserved for itself the authority to interpret the Constitution, and strike down laws as unconstitutional if necessary, the other branches insisted on the right to have their own constitutional interpretations. So for instance, when Andrew Jackson vetoed the charter extension for the Second Bank of the United States in 1832, he did so with a message explaining why he understood the Bank to be unconstitutional—notwithstanding the Supreme Court's contrary opinion in *McCulloch v. Maryland*.[22]

These points are important to the argument I advance in the last section of this chapter and the first section of the next: when the Reconstruction Amendments brought important new rights online, there was ample support in the American constitutional tradition for a jurisprudence in which rights

22. 17 U.S. 316 (1819); see Brest et al. (2006, 74–77).

could require affirmative acts from the states to regulate private-party relations, and Congress could play a role in defining their terms. I explain why, instead, the Supreme Court took a strictly vertical and court-centric approach to rights.

While the original text of the U.S. Constitution, as drafted by the delegates to the Philadelphia Convention during the summer of 1787, contained no charter of rights, it did provide guarantees against certain government abuses, including ex post facto laws, bills of attainder, and (except in cases of emergency) suspension of habeas corpus.[23] But the absence of more explicit rights protections quickly became one of the key flashpoints in the effort to get the Constitution ratified. Though the Constitution's promoters offered assurances that explicit rights protection was unnecessary, as the Constitution's built-in limitations on the national government's power preserved an ample sphere of freedom,[24] several state ratifying conventions demanded amendments that explicitly added in rights.

The first Congress obliged, and James Madison drafted nineteen amendments, which were winnowed and edited in Congress to a slate of twelve. Two of these were not ratified by the requisite three-fourths of state legislatures, but those that were became the first ten amendments to the Constitution in 1791.

The Bill of Rights reads, to us, like the prototypical liberal charter of rights. All of the usual suspects seem to be here: freedom of speech, the press, assembly, and belief; protections of the person, home, and property against unreasonable searches, seizures, and treatment; rights to fair process in both criminal and civil matters. In addition, there appear some other elements less consonant with the liberal creed: the right to bear arms, and what appears to be a fetish for juries.

In fact, the original ten amendments are less familiar than they seem at first blush. First, as Akhil Amar has argued, the first amendments to the Constitution have at least as much to say about the structures and processes of government as about individual liberties (Amar 2000, 2012). The free press guarantee, for instance, was valued not least for its instrumental role as a check on government abuses that could be punished at the ballot box. And the insistence on juries and citizen militias both speak to ensuring public access to the levers of power through popular participation in the processes of government.

Some rights also speak to the vertical separation of powers between national and state governments. In declaring that Congress can make no law respecting an establishment of religion, the First Amendment leaves the states free to establish official churches without federal interference—which many of them

23. U.S. Const., art. I, sec. 9.

24. See, for instance, The Federalist No. 84 (Alexander Hamilton).

had done. Nor are the rights all individual rights. Juries and militias are groups of citizens acting together, and the First Amendment's "right of the people peaceably to assemble" is a right explicitly granted to "the people" (Bhagwat 2010, 30–36; Primus 2007, 85–88).

And importantly, prior to *Marbury v. Madison*, it was by no means obvious that federal courts would be freely exercising a general power of judicial review, to test government actions for conformity with the Constitution.[25] The Bill of Rights represented something more than, and also less than, a charter of rights as we understand the term: a set of justiciable, individual, defensive rights. (Indeed, the first time the Supreme Court used the term "Bill of Rights" to refer to the first ten amendments was in the *Slaughterhouse Cases*, after the Civil War.[26])

Moreover, the rights guaranteed in the amendments were intended not to create new entitlements to government forbearance so much as to restate, and express commitment to, norms already in effect. In Akhil Amar's words, Madison "generally endorsed clauses . . . that clarified limits that federalists had claimed were implicit in their plan all along, or that codified principles that were common practice among the states" (2012, 319). In asking Congress to adopt the amendments in his first inaugural address, George Washington urged Congress to enshrine "the characteristic rights of freemen" (Amar 2012, 318).

And importantly, the whole constitutional project played out against the backdrop of a common law that was understood to provide substantial protection for individuals' basic rights (Chemerinsky 1985, 506). Prerevolutionary polemicists frequently invoked the English common law as the treasured heritage of the colonies, the repository of "the rights and liberties of Englishmen that were claimed as an indefeasible birthright" (Goebel 1964, 11) but denied by the actions of the Crown. "These appeals to the common law . . . created a regard for its virtues that seems almost mystical," and this aura carried over into the early republic. Even before the Constitution was drafted, most states had already passed reception statutes that formally adopted the English common

25. In an important article, Michael Treanor has argued that U.S. courts prior to *Marbury* exercised a power of judicial review far more often than typically appreciated (2005). Significantly, Treanor finds that courts generally used that power to overturn statutes only when separation of powers issues were implicated or when states trenched on federal powers. More broadly, Philip Hamburger has argued that what we call the power of judicial review was a necessary incident of the common law conception of the judicial role (2008). But what Hamburger describes is not identical to modern judicial review. Also, his book says little about how a written constitution might have altered that older conception (White 2010; Steinfeld 2010).

26. 83 U.S. 36, 109 (1872).

law as providing the default rules of decision, subject to statutory alteration (Horwitz 1977, 4).

Indeed, the common law functioned in some respects as the constitutional law of the early republic.[27] First, the common law was in an important sense the fundamental law of the country, predating the written Constitution. For legal theorists of the early nineteenth century, "constitutionalism was derived from and always secondary to an older body of law that remained the 'national law' of the Union and the individual states—'the general law of the land'" (Novak 1996, 38).[28] Furthermore, the common law defined individual rights—and not only "political" rights but "the more general 'civil rights and obligations of the citizen': 'the relations between man and man'"(Novak 1996, 37).[29]

Although thinking about the nature of common law evolved in the early Republic,[30] the common law remained a pervasive regulatory regime through the first half of the nineteenth century, through which courts—primarily state courts—provided the rules that a well-regulated society required. The common law functioned as the primary matrix within which individuals' competing rights claims were asserted, assessed, and negotiated.

The law of nuisance, for instance, was the site where courts mediated between competing interests, both private and public, by adjudicating claims about the scope and limits of property rights. In the words of Horace Wood's influential treatise on the law of nuisance, "every enjoyment by one of his own property, which violates the rights of another in an essential degree, is a nuisance, and actionable as such at the suit of the party injured thereby" (Wood 1875, 2). Nuisance law placed limits on personal liberty as well, and Wood's treatise offers, among many others, keeping a disorderly house, calling together large and disorderly crowds, eavesdropping, and indecent exposure as examples of nuisances. The law of nuisance furnished a basis for the regulation of public health and public morals—indeed, it was "one of the most important regulatory

27. See Eskridge and Ferejohn (2010, 209) ("At the founding, America's small 'c' constitution consisted, in large part, of state common law.").

28. Novak is quoting Henry Baldwin and Peter Du Ponceau.

29. Here Novak quotes Francis Hilliard.

30. Morton Horwitz has argued that what the common law represented in the United States changed between the late eighteenth century and the early nineteenth century. Between 1780 and the 1820, Americans came to regard the common law less as the distillation of "natural principles of justice" and more as "an instrument of will," justified by consent and social utility (Horwitz 1977, 7, 22). The common law was not frozen in time but continually adapting to meet evolving needs. James Wilson praised its "accommodating spirit," which permitted it to "adjust itself to every grade and species of improvement by practice, commerce, observation, study, and refinement" (Novak 1996, 40).

tools of the nineteenth-century American state" (Novak 1996, 44). The touchstone for the limits of individual rights in the law of nuisance was the maxim *sic utere tuo ut alienum non laedas*: use your own so as not to harm another. Nineteenth-century state courts proceeded under this banner to define the scope and limits of individual rights.

Moreover, Americans were not always punctilious about distinguishing between the written Constitution and the common law. The term "constitution" was often used in the founding era to refer to fundamental rights derived from natural law or English historical practice (Chemerinsky 1985, 514 n.50).

The quasi-constitutional character of the common law is also reflected in its relationship to legislation. According to the famous canon of statutory interpretation, statutes in derogation of the common law are to be construed narrowly (Novak 1996, 267 n.95). Accordingly, the common law acted as a kind of force field that shaped how legislation was received by courts.

JUDICIAL POWER AND FEDERALISM

The prominence of the common law in the founding period helps explain both the constitutional division of labor between federal and state courts, and state governments' exemption from the rights contained in the first ten amendments.

The constitutional relationship between the jurisdiction of federal and state courts, as codified in Article III, mimics the structure of American federalism more generally: the national bodies, both legislative and judicial, have power over a narrowly defined set of subject matters, while their state counterparts operate under almost no subject matter restrictions—but valid acts of the national institutions trump the states. Article I, Section 8 confines the legislative competence of Congress to limited areas, but under Article VI, federal law is supreme over state law within those areas. Similarly, Article III, Section 2 provides that "[t]he judicial power [of the United States] shall extend to" nine different classes of "cases and controversies," including cases arising under federal law and the Constitution, cases between citizens of different states, and controversies where the United States is a party. Rulings of federal courts trump state courts within those areas; state court rulings may be appealed to federal courts, but not the other way around.[31]

Critically, the Constitution left underdetermined the scope of federal judicial power in two respects. First, the Constitution itself only established one federal court: the Supreme Court. Article III, Section 1 declared that "[t]he Judicial Power of the United States, shall be vested in one Supreme Court, and in such

31. See Martin v. Hunter's Lessee, 14 U.S. 304 (1816).

inferior courts as the Congress shall from time to time ordain and establish." Because the Constitution granted the Supreme Court original jurisdiction only over the rare cases involving ambassadors and public ministers and those to which a state was a party, had Congress declined to "ordain and establish" federal trial courts, federal judicial power would be exercised exclusively by the Supreme Court, primarily on appeal from decisions by state courts. Second, while Article III made it constitutional for federal courts to exercise jurisdiction in the named classes of cases, it did not compel Congress to grant courts jurisdiction over all these cases. Indeed, Article III, Section 2 explicitly makes the Supreme Court's appellate jurisdiction subject to "such exceptions, and under such regulations as the Congress shall make."

In fact, the first Congress did establish lower federal courts, in the Judiciary Act of 1789: both trial courts ("district courts") and intermediate "circuit" courts, which were to be staffed by a combination of Supreme Court Justices "riding circuit" and district court judges. But the first Congress did not vest the newly created courts with the full jurisdiction permissible under the Constitution, or anything close to it. The Act did grant federal trial courts diversity jurisdiction—original jurisdiction over actions where the parties are citizens of different states. However, the Act did not establish general federal question jurisdiction. In other words, a claim that raised a question under federal law was not, without more, a ticket into a federal court.

The 1789 Act did establish some islands of specialized federal question jurisdiction over certain kinds of cases, including federal felony cases.[32] The Act also vested the Supreme Court with appellate jurisdiction over certain federal law rulings by states' highest courts. Specifically, Section 25 gave the Supreme Court the power to review state court decisions (1) invalidating federal statutes, treaties, or actions; (2) upholding state statutes or acts against claims of violating federal law, the Constitution, or treaties; and (3) denying claims made under the Constitution or federal statutes, treaties, or commissions. At least in these critical contexts, when state courts limited federal power, expanded state power at the expense of federal claims, or limited rights under federal law, the 1789 Act gave a federal court jurisdiction to review. Outside of these circumstances, however, the 1789 Act contemplated that questions of federal law would be decided by state courts and not subject to review in any federal court.[33] Moreover, the

32. Judiciary Act of 1789, 1 Stat. 73, § 9. Federal district courts had exclusive jurisdiction over those matters and shared concurrent jurisdiction with state courts over others, including tort claims brought by aliens for violations of the law of nations or treaties.

33. Not counting a short-lived effort to expand federal question jurisdiction by the outgoing Federalist Congress in 1801, Congress would only establish general federal question jurisdiction with the Jurisdiction and Removal Act of 1875.

Judiciary Act permitted cases subject to the concurrent jurisdiction of both state and federal courts, but actually filed by plaintiffs in state court, to be removed to federal court only in limited circumstances.[34]

The regime envisioned by the first Judiciary Act was thus one in which the tasks of interpreting federal law and the Constitution would be shared by state and federal courts, with the former doing the lion's share of the work. Ironically to modern sensibilities, federal courts are valuable in this vision mostly for their role in deciding what we would consider questions of state law, as neutral fora for the resolution of diversity disputes.[35] The 1789 Act equipped federal courts with limited levers for steering or coordinating state court interpretations of federal law and the Constitution. The Supreme Court could overturn state supreme court decisions that favored state law claims over federal law claims in the event of a conflict, but such conflicts and hence such decisions would be relatively rare, given the limited scope of federal legislation in the early republic.

Constitutional rights were also a potential source for federal judicial power, but only a weak one, since the Supreme Court held in *Barron v. Baltimore* that the constitutional rights contained in the first ten amendments do not apply against state governments.[36] As Chief Justice Marshall explained, the amendments were adopted owing to concern that "those powers which the patriot statesmen who then watched over the interests of our country deemed essential to union, and to the attainment of those invaluable objects for which union was sought,"—that is, the powers of the national government—"might be exercised in a manner dangerous to liberty."[37] Accordingly, the amendments "demanded security against the apprehended encroachments of the General Government—not against those of the local governments."[38]

The fact that state governments were largely exempted from constitutional rights review in federal courts was not regarded as a cause of concern in the early republic, and not only because state governments were considered to be closer to the people and therefore less of a threat to their liberty.[39] It was also the case,

34. Judiciary Act of 1789, 1 Stat. 73, § 12.

35. It was not obvious to nineteenth-century lawyers that the common law was state law and not federal law; indeed, whether it was federal or state law was the subject of an important and long-running debate (Amar 2000, 147).

36. 32 U.S. 243 (1833).

37. *Id.* at 250.

38. *Id.*

39. State governments were not entirely exempted: Article I, Section 10 of the Constitution contains prohibitions against the states—for instance, a ban on ex post facto laws—that could be the basis for litigation.

as Chief Justice Marshall observed, that the states were bound by state constitutions that predated the federal Constitution and restrained state power.[40] And importantly, as discussed above, the common law was understood to provide substantial protection for individuals' basic rights. The common law, with state courts as its stewards, offered the founding generation some assurance against gross abuses in the states.

Plainly, empowering federal courts to secure federal rights in the states was not a high priority for either the framers of the Constitution or the Congress that passed the 1789 Judiciary Act. Federal courts did perform a steering and coordinating function with respect to the law applied in the states, but they did so in large part through superintending the development of the common law. We see this in the 1842 case *Swift v. Tyson*, which illustrates the fundamental character of the common law as well as its implications for federalism and jurisdiction.[41]

The outcome in *Swift* turned on the enforceability of a note which had been endorsed to the plaintiff (Swift) in exchange for the cancellation of a debt. The note had been presented for payment and then dishonored in New York, and Swift brought his complaint in New York state court. Under the common law of contracts as applied in New York, such a note was unenforceable, because a preexisting debt did not count as consideration. Accordingly, Swift lost in the Court of New York and sought review in the U.S. Supreme Court on the basis of diversity: he was a citizen of Maine, and Tyson a citizen of New York.

The Supreme Court declined to follow the New York rule, notwithstanding the Rules of Decision Act, which instructed federal courts to apply "the laws of the several states" in diversity cases. Instead, the Supreme Court adopted the rule that it found to accord better with "the principles established in the general commercial law."[42] As Justice Story explained, the law of negotiable instruments was not the law of any one place; rather, it was law "of the commercial world."[43] The common law rulings handed down in New York courtrooms were not in any sense the law of New York; rather, they reflected the efforts of New York judges to apply law held in common. With respect to this body of law, "the state tribunals are called upon to perform the like functions as ourselves, that is, to ascertain, upon general reasoning and legal analogies, what is the true exposition of the contract or instrument, or what is the just rule furnished by

40. 32 U.S. at 247.

41. 41 U.S. 1 (1842).

42. *Id.* at 18.

43. *Id.* at 19.

the principles of commercial law to govern the case."[44] In *Swift*, the general commercial law, and the common law more generally, is something bigger than state law: it is, in Justice Holmes's derisive phrase from decades later, a "brooding omnipresence in the sky."[45]

THE CONSTITUTIONAL POLITICS OF RECONSTRUCTION AND THE STATE ACTION DOCTRINE

The world of American law changed with the Civil War and Reconstruction. The war, emancipation, and the Reconstruction Amendments fundamentally altered what "the United States" meant, transforming the relation of the parts to the whole and the nature of the American enterprise of self-government. And the idea of rights was at the heart of this transformation.

There were different paths the Supreme Court could have taken in giving content to the new rights guaranteed against the states by the Reconstruction Amendments. The Court could have concluded that these rights, even if not directly binding on private parties, nonetheless did produce an effect on private-party legal relations. The private law is maintained and enforced by the states, and the states are directly bound by rights: therefore, the states are bound to regulate the private law in a manner consistent with their rights obligations. Such an approach would amount to a version of indirect horizontal effect.

But this way of thinking about rights also resonates with antebellum American practice. The common law vision of the well-regulated society, in which the state is expected to intervene in private law orderings to mediate between the competing rights of different citizens, is congenial to it. What is more, this conception of the Reconstruction rights had substantial purchase when the amendments were still new. For a time, it was common ground between a majority in Congress and the Supreme Court that the states' failure to provide protection against at least some forms of discrimination was actionable under the Fourteenth Amendment, as explained below. This approach to the Reconstruction Amendments would also justify, as legislation to enforce the amendments, federal statutes targeting private discrimination.

Ultimately, though, the Court took a different path, inaugurating the state action doctrine in the *Civil Rights Cases*. As declining support for the Reconstruction project from the other branches of government and the broader public made an expansive approach to constitutional rights untenable, the Court retrenched. Its decisions of the 1870s and 1880s delimited the scope of constitutional rights and

44. *Id.*

45. Southern Pacific Co. v. Jensen, 244 U.S. 205, 222 (1917) (Holmes, J., dissenting).

more sharply distinguished them from nonconstitutional rights. These elements of the Court's postwar constitutional settlement both limited the relevance of constitutional rights in relations among nonstate actors and consolidated the Supreme Court's own role as master of the Constitution's meaning. This section analyzes the normative and strategic context in which the Court was operating in the years leading up to that decision, which is discussed in the following chapter.

The Postwar Legal Order

Three changes reshaped public law and federalism in the postwar legal order: the Reconstruction Amendments, enforcement legislation from Congress, and the expansion of the jurisdiction of federal courts. They are discussed in turn below.

Reconstruction Amendments

Not all provisions of the Reconstruction Amendments—the Thirteenth, Fourteenth, and Fifteenth—sounded in rights: Section 3 of the Fourteenth Amendment, for instance, bars former Confederates from serving in official capacities in the national government, subject to removal of the disability by Congress. But for the most part, the reconstruction of the three-point relationship between national government, state governments, and citizens was accomplished by means of rights. The Thirteenth Amendment declared that "[n]either slavery nor involuntary servitude, except as a punishment for crime whereof the party shall have been duly convicted, shall exist within the United States, or any place subject to their jurisdiction." This established a right not to be enslaved that was truly *erga omnes*, binding by its terms not only against state and national governments but against individuals as well.

After establishing birthright citizenship, Section 1 of the Fourteenth Amendment went on to declare that "[n]o State shall make or enforce any law which shall abridge the privileges or immunities of citizens of the United States" and to guarantee against the states rights of due process and the equal protection of the laws to all persons within their jurisdictions. Section 2 used the threat of reduced representation in Congress to induce states to secure the right to vote. The Fifteenth Amendment, ratified two years after the Fourteenth, afforded voting rights still stronger protection, flatly barring both states and national government from denying the right to vote "on account of race, color, or previous condition of servitude."

And crucially, Congress did not leave these rights to judicial enforcement alone but made them the platform for a broader structural and institutional transformation. All three of the amendments contained enforcement clauses, authorizing Congress to enforce the substantive provisions "by appropriate legislation." Congress thus reserved for itself a role in determining concretely what respecting rights would mean in the states, giving it newfound powers to legislate for the states.

What exactly were the rights that the states were newly obliged to respect? In particular, what exactly were the "privileges and immunities of citizens of the United States" that were binding on states by virtue of the Fourteenth Amendment? This debate has roiled mightily for many decades, both on and off the Court.[46] At the very least, it seems clear that the Privileges and Immunities Clause was understood at the time of its passage to encompass the individual rights textually guaranteed by the Constitution and its amendments, whatever else it might contain.

Another important question concerns the other rights innovation of the Fourteenth Amendment, the newly minted right to equal protection. The amendment declares that "no State shall . . . deny to any person within its jurisdiction the equal protection of the laws." What obligations exactly does this impose on the state?

Pamela Brandwein has argued persuasively that the equal protection rights of the Fourteenth Amendment originally was understood not only to bar the states from treating persons differently on the basis of race but also to obligate the states to provide affirmative protection against certain kinds of discriminatory abuses initiated by private actors. According to Brandwein, the Reconstruction Congresses and the Supreme Court alike spoke a "lost language of state neglect."[47]

For politicians and jurists with mainstream views (as opposed to Democrats on one side and radical Republicans on the other), the states were obligated to protect an important set of rights. More specifically, they must protect "those rights that a Republican consensus regarded as fundamental": those "deemed essential for blacks to become 'free laborers' on terms equal with whites" (Brandwein 2006, 276). These were civil rights, but not social rights. There

46. Notably, Akhil Amar has advanced an influential theory of "refined incorporation," according to which the Fourteenth Amendment obliges the states to respect all those individual rights guaranteed against the federal government, as found within the first eight amendments of the Bill of Rights, as well as elsewhere in the Constitution, plus a set of unenumerated common-law rights understood to be fundamental, including those named in the antebellum case *Corfield v. Coryell*, which interpreted the "privileges and immunities" clause found in Article IV of the Constitution (Amar 2000, 177–78). More recently, Kurt Lash has further refined refined incorporation, by drawing a sharp distinction between the "privileges and immunities of citizens of the United States" (in the Fourteenth Amendment) and the "privileges and immunities of citizens in the several States" (in Article IV). Lash argues that the former excludes any unenumerated rights: the states are bound to respect the textually secured individual constitutional rights only (2014, 278). For a brief overview of the controversies, see Lash (2014, vii–xi).

47. For details, see Brandwein (2006, 287–93).

were differences of opinion over which rights counted as fundamental (i.e., civil) rights: radical Republicans, for instance, would include rights of equal access to public accommodations, while most moderates would not.[48] But the idea that rights imposed on the states some duty to protect was common ground. Moreover, state neglect created an opening for federal action, under the enforcement structure of the Fourteenth Amendment: "The state's failure was a rights violation ('state action') within the meaning of the Fourteenth Amendment and Congress had the power to provide a remedy under Section 5 of that Amendment: the federal prosecution of individuals who remained unpunished" (Brandwein 2006, 276).

The state neglect concept was a "legal idiom . . . associated with nineteenth-century conceptions of rights and rights protections" (Brandwein 2006, 275). Indeed, the idea that the right to equal protection is more than a purely negative liberty—that is a right to be *protected*—fit comfortably with the open-textured and expansive antebellum conception of common law rights, as described above. Brandwein and other scholars have presented evidence that this understanding of the equal protection right was conventional early in Reconstruction.[49] For instance, in correspondence over a case pending in circuit court in early 1871, Justice (and eventual author of the *Civil Rights Cases*) Joseph Bradley explained his understanding of the scope of equal protection to Judge (and future Justice) William Woods as follows: "Denying includes inaction as well as action. And denying the equal protection of the laws includes the omission to protect as well as the omission to pass laws for protection. . . ."[50] Judge Woods reproduced Bradley's language nearly verbatim in his opinion in the case.[51]

Enforcement Legislation

In the decade after the Civil War, Congress passed a string of statutes to combat persistent violence and discrimination against African Americans in the

48. Richard Primus cautions modern scholars against taking too seriously the distinctions drawn between civil, social, and political rights in the Reconstruction period. Rather than reflecting a coherent and consistent typology, Primus argues that "particular rights moved about among the categories in a kind of constitutional shell game depending on whether legislators or judges wanted to confer those rights on blacks" (2007, 128).

49. In addition to Brandwein, see Frantz (1964). Brandwein's scholarship is more easily reconciled with the Supreme Court's jurisprudence than some other scholars', because she emphasizes the distinction between fundamental civil rights, which the state is obligated to protect, and social rights, which the state is not obligated to protect. See Brandwein (2006, 285–86). For a dissenting view, see Benedict (1978, 45).

50. Quoted in Brandwein (2014, 48).

51. United States v. Hall, 26 F. Cas. 79, 81 (C.C.S.D. Ala. 1871) (No. 15,282).

South. When the Civil Rights Act of 1866 provided insufficient protection, Congress enacted the Enforcement Acts and the Ku Klux Klan Act, as well as the Fifteenth Amendment, between 1870 and 1871. Vigorous enforcement of the Ku Klux Klan Act did reduce violence against African Americans, at least for a time (Foner 2002, 458–59). But it also exhausted Congress's appetite for Reconstruction.[52] Many Republicans hoped that the legislative efforts of the 41st Congress, culminating with the Fifteenth Amendment, would be Reconstruction's grand finale and justify them in washing their hands of the problems of African Americans. In the words of then-Congressman James A. Garfield, "The Fifteenth Amendment confers upon the African race the care of its own destiny. It places their fortunes in their own hands" (Foner 2002, 449).

By 1874 and 1875, violence and repression in the South were on the rise again, but this time, the federal government did not offer effective aid. As a new Democratic majority prepared to retake control of the House, the 43rd Congress did pass a final Civil Rights Act in 1875, but only "after bitter divisions among the Republicans themselves" (Kutler 1968, 159). By its terms, the 1875 Act was far-reaching. It declared, among other things, a right "to the full and equal enjoyment of the accommodations, advantages, facilities, and privileges of inns, public conveyances on land or water, theaters, and other places of public amusement," without regard to race or previous condition of servitude. The Act made violation a misdemeanor, punishable by fine and jail time, and also created a private right of action to sue in federal court for a $500 fine.

Federal Jurisdiction

Significantly, the same lame duck Congress also enacted the Jurisdiction and Removal Act of 1875. For the first time, this statute created general federal question jurisdiction: in other words, it gave federal trial courts original jurisdiction over all actions "arising under" federal law. Equally important, the Act provided for the removal of federal question actions to federal court. That is, a plaintiff could not defeat federal jurisdiction just by initiating an action in state court: the defendant could transfer the case to federal court. The statute

52. Already by the late 1860s, political enthusiasm for the Reconstruction project had begun to fade. Even President Ulysses S. Grant's 1868 campaign slogan, "Let Us Have Peace," conveyed exhaustion with the years of sectional conflict, and his exceptionally mediocre cabinet seemed "oddly detached from the debates over Reconstruction" (Foner 2002, 445). A string of Democratic victories in Southern states between 1869 and 1871 and the rise of the Ku Klux Klan during those same years undermined many of the gains freedmen had made since Appomattox (Foner 2002, 423–43).

expanded on more modest efforts to expand the federal courts' removal jurisdiction in 1866 and 1867 (Kutler 1968, 154).

The Jurisdiction and Removal Act ended the antebellum regime in which state courts played a lead role in applying federal law and elevated the federal courts in the American political economy. The 1875 statute and its predecessors represented "the greatest legislative expansion of jurisdiction since 1789" (Kutler 1968, 143). One significant driver behind Congress's consolidation of federal judicial power was "the objective of making federal courts into agents of economic nationalism": the parochialism of state courts was a threat to the growth of a national industrialized economy (Crowe 2007, 163). But coupled with the Civil Rights Act 1875, the jurisdictional reform had the effect of offloading responsibility for civil rights from Congress to the courts. With the restoration of "home rule" in the South following the disputed presidential election of 1876, the political branches' abandonment of the Reconstruction project was official and complete. The only real option for aggrieved citizens was to bring their claims of rights violations directly to federal courts, which could provide judicial remedies. The courts alone were left to make good on the promise that all citizens would enjoy the rights of national citizenship and equal protection of the laws.

Reconstruction Politics and the Supreme Court

And when the Court addressed these developments in the law, it did so from a position of institutional weakness. Since the Civil War, the Supreme Court had found itself in an extraordinarily delicate position. To the Republican majorities in both houses of Congress and the Republican president who took office in 1861, the Taney Court, indelibly identified with *Dred Scott*, was deeply suspect. Abraham Lincoln set about remaking the Court, appointing five new Justices (including Chief Justice Salmon Chase) between 1862 and 1864. The Republican Congress expected the judicial branch, post-Taney, to be a faithful agent of Reconstruction: it was not at all inclined to tolerate the Court throwing up obstacles to its wartime or Reconstruction plans, nor did it feel obliged to make a great show of respecting judicial independence.

Congress launched one shot across the Court's bow when it reduced the number of Justices from ten to seven in 1866, to prevent Andrew Jackson from making appointments, and a second when it stripped the Court of habeas corpus jurisdiction over military commissions in 1868, so as to deny the Court a chance to rule on the validity of the Reconstruction Acts. Meanwhile, Democrats looked to the Court as the guardian of the Constitution in the face of Republican overreaching. By repeatedly invoking the Constitution against Reconstruction policies, Democrats drew the Court straight into the white-hot political controversies of the day (Kutler 1968, 30).

The Court picked its way through the minefield of Reconstruction politics with great care.[53] The Court's rulings from the 1870s and 1880s helped to inter the increasingly unpopular Reconstruction project by constricting the scope of the constitutional rights that freedmen could claim or that could justify civil rights legislation from Congress. In 1872's *Slaughterhouse Cases*, the Court minimized the significance in the structural change in federal-state relations the Fourteenth Amendment had wrought and reduced the privileges and immunities of national citizenship to trivialities. The privileges and immunities guaranteed by the Fourteenth Amendment could not include fundamental civil rights, the Court reasoned, since that construction would "radically chang[e] the whole theory of the relations of the State and Federal governments to each other and of both these governments to the people."[54]

Four years later, in *United States v. Cruikshank*,[55] the Court threw out convictions under the 1870 Enforcement Act of three participants in the notorious Colfax Massacre.[56] The Enforcement Act made it unlawful for any persons to "band or conspire together . . . with intent to prevent or hinder [any citizen's] free exercise and enjoyment of any right or privilege granted or secured to him by the constitution or laws of the United States." The Court held the Act could not reach the offenses charged against the defendants. In an opinion by Justice Bradley, the Court relied on the logic of the *Slaughterhouse Cases* and stressed the distinction between natural rights and constitutional rights to hold that none of the conduct alleged against the defendants, in fact, violated rights of the United States.[57]

53. The Court avoided direct provocations whenever possible. The Court bowed to Congress's jurisdiction-stripping in *Ex parte McCardle*, 74 U.S. 506 (1869), but framed Congress's move as something less than a complete suspension of habeas (Kutler 1968, 104–08). On the other hand, the Court limited the conditions under which military commissions could be established and operate in *Ex parte Milligan*, 71 U.S. 2 (1866). In 1867 and 1868, the Court declined to pass on the constitutionality of Reconstruction, and in 1869, it upheld Reconstruction as a valid effort to enforce the constitutional guarantee of a republican form of government in each state. Mississippi v. Johnson, 71 U.S. 475 (1867); Georgia v. Stanton, 73 U.S. 50 (1868); Texas v. White, 74 U.S. 700 (1869).

54. Slaughterhouse Cases, 83 U.S. 36, 78 (1872).

55. 92 U.S. 542 (1876).

56. Following a dispute over local and state election results in 1872, a white paramilitary group numbering over three hundred attacked black supporters of the Republican candidate at the Grant Parish courthouse in Colfax, Louisiana, killing over one hundred.

57. As Pamela Brandwein has noted, the Court's opinion did not decisively close the door on the idea that the right to equal protection might oblige the state to take steps to protect citizens against discrimination *on the basis of race*; the opinion suggests in places that the indictment was defective because it did not clearly allege that race was the basis for the abuses at Colfax. The circuit court opinion, also written by Justice Bradley, made this point more clearly (Brandwein 2006, 293–95).

In short, then, already in the first decade after the end of the Civil War, the Supreme Court had done much to hollow out the protections offered by the new constitutional rights. It is against that backdrop that the Court would have the chance to decide in a few years' time what those rights meant for private-party legal relations.

5

State Action and Constitutional Containment

BIRTH OF THE STATE ACTION RULE

Coming not long after a stepped-up enforcement bill failed in Congress and President Ulysses S. Grant declined to send federal troops to Mississippi to stop violence against freedmen, the *Cruikshank* decision completed a troika of events that dramatically illustrated the abandonment of Reconstruction by all three branches of the national government (Foner 2002).[1] But *Cruikshank* is important also because it contained the seeds of the state action doctrine that the Court more fully developed in the *Civil Rights Cases*.[2] The *Civil Rights Cases* mark the most important moment in the Court's postwar constitutional settlement, and they are worth examining in some detail.

In March 1883, the Court heard five consolidated cases that involved the exclusion of African Americans from inns, theaters, and the railroad, in violation of the Civil Rights Act of 1875. Only one of the cases came from the Deep South, where the Act was going effectively unenforced (Goldstone 2012, 104, 118).

The central question for the Court, wrote Justice Bradley, was whether Congress had the power to pass the law. The statute's defenders relied principally on the Fourteenth Amendment. While acknowledging that Section 1's litany of things that "no State shall" do is "prohibitory in its character, and prohibitory upon the States," Justice Bradley noted that "[i]t is State action of a particular character that is prohibited. Individual invasion of individual rights

1. For details on the so-called Force Bill, see Gillette (1980, 280–99).

2. See, for instance, 92 U.S. at 554 ("The fourteenth amendment prohibits a State from depriving any person of life, liberty, or property, without due process of law; but this adds nothing to the rights of one citizen as against another. It simply furnishes an additional guaranty against any encroachment by the States upon the fundamental rights which belong to every citizen as a member of society.").

is not the subject-matter of the amendment."[3] The contours of the right guaranteed by Section 1 of the Fourteenth Amendment also circumscribe the scope of Congress's power to enforce the amendment under Section 5:

> [T]he last section of the amendment invests Congress with power to enforce it by appropriate legislation. To enforce what? To enforce the prohibition. To adopt appropriate legislation for correcting the effects of such prohibited State law and State acts, and thus to render them effectually null, void, and innocuous. This is the legislative power conferred upon Congress, and this is the whole of it.[4]

Congress cannot act here, precisely because the requisite state action is lacking:

> [U]ntil some State law has been passed, or some State action through its officers or agents has been taken, adverse to the rights of citizens sought to be protected by the Fourteenth Amendment, no legislation of the United States under said amendment, nor any proceeding under such legislation, can be called into activity.[5]

Congress may not use the Fourteenth Amendment to pass legislation that "cover[s] the whole domain of rights appertaining to life, liberty, and property, defining them and providing for their vindication. That would be to establish a code of municipal law regulative of all private rights between man and man in society."[6] The Civil Rights Act "does not profess to be corrective of any constitutional wrong committed by the States," but "proceeds *ex directo* to declare that certain acts committed by individuals shall be deemed offenses, and shall be prosecuted and punished by proceedings in the courts of the United States."[7] Hence, it exceeds the scope of Congress's power under the amendment.[8]

The *Civil Rights Cases* were recognized at the time, and have been recognized since, as a watershed in American rights jurisprudence.[9] As a matter of

3. *Civil Rights Cases*, 109 U.S. 3, 11 (1883).

4. *Id.*

5. *Id.* at 13.

6. *Id.*

7. *Id.* at 14.

8. The Court went on to hold that the Thirteenth Amendment did not authorize the Civil Rights Act either.

9. See Fairman (2009, 568–85) (describing contemporaneous media responses to the decision).

black letter constitutional law, the *Civil Rights Cases* are recognized as the origin of the state action rule, even if the decision did not explicitly reject the state neglect concept. A standard contemporary hornbook for law students offers the following lapidary formulation of this rule: "Nearly all of the rights guaranteed by the Constitution to individuals are protected only against interference *by government*" (Emanuel 2012, 435). But the *Civil Rights Cases* decision is not as straightforward as it might appear at first glance.

Start with the term "state action" itself. The natural question to ask is, "state action" as opposed to what: what is the alternative? Logically, there are two: there is *nonstate* action, and there is state *inaction* (West 2003). Statements in the *Civil Rights Cases* such as "[i]ndividual invasion of individual rights is not the subject-matter of the amendment" draw the reader's focus to the first of these oppositions, contrasting action *of the state* to action *of nonstate actors*. In other words, they suggest that the Court must choose between holding that the U.S. Constitution may be violated by actions of the state only and holding that the Constitution may be violated by both state action and the acts of nonstate actors. Framed in this way, the U.S. Supreme Court's judgment amounts only to a rejection of *direct* horizontal effect and seems uncontroversial.

But this framing obscures the second opposition, between state action and state *inaction*. In this framing, the question becomes: may the Constitution be violated by state action only, or also by state inaction? Or, to particularize it to the issue in the *Civil Rights Cases*, can the right to equal protection of the laws impose on the state affirmative obligations: for instance, to proscribe or punish certain forms of discriminatory treatment? This question is trickier. As described above, the contemporaneous conventional wisdom seemed to be that the Fourteenth Amendment encompassed state neglect: that state inaction could be, in a word, actionable under the Fourteenth Amendment.

The question of just how far the state's obligations ran, however, was more controverted, as discussed above. But Justice Bradley framed matters in the *Civil Rights Cases* in a way that permitted the Court to sidestep these difficult issues. In his opinion, Justice Bradley nowhere explicitly repudiated the statement he had made to Judge Woods a dozen years earlier: that "denying the equal protection of the laws includes the omission to protect as well as the omission to pass laws for protection." Rather, he changed the conversation, shifting the focus from the role of the state to the proximate source of the injuries for which redress was sought (here, the owners of private establishments who denied entry to African Americans). In this way, the *Civil Rights Cases* prefigure the peculiarities of *Flagg Brothers* a century later. The Court in *Flagg Brothers* focused on whether the actions of the warehousemen could be attributed to the state, rather than asking whether the challenged statute, which was undeniably an action of the state, was consistent with the Constitution.

The state action rule, as introduced in the *Civil Rights Cases*, reduced the potency of rights as a tool for challenging unequal institutions and practices. It marks an important moment in more than one narrative of institutional and moral failure in American history. It is the culmination of the judicial abandonment of the Reconstruction project, and the recently freed slaves it had sought to help, which was part of the abandonment by each of the branches of the national government.[10] It also anticipated the Supreme Court's wholesale capitulation to the rise of Jim Crow in the South more than a decade later, in *Plessy v. Ferguson*.[11]

But even if the Court had wanted to pursue an equality agenda, it is by no means clear how successful it would have been in the face of widespread hostility by the governments of the South and without support from the political branches of the federal government.[12] Political support for enforcing Reconstruction rights was spent well before the *Civil Rights Cases* were argued to the Court. As Pamela Brandwein has argued,

> It seems clear that the Court, in this highly unstable political environment, lacked the clout to lead with an assertive racial egalitarianism. The Court faced institutional concerns regarding the preservation of its legitimacy. Recounting *Colfax* or repeating Justice Woods would have highlighted Southern maladministration of law as a rights denial. And as events made plain, the Court could not count on the executive branch to undertake the broad prosecutorial efforts necessary to remedy this rights denial, *i.e.*, to enforce the Court's rules. By recounting *Colfax* or repeating Justice Woods, the Court thus risked appearing ineffectual. The Court's modulated expression of state neglect, then, can be seen as an "available device for not doing"; that is, for not putting itself out in front of the political branches during a period of instability when four Republican presidents (Grant, Hayes, Arthur, Harrison) tacked away and then back toward rights enforcement. This secured key legal principles without risking the influence of the Court (Brandwein 2007, 372) (internal citation omitted).

10. Justice Bradley's eagerness to turn the page on Reconstruction is almost palpable in the *Civil Rights Cases*. He writes: "When a man has emerged from slavery, and by the aid of beneficent legislation has shaken off the inseparable concomitants of that state, there must be some stage in the progress of his elevation when he takes the rank of a mere citizen, and ceases to be the special favorite of the laws, and when his rights as a citizen, or a man, are to be protected in the ordinary modes by which other men's rights are protected." 109 U.S. at 25.

11. 163 U.S. 537 (1896).

12. See generally Rosenberg (2008).

The Court "risked appearing ineffectual" if it declared that citizens were entitled to rights that the state governments violated at every turn with the tacit acquiescence of federal law enforcement. Instead, the Court declared "mission accomplished" and left the field, asserting that the abuses in the South did not implicate constitutional rights.[13]

Taking a more expansive approach to constitutional rights would also have reduced the Supreme Court's control over the interpretation and application of those rights. Suppose the Supreme Court had signaled in the *Civil Rights Cases* that the Fourteenth Amendment imposed some affirmative duties on the states to protect citizens against discrimination. Questions about what the Constitution concretely required of the states would be litigated not only in federal but also state courts, with limited opportunities for federal review.[14] The Supreme Court could have substantial difficulty corralling disparate views on the reach of rights into coherent doctrine, as it might also had it afforded Congress broad latitude to use its Fourteenth Amendment enforcement power to define the meaning of the equality right in its own terms. Competing constructions of rights could both challenge the Court's cassational capacity and drag it into contentious conflicts it would prefer to avoid in an era of highly charged politics.

The state action doctrine helped the Supreme Court to consolidate its interpretative authority over the Constitution. Other moves the Court made during this same period also strengthened its position. In particular, the Supreme Court had normalized judicial review of federal statutes in the years immediately after the Civil War. Even as the Supreme Court bobbed and weaved on the most high-profile issues concerning the war and Reconstruction, it struck down ten federal statutes in whole or part between 1865 and 1873, in contrast to only two previously (in *Marbury* and *Dred Scott*)[15] (Kutler 1968, 114; Horwitz

13. Intimidation already reduced the number of claims brought under the Civil Rights Act to a handful, rendering it a "dead letter" even before the Supreme Court issued its opinion (Foner 2002, 552). The Supreme Court's decision spared the national government the embarrassment of having the law on the books any more.

14. These questions could end up decided by a state court depending on the manner in which they were raised. As the Supreme Court first held in *Metcalf v. City of Watertown*, 128 U.S. 586 (1888), a case only "arises under" federal law for the purposes of the federal subject matter jurisdiction statute if federal law is a necessary element of the plaintiff's case. So if, for instance, a defendant in a trespass action asserted that his ejection from an inn on account of his race was unconstitutional, he would have to litigate the issue in state court, since the federal (constitutional) issue only arises as part of the defense. The Supreme Court would be the only federal court that could exercise jurisdiction, and it could only do so after the state appeals process had run its course.

15. Dred Scott v. Sandford, 60 U.S. 393 (1857).

1992, 19). The cases included *United States v. Dewitt*,[16] the first case in which the Court struck down a federal law on Commerce Clause grounds, and *Hepburn v. Griswold*,[17] which invalidated the issuance of paper money as inconsistent, not with any specific provision, but with the "spirit" of the Constitution.

In any other period of U.S. history, these cases probably would have received more attention because they raised important issues of federal-state relations and the separation of powers. But with war and Reconstruction cases drawing disproportionate scrutiny, the Court quietly laid the groundwork for judicial supremacy in these and other rulings.[18] The Court was laying to rest the departmentalist views of constitutional interpretation that had had such currency in the antebellum years.

The Court also marked out the borders of its bailiwick by sharpening the hitherto hazy distinction between the law of the U.S. Constitution and what it called "general constitutional law." In *Loan Association v. Topeka*, from 1874, the Supreme Court was still willing to invalidate a state tax imposed for the benefit of a private business, not because it violated any textual provision of the Constitution but because "there are such rights in every free government beyond the control of the State. . . . The theory of our governments, State and National, is opposed to the deposit of unlimited powers anywhere."[19] But just four years later, the Court was far more punctilious about the nature of federal constitutional law. In *Davidson v. Louisiana*, the Court declined to strike down a state tax as a violation of due process.[20] The Court distinguished its resort to the general common law in *Loan Association* on the ground that the Court had been reviewing a lower federal court, not a state court, in the earlier case. The

16. 76 U.S. 41 (1870).

17. 75 U.S. 603 (1870), overruled by the *Legal Tender Cases*, 79 U.S. 457 (1871).

18. Stanley Kutler's summation of these developments is worth quoting at some length:

> Perhaps the greatest relevance of the judicial review cases is as an adumbration of future developments. The role and record of the Supreme Court as a legislative censor in the late nineteenth century are clearly established. The activities of the post–Civil War decade, however, might be seen as a foundation for the Court's later behavior and character. The regular pattern of asserting the propriety of judicial review, the willingness to examine legislative purpose, and the perfection of vested rights characterized the Chase Court's decisions almost as much as those of later years. While the history of judicial review properly goes back to *Marbury v. Madison*, and beyond, the Court's performance from 1865 to 1873 marked a significant deviation. The sheer volume alone is different. But more important was the political and public acceptance of this judicial function as a standard for measuring the legitimacy of power (Kutler 1968, 125).

19. 87 U.S. 655, 662, 663 (1874).

20. 96 U.S. 97, 105 (1878).

Court's ostensible restraint in *Davidson* at the same time underlines the idea, commonplace now but not at the time, that the law of the U.S. Constitution is a body of positive law, which is distinct and separate from general principles and inherited legal traditions and over which the Supreme Court has final interpretive authority.

When first confronted with the opportunity to give horizontal effect to constitutional rights, the U.S. Supreme Court demurred. The Court framed the issue in terms of a dichotomy between state action and nonstate action and held categorically that constitutional rights did not apply to the latter. The discriminatory treatment African Americans endured, especially in the South, fell far short of the constitutional values embodied in the Reconstruction Amendments, and using rights to bridge the gap would have been consistent with the widespread contemporary understanding that rights could require positive action by the state. But in the context of post-Reconstruction politics, doing so was not in the Court's interest. While federal courts had new formal powers to control how federal law was applied in the states, owing to the postwar expansions of federal jurisdiction, there was no political support for advancing the protection of civil rights. A broad declaration of the scope of rights would be undercut by the intransigence of Southern states and the indifference of the Congress and the President.

By contrast, the state action rule yielded functional advantages for the Court. By framing the question of rights' horizontal effect in terms of an opposition between state action and nonstate action, the Court altogether avoided entanglement in difficult, contentious questions about when state *inaction* might be constitutionally actionable. And confining the effect of rights to the vertical citizen-state relationship aided the Court in its efforts to differentiate constitutional law from common law and establish itself as the ultimate authority on the former.

STATE ACTION UNDER PRESSURE

In the decades after the *Civil Rights Cases*, the state action rule effectively shut down any and all claims that the states bore obligations, derived from constitutional rights, to protect the interests of individuals against the acts of other nonstate actors. Under the banner of the state action rule, the Supreme Court held not only that states were not *required* to take action to protect individuals against unequal treatment but also that the federal government was not *permitted* to protect individuals against such treatment.[21] The doctrine, only

21. See, e.g., Hodges v. United States, 203 U.S. 1 (1906).

rarely subjected to critical examination, served for many years as a powerful constitutional containment device.[22] The point is not that the Supreme Court was categorically hostile to new rights claims; after all, the "Lochnerism" of the early twentieth century depended on finding new rights to economic liberty in the Fourteenth Amendment. Rather, the state action requirement blocked rights claims to—as opposed to rights claims *against*—state interventions in private orderings. And by preemptively ruling out of bounds many potential rights claims as well as many potential uses of the congressional enforcement powers, it helped ensure that the Supreme Court would dictate the course of constitutional change.

In the years following World War II, however, the Court's state action framework came under increasing pressure. In the wake of a war against Nazi and fascist enemies, and in the context of a Cold War against a repressive Soviet state, a civil liberties and equal rights agenda gained political ground in the United States. Popular opposition mounted to racial discrimination in particular, championed by an active civil rights movement. The Supreme Court played an important role in pushing the national debate on civil rights forward, most explosively with its 1954 decision in *Brown v. Board of Education*. Since the Supreme Court gave up its role as legislative censor in the social and economic field in the late 1930s, it had begun defining its identity, with increasing clarity, as a rights-protecting court.

The Court was in the vanguard of the broader attitudinal and political changes, in particular with respect to racial equality. Mid-century opinion polls show a steady increase among Americans sympathetic to civil rights from the 1940s until the 1960s (Best and Radcliff 2005, 84–85). The political branches also took action. Soon after the war's end, President Harry S. Truman advanced the cause of civil rights with an executive order ending racial discrimination in the military, which was largely executed by President Dwight D. Eisenhower (Nichols 2007).[23] Congress passed its first civil rights legislation in over eighty years in 1957, after years of hard-fought effort by liberal Democrats that finally overcame the opposition of Southern Democrats.

Indeed, political divides over civil rights and civil liberties increasingly (though not exclusively) broke along sectional lines. More and more, the South played the role of a regional holdout from an emerging national consensus in favor of greater rights protections. And the structure of American federalism

22. In the 1920s, Robert Hale voiced criticisms of the state action doctrine that would find a wider hearing only decades later (1923).

23. As Nichols notes, Eisenhower may have made his most lasting contribution to civil rights through his appointments to the federal bench, including the Supreme Court.

constrained national institutions in their ability to bring recalcitrant states and localities in line with national norms. Congress's reach was restricted by the limitation of its legislative powers to those subjects enumerated in Article I of the Constitution plus the Reconstruction Amendments. Congress would famously overcome these limitations to some extent through an expansive construction of its Commerce Clause power, aided and abetted by the Supreme Court. But even the power to regulate interstate commerce would not permit Congress to penetrate the innermost citadels of the private law with legislation that gave concrete expression to the values of freedom and equality.

Federal courts likewise had a limited capacity to countermand state practices. State courts were the final authorities of matters on state law, and in the absence of federal legislation, only the Constitution trumped state law and the decisions of state courts.[24] And so, the Supreme Court increasingly turned to the Constitution. Starting after the end of the Second World War, the Supreme Court began selectively deploying constitutional rights horizontally to fill the normative gap between national standards and local (principally Southern) outliers.

The Supreme Court's softening of the strong state action norm is an important part of what I call the second postwar constitutional settlement.[25] In judicial decisions and political discourse alike, American constitutionalism came to be increasingly identified with the protection of individual rights. Richard Primus emphasizes how the postwar valorization of human rights, and their identification with constitutional rights, served to distinguish the United States from its international foes, the Nazis and Soviets (Primus 1999, 177–203). Interestingly, in the United States, the threats to rights came primarily from subnational political units: the states and, in particular, Southern states. Accordingly, promoting rights in the United States meant nationalizing the protection of rights. The Supreme Court did this, not least, by formally extending the reach of rights to the states. Between 1948 and 1969, the Supreme Court handed down eleven decisions "incorporating" rights in the first eight amendments to the Constitution

24. The Supreme Court's epic 1938 decision *Erie Railroad Co. v. Tompkins*, 304 U.S. 64, had a role to play in this as well. As discussed above, under *Swift v. Tyson*, federal courts sitting in diversity jurisdiction (i.e., hearing nonfederal claims between citizens of different states) would resolve those disputes with reference to federal common law: that is, federal courts would decide for themselves the appropriate common law rule of decision in the case. In *Erie*, the Supreme Court overruled *Swift*, rejecting the idea that there is any such thing as general federal common law, with the result that diversity cases would have to be decided with reference to the state law rules.

25. Richard Primus refers to it as the "third transformation" in the history of American rights, which played out between 1948 and 1969. This third transformation was in part a "struggle over the meaning of the first two"—namely, the Bill of Rights and Reconstruction (Primus 1999, 70).

against the states through the operation of the Fourteenth Amendment Due Process Clause (Primus 1999, 69). Granting Congress more leeway to legislate under the banner of rights and relaxing the state action requirement reinforced the conception of the Constitution as a rights-protecting pact and the conception of the Supreme Court as a rights-protecting court.

The postwar emphasis on rights, and the Supreme Court's close identification with rights protection, also provided a new rationale for judicial supremacy. The Supreme Court must have the last word on the meaning of rights to prohibit other actors, particularly at the state level, from defining rights down. The twinning of judicial supremacy and rights protection in the Court's normative narrative came through vividly in the iconic 1958 decision *Cooper v. Aaron*.[26] When the governor and legislature of Arkansas denied that they were bound by the Supreme Court's decision in *Brown v. Board of Education* that school segregation was unconstitutional, the Court emphatically rejected the claim. In a decision signed by each Justice individually, the Court declared not only that the Constitution was the supreme law by virtue of Article VI, but that "the federal judiciary is supreme in the exposition of the law of the Constitution."[27] And in the conclusion of the opinion, the Court asserted that extending the mantle of supremacy from the Constitution to the Court was essential to the realization of rights:

> The principles announced in that decision and the obedience of the States to them, according to the command of the Constitution, are indispensable for the protection of the freedoms guaranteed by our fundamental charter for all of us. Our constitutional ideal of equal justice under law is thus made a living truth.[28]

A tide of judicial decisions and legislative actions advanced antidiscrimination and civil liberties norms for a generation after the end of World War II. And—most relevant for present purposes—the Supreme Court made a series of ad hoc alterations to the state action rule during that same period, to reach and remedy the increasingly anomalous sectional divergences that otherwise lay beyond the reach of federal powers. Because these alterations were ad hoc, the Supreme Court never articulated a theory of what, exactly, rights entitled citizens to under the law. It is the ad hoc quality of the Court's doctrinal excrescences that earned state action doctrine the sobriquet of a "conceptual disaster area."

26. 358 U.S. 1.

27. *Id.* at 18.

28. *Id.* at 19–20.

But the lack of a general theory that would explain when the effects of rights would reach into the private law also permitted the state action norm to continue to function as a constitutional containment device, which reinforced the Court's supremacy. The Court did not hem itself in with a theory: instead, rights would reach into the private law when the Court said they would.

The variation in how the Supreme Court approached state action over time furnishes material for a comparison. Why was it that the Supreme Court used constitutional rights to intercede in matters governed by private law following the Second World War but not the Civil War? Of course, much had changed between the early 1880s (when the Supreme Court first rejected the horizontal effect of rights in the *Civil Rights Cases*) and the late 1940s (when the Court first blocked judicial enforcement of private discrimination). But the key, I argue, is that the strategic logic to the Court's use of constitutional rights changed dramatically in that period.

After Reconstruction, granting horizontal effect to rights meant taking on a mission the weakened Court could not accomplish: to root out discrimination in the South, without the backing of the other branches of government or a powerful public constituency. After World War II, and especially as the Civil Rights movement gained traction, the Supreme Court was in the vanguard of a broader political and social change in the politics of civil rights and civil liberties. The cause of robust rights protection attracted significant constituencies, inside and out of government. As the Supreme Court got out of the business of policing economic regulation, it made rights central to its agenda and identity. Among national institutions, it was only the Supreme Court that could reach and rectify local discrimination under the auspices of the private law, and only through resort to constitutional rights. When the Court did so, it demonstrated its unique value-added to American government while advancing its agenda.

The next sections illustrate developments in state action doctrine and in processes of lawmaking, in three areas. The first section, devoted to the horizontal application of equality rights, is the longest, because this is the area in which the Supreme Court has deviated most from the state action requirement. I argue that this is where we should expect to see rights given horizontal effect, since states were blocking the advance of a civil rights agenda that had the Court's support, and only resort to constitutional rights could breach the fortress of federalism. Still, the Court did not formally jettison the state action rule, but worked around it, avoiding a still broader transformation in how constitutional law is made. I discuss how the Court did this with a focus on voting and housing discrimination. The Court also licensed a degree of legislative constitutionalism in this area, allowing Congress some latitude to legislate in the service of equality values, and I discuss the key decisions on Congress's enforcement powers, which transformed the restrictive approach the Court had taken in the *Civil Rights Cases*. But here as well, the Court's tolerance for constitutional pluralism was limited, and I argue that the Court justified antidiscrimination legislation with reference to the rights enforcement powers of Congress only when no other avenue was open.

There are a number of areas where private legal arrangements can implicate the freedom of expression, but the Supreme Court has most decisively brought constitutional rights to play in the context of libel law. This also makes sense, I argue, since libel law more directly implicates the Court's civil libertarian concerns than the others. The discussion here focuses on the Supreme Court's landmark *New York Times v. Sullivan* case, and its transformation of libel law. By contrast, I argue, the Court has no incentive to constitutionalize internal family legal relations, and the Court has not done so. The *DeShaney* case illustrates how the Court has left the regulation of this area to state lawmakers. The Court will bring the Constitution to bear on family law matters only when an alleged rights violation can be traced directly back to the act of a state—for instance, state law's exclusion of same-sex couples from marriage rights.

EQUALITY

It is not surprising that cases involving racial discrimination play an outsized role in American state action doctrine. Here is an area where the normative gap between localized practices (especially in the Jim Crow South) and emerging national equality norms yawned especially wide. Moreover, the constitutional guarantee of equal protection could be plausibly interposed to fill this gap. And crucially, the Supreme Court could draw on institutional and popular support for expanding the rights agenda to combat discrimination.

The Supreme Court began moving into the civil rights space, slowly at first, in the 1940s. In the 1960s the Court gave its blessing to a far-reaching legislative antidiscrimination agenda that transformed state and local law. But the legislation left some private-party relationships under the law untouched. And in these areas, the Supreme Court repeatedly used constitutional rights to remedy these wrongs, adding twists and turns to state action doctrine in the process.

The discussion here of the Court's state action jurisprudence in the antidiscrimination context is necessarily selective, given how much of the development of state action doctrine was driven by racial discrimination cases. I focus here on landmark cases and the relationship between the Court's state action doctrine and the legislative antidiscrimination agenda. I argue that the Court promoted substantive equality values, and at the same time maintained its own privileged position with respect to rights, by using rights selectively to ground its decisions when no other source of law would, and seeking nonrights sources for congressional power to promote equality when possible.

White Primaries

The first major crack in the state action rule appeared in the context of a long-running series of conflicts over the "white primaries" in Texas. Because the state Republican parties in the South had collapsed in the wake of Reconstruction, the Democratic primaries were the only real competitive elections in many Southern states. A 1923 statute in Texas expressly excluded blacks from participating in the primaries. In the unanimous 1927 decision *Nixon v. Herndon*, the Supreme Court struck down the statute, ruling that it violated the Fourteenth Amendment.[29]

Nixon v. Herndon did not pose a difficult state action problem: the target of the challenge was a statute, and it was unambiguously discriminatory. But the state's efforts to circumvent *Herndon* required the Court to confront successively more difficult state action issues. In the wake of *Herndon*, the Texas legislature rewrote the statute to provide that the executive committee of each party could set eligibility requirements for primary voting. In 1932, the Supreme Court struck down this arrangement as well. Justice Cardozo wrote for the unanimous Court that state parties, in prescribing eligibility requirements for voting, were exercising power delegated by the state, and therefore subject to the Fourteenth Amendment.[30] Within a month of the Supreme Court's decision, the state Democratic convention of Texas had adopted on its own volition a resolution limiting membership in the party, and participation in the primary, to whites.

The state Democratic Party had taken up where the legislature had left off. The effect was exactly the same—only whites could vote in the primary—but since the discrimination was now effected by a voluntary political association, the Court could reach it only by rejecting, ignoring, or finessing the state action doctrine. At first, the Court blinked. In the 1935 case *Grovey v. Townsend*, a unanimous Court held that the Fourteenth Amendment did not reach the party's regulation of its own membership.[31]

But significantly, nine years later, the Court did an about-face. In *Smith v. Allwright*, the Court overruled *Grovey* and invalidated the Texas Democratic Party's exclusion of nonwhites from primary participation.[32] The Court now found that rules restricting participation in primaries fell within the ambit

29. 273 U.S. 536. Oliver Wendell Holmes wrote for the Court. The Court did not reach the question whether the Fifteenth Amendment applied to primaries.

30. 286 U.S. 73 (1932).

31. 295 U.S. 45 (1935).

32. 321 U.S. 649 (1944).

of state action, even if imposed by parties, owing to the primaries' tight integration into the machinery of public elections. In Justice Reed's words for the Court, "this statutory system for the selection of party nominees for inclusion on the general election ballot makes the party which is required to follow these legislative directions *an agency of the state* in so far as it determines the participants in a primary election."[33]

Why the switch between *Grovey* and *Allwright*? The nine years separating the cases nicely illustrate some of the political and institutional currents that were beginning to change the logic of requiring state action in the context of racial discrimination. For starters, institutional support for dismantling race restrictions on voting was growing within the executive branch. Frank Murphy, who became Attorney General in 1939, established a Civil Liberties Unit within the Department of Justice (DOJ). The Civil Liberties Unit undertook a long-term, incremental litigation strategy to rooting out voting discrimination (Valelly 2004, 160). Among other things, the DOJ persuaded the Supreme Court that the Fifteenth Amendment did apply to primaries in the 1941 case *United States v. Classic*,[34] a decision that provided important support for the Court's holding in *Allwright*. At the same time, interest group and social movement pressure was beginning to grow, resulting in more litigation and refinements to the legal arguments. Thurgood Marshall, who led the NAACP's litigation strategy against white primaries and argued *Smith v. Allwright*, hammered home the argument that the white primary was an "integral part of the election machinery of Texas" (Valelly 2004, 161). And the Court itself was changing. Remarkably, between 1935 and 1944, Franklin Roosevelt made eight appointments to the Supreme Court. Roosevelt's appointments included Justices "determined to deepen the Court's civil liberties and civil rights orientation" (Valelly 2004, 158).

The nascent civil rights agenda became even more mainstream, and more politically institutionalized, in the second half of the 1940s. Encouraged by his advisers to reach out to black voters or else lose the 1948 election, President Truman began pushing a civil rights agenda near the midpoint of his first term (Valelly 2004, 165). The landmark report of Truman's Committee on Civil Rights, released in 1947, identified elements of racial hierarchy throughout American society and the economy, and urged their abolition. Truman announced the policy to end segregation within the armed forces and civil service in 1948. At the 1948 convention, liberal Democrats seized the momentum and won acceptance for an aggressive civil rights plank in the party's platform, precipitating a walkout by the Southern "Dixiecrats." These moves catalyzed

33. *Id.* at 663 (emphasis added).

34. 313 U.S. 299 (1941).

a broader realignment that made African Americans a crucial constituency of the national Democratic Party. The politics of civil rights were thus changing fast. As a result, and unlike after Reconstruction, efforts by the Supreme Court to make civil rights—and especially voting rights—effective for African Americans would henceforth find substantial constituencies within the political branches.

Against this backdrop, the Supreme Court decided its final "white primary" case in 1953. In *Terry v. Adams*, stopping race-based exclusion from voting required the Court to deviate still further from strict adherence to the state action rule. In Fort Bend County, Texas, the Jaybird Democratic Association, "a self-governing voluntary club," held pre-primary elections prior to the official Democratic primaries.[35] Since 1889, the winner of the Jaybird primary almost invariably went on to enter the Democratic primary, to run without opposition, and to win the general election. Black voters in Ford Bend County challenged their exclusion from the Jaybird primary under the Fifteenth Amendment.

The Court sustained the challenge, but divided on the reasoning. Writing for himself and two others, Justice Black seemed to toggle between two rationales, neither stated with precision. The first was that the Jaybird primary itself constituted state action. By virtue of its decisive role in selecting public officials, the Jaybird primary was an "election" within the meaning of Fifteenth Amendment.[36] The second was that the Fifteenth Amendment imposed an affirmative duty on the state to bar the discrimination practiced by the Jaybird club:

> For a state to permit such a duplication of its election processes is to permit a flagrant abuse of those processes to defeat the purposes of the Fifteenth Amendment. . . . It violates the Fifteenth Amendment for a state, by such circumvention, to permit within its borders the use of any device that produces an equivalent of the prohibited election.[37]

Writing for himself and three others, Justice Clark concluded that the Jaybird club constituted a political party, so that the case was covered by *Allwright*. Justice Frankfurter found that the state action requirement was met because some county officials participated in the Jaybird primary, and Justice Minton dissented, finding no state action present.

The white primary cases together illustrate how the growing political and legal potency of civil rights claims put pressure on the state action requirement.

35. 345 U.S. 461, 463 (1953).

36. *Id.* at 468.

37. *Id.* at 469.

The successive rounds of litigation amounted to a dialectical process, wherein Texas distanced its official state institutions further and further from voting exclusion, drawing the Court deeper and deeper into private associations in an effort to root out discrimination. And importantly, the Court was not alone in pushing civil rights into new terrain. Private and public streams of litigation, ably tended by the NAACP and the Justice Department, fed the Court a steady diet of arguments and incrementally built an infrastructure of useful precedents. More broadly, by the early 1950s, the cause of civil rights was beginning to find both partisan and popular constituencies.

In going after discrimination outsourced to private associations, the Supreme Court did not abandon the venerable state action framework, unleashing consequences that would be hard to predict and control. Rather, the Court produced ad hoc rationalizations of its results, generating confusion along the way. In the *Terry* opinions alone, we can discern four distinct arguments why the state action requirement is met—and one why it is not.

In some respects, *Terry* showcased rights' profound disruptive potential. The Court permitted the Fifteenth Amendment voting right to be used not just as a shield but as a sword and, moreover, a sword wielded against a private party. The defendant Adams was president of the Jaybirds. The suit against him sought damages as well as injunctive relief.[38] Moreover, the Court treated the right against race-based voting discrimination as an entitlement, not a value. Once the right is implicated, it's not subject to balancing against other interests: it dictates the outcome of the case.

But at the same time, the broader impact of the decision was blunted by the Court's failure to embed it in a satisfactory theory to explain why, when, and how constitutional rights could have horizontal effect. The Court did not provide much of a guide for lower courts, legislatures, or litigants to use in further elaborating what rights meant for the interactions of private individuals. Ultimately, the impact of *Terry* did not extend far beyond the peculiar phenomenon of the Jaybird club and similar organizations.[39]

Racially Restrictive Covenants

Terry shows the Supreme Court at mid-century reaching out to strike down consequential acts of discrimination initiated by private actors without reconceiving the state action framework inherited from the *Civil Rights Cases*, but by

38. The trial court concluded that the plaintiffs had waived their claim for damages, and the plaintiffs did not appeal on this point. Terry v. Adams, 90 F. Supp. 595 (S.D. Tex. 1950).

39. The Democratic Clubs of South Carolina, for one, had functioned much like the Jaybird club. See Baskin v. Brown, 174 F.2d 391 (4th Cir. 1949).

making ad hoc exceptions to it. The Court's most famous state action decision, *Shelley v. Kraemer*, offers an even better illustration of the phenomenon.

The case played out against the background of racial residential segregation in the United States, a phenomenon the Supreme Court itself had played some part in shaping. In the 1917 case *Buchanan v. Worley*, the Supreme Court struck down, as violating the Fourteenth Amendment, a Louisville, Kentucky, ordinance that made it unlawful for "any colored person" to move into a block with a majority of white residents.[40] Racially restrictive covenants—agreements inserted into deeds that barred the sale of property to African Americans or other minority groups—were a private law alternative to municipal ordinances. Restrictive covenants existed before *Buchanan* was decided, but their adoption spread in the 1920s, not just through the South but through the North and Midwest, especially in cities that received large numbers of African Americans who left the South as part of the Great Migration (Jones-Correa 2000, 551–59). The Supreme Court declined to hear a challenge to the constitutionality of restrictive covenants in 1926, on the grounds that the record did not present a substantial question of constitutional law, in *Corrigan v. Buckley*.[41] Residential segregation was bolstered by the federal government dating back to the New Deal, when the Home Owners Loan Corporation, a forerunner to the Federal Housing Administration, made neighborhood "stability" (including racial homogeneity) a key desideratum for federal mortgage underwriting standards (Jones-Correa 2000, 565–66).

Two decades after *Corrigan*, the Court granted review of two state supreme court decisions, one from Missouri and the other from Michigan, that upheld restrictive covenants against constitutional challenge. Both of the state supreme courts had sustained the validity of the covenants on the grounds that state action was lacking: the covenants represented merely private agreements.[42] Both state supreme courts had also rejected arguments that the covenants were invalid as contrary to public policy.

Overturning the rulings on the basis that this latter conclusion was wrong—in other words, holding racially restrictive covenants to be incompatible with

40. 245 U.S. 60 (1917). Incidentally, *Buchanan* was the first major victory of the NAACP.

41. 271 U.S. 323 (1926). *Corrigan* concerned the enforcement of a restrictive covenant in Washington, D.C., which was considered exempt from the Fourteenth Amendment's commands to the states.

42. Kraemer v. Shelley, 355 Mo. 814 (1947); Sipes v. McGhee, 316 Mich. 614 (1947). In *Kraemer*, the plaintiffs had sought an injunction to block a pending sale of a property to an African American family through a white intermediary. In *Sipes*, the plaintiffs sought to have the covenant enforced against an African American family that had already purchased and begun occupying the property in question.

public policy—was not an option for the U.S. Supreme Court. The supreme courts of Missouri and Michigan are the final authorities on the law of Missouri and Michigan, respectively, and the content of public policy is a matter of state law. The U.S. Supreme Court could trump their rulings only by bringing the Constitution into play. Accordingly, the briefs of the petitioners and a number of amici curiae, including the United States, furnished the Court with arguments why the enforcement of such covenants ran afoul of the Constitution.

In his opinion for a unanimous (if short-staffed) Court,[43] Chief Justice Vinson ruled that the Constitution forbade the enforcement of the racially restrictive covenants. Vinson's opinion addressed the state action issue head on. Citing to *Buchanan*, Vinson observed that racial restrictions on the sale of property would be clearly unconstitutional if adopted by state statute or local ordinance. By contrast, these privately adopted covenants by themselves would not violate the Constitution, if "effectuated by voluntary adherence to their terms."[44] Here, however, "there was more": "These are cases in which the purposes of the agreements were secured only by judicial enforcement by state courts of the restrictive terms of the agreements."[45] As the Court framed it, the central question in the case became whether judicial enforcement of the covenants counted as "state action."

Framed this way, the Court's question was easy to answer in the affirmative. The Court unleashed a cavalcade of quotations and citations to the effect that judicial action is state action.

But this conclusion is equal parts uncontroversial and irrelevant. The discriminatory choice at the root of the constitutional violation here is the action of private parties: it is the inclusion of a racially restrictive covenant in the deed. It can't be that judicial involvement introduces the element of state action into every legal relationship of private parties, such that the norms governing the parties are attributed to the state, or else the state action requirement becomes a nullity.

So why, then, is judicial enforcement of a racially restrictive covenant unconstitutional? This is the real question at the heart of the case, and the Court dodges it, using the state action doctrine in a kind of sleight of hand. In this respect, *Shelley* resembles *Flagg Brothers*, though the misdirection works to opposite ends in the two cases. In *Flagg Brothers*, the Court rested its ruling on the common-sensical proposition that the warehouseman's sale of property

43. Justices Reed, Jackson, and Rutledge recused themselves, presumably because they owned property subject to racially restrictive covenants.

44. Shelley v. Kraemer, 334 U.S. 1, 13 (1948).

45. *Id.* at 14.

is not an action of the state, drawing attention away from what the state *did* do: authorizing the sale under statute. In *Shelley*, the Court points to judicial enforcement of the covenant to unleash the horizontal effect of the Fourteenth Amendment. But what is lacking is a substantive theory of the equality right to explain *why* it bars enforcement of discriminatory agreements drafted by private parties and to indicate prospectively when the logic of *Shelley* does and does not apply. The Court's ruling here is strong medicine—it overwrites the content of agreements whose validity is unimpeached within the terms of private law—but it is administered without prescription.

Legislative Constitutionalism and Its Limits

The cause of civil rights gained significant political traction in the 1960s, finding champions in the White House and winning the support of majorities in Congress. In the same years, the Supreme Court advanced civil rights judicially in ways that complemented and, to some extent, went beyond the efforts of the political branches. The Court's role involved, first of all, getting out of Congress's way. To an unprecedented degree, the Court permitted Congress to use its enforcement power under the Reconstruction Amendments to define what constitutional equality rights would mean on the ground. But even so, the Court was only willing to let Congress share in the task of constitutional construction within limits. Also in this period, the Court invoked more exceptions to the state action norm, without ever abandoning the state action framing, to reach pockets of racial discrimination beyond the scope of federal legislation.

As I argued above, introducing the state action doctrine had originally allowed the Supreme Court to contain the disruptive potential of constitutional rights and to consolidate its own authority in a period of institutional vulnerability. Rights were easier to manage when they operated in one dimension only: the vertical dimension, containing the relationship between citizen and state. Bringing rights to heel ex ante, by narrowing their scope of application, kept the Court from being dragged, through litigation, into unwelcome disputes over discriminatory social institutions. It also helped the Court establish a strong brand of judicial supremacy, in which rights functioned as entitlements with determinant content and the Court was the authoritative arbiter of that content.

In its 1960s decisions on Congress's power to enforce the Reconstruction Amendments, the Court relaxed, to some degree, its monopoly over authoritative constitutional interpretation. The Court did so most consequentially in the context of the Voting Rights Act of 1965 (VRA). The disenfranchisement of African Americans in the former states of the Confederacy was extensive and enduring: in many places, voting rolls in the early 1960s were nearly as lily-white as they had been in the 1890s. Southern states used numerous means to block access to the ballot, including literacy tests and other voting requirements that were facially neutral but applied in a discriminatory fashion. An earlier legislative effort, the Civil Rights Act of 1957, had limited success in rooting out these practices. The 1965 Act went further, effectively putting elections in the South into federal receivership. In addition to banning the use of any voting qualification, standard, practice, or procedure resulting in the denial or dilution of the right to vote on account of race, including a number of specified procedures, the VRA required that jurisdictions meeting certain criteria have any changes to their voting rules precleared by the Justice Department to ensure against discriminatory effects. The states originally covered by the preclearance formula, which hinged on voting practices and participation rates, included most of the states of the former Confederacy, and none outside of it.

In two important cases from 1966, the Supreme Court upheld the VRA against claims that it exceeded Congress's authority. In *South Carolina v. Katzenbach*, the Court held that Congress was authorized under the enforcement clause of the Fifteenth Amendment even to ban practices that the Court itself had held *did not* violate the right to vote.[46] South Carolina invoked the Supreme Court's original jurisdiction to challenge the preclearance provisions, arguing that the VRA was not "appropriate" legislation to enforce voting rights within the meaning of Section 2 of the Fifteenth Amendment, because it proscribed more than denials of the vote based on race. Chief Justice Warren's opinion for the Court rejected that argument. After recounting Congress's difficulties in securing effective voting rights in the face of Southern efforts to undermine them, the Court concluded that Congress must have broad discretion in choosing the means to secure the right. Chief Justice Warren invoked the Supreme Court's most famous case about the powers of Congress:

> The basic test to be applied in a case involving § 2 of the Fifteenth Amendment is the same as in all cases concerning the express powers of Congress with relation to the reserved powers of the States. Chief Justice Marshall laid down the classic formulation, 50 years before the Fifteenth Amendment was ratified:
>
> > "Let the end be legitimate, let it be within the scope of the constitution, and all means which are appropriate which are plainly adapted to that end, which are not prohibited, but consist with the letter and spirit of the constitution, are constitutional."[47]

46. 383 U.S. 301 (1966).

47. *Id.* at 326 (citing McCulloch v. Maryland, 17 U.S. 316, 421 (1819)).

The message was clear: the Court would judge Congress's choice of means in enforcing rights just as with respect to Congress's other enumerated powers: with ample deference.

Katzenbach v. Morgan raised a challenge to VRA Section 4(e), which barred the use of literacy tests as voting qualifications against persons educated in Puerto Rico.[48] The complication here was that the Supreme Court had recently ruled that literacy tests do not violate the Fourteenth Amendment.[49] The question was whether Congress was nonetheless authorized to ban the use of literacy tests under its power to enforce the Fourteenth Amendment.[50] In order to answer yes, the Court could not rely on the logic of *South Carolina*: that Congress could create a protective buffer, in order to protect the right at its core. The Fifteenth Amendment guarantees a right to vote without regard to race, and to safeguard that right, Congress could proscribe facially neutral practices that had been used to undercut that right. But by contrast, the Supreme Court had ruled that the Constitution *permitted* literacy tests as voting qualifications. Banning the use of literacy tests against those schooled in Puerto Rico did not obviously serve to vindicate any constitutional right as identified by the Supreme Court. Sustaining Section 4(e) would seem to require granting Congress some latitude to define the Equal Protection right for itself, in opposition to the Supreme Court's law on point.

The Supreme Court turned back the challenge to the law. In places, Justice Brennan's opinion for the Court suggests that Congress might get to decide for itself what the right to equal protection required. Congress might have good reasons for restricting the use of literacy tests, according to Justice Brennan. Congress could have questioned whether New York's test was in fact motivated by prejudice, or "whether denial of a right deemed so precious and fundamental in our society was a necessary or appropriate means of encouraging persons to learn English, or of furthering the goal of an intelligent exercise of the franchise."[51] Elsewhere in the opinion, Justice Brennan links the ban on literacy tests, somewhat tenuously, back to other Fourteenth Amendment concerns. Broader ballot access for Puerto Ricans could translate into "enhanced political power," which would in turn "be helpful in gaining nondiscriminatory treatment in public services for the entire Puerto Rican community."[52]

48. 384 U.S. 641 (1966).

49. Lassiter v. Northampton County Board of Elections, 360 U.S. 45 (1959).

50. The Fourteenth Amendment was implicated and not the Fifteenth because literacy tests did not implicate a denial of the right to vote on account of race.

51. 384 U.S. at 654.

52. *Id.* at 653.

Justice Harlan, joined by Justice Stewart, dissented. In proscribing a practice the Court had found consistent with the Fourteenth Amendment, Congress was not enforcing the amendment but "defin[ing] the substantive scope of the Amendment."[53] And this Congress could not do: "That question [whether a practice violates equal protection] is one for the judicial branch ultimately to determine."[54]

Arguably *Jones v. Alfred H. Meyer Co.*, decided in 1968, represented the high-water mark for the Court's tolerance of legislative constitutionalism.[55] The case concerned a challenge to Section 1 of the Civil Rights Act of 1866, since codified as 42 U.S.C. Section 1982. Section 1982 guaranteed "all citizens . . . the same right, in every State and Territory, as is enjoyed by white citizens thereof to inherit, purchase, lease, sell, hold, and convey real and personal property." When Joseph Jones and his wife were refused the chance to purchase a home in a St. Louis subdivision because they were black, they sued for damages and injunctive relief under Section 1982. In *Hurd v. Hodge*,[56] a companion case to *Shelley v. Kraemer*, the Supreme Court had ruled that Section 1982 could be used as a shield, to block the rescission of a home sale to African American buyers.[57] *Hurd* relied on the *Shelley* logic, that the judicial enforcement of a restrictive covenant added the element of state action. But that rationale was not available here, since the plaintiffs were attempting to use Section 1982 as a sword not a shield. Section 1982 was the basis for a lawsuit brought by one private party against another, for damages and injunctive relief. And the claimed source for Congress's authority to pass this provision was the Thirteenth Amendment enforcement power. The Thirteenth Amendment abolished slavery and involuntary servitude. Obviously, housing discrimination was not slavery. The Supreme Court could sustain the law only by giving Congress a fairly free hand in legislating under the banner of rights.

And in an opinion by Justice Stewart, the Court did. First, the Court addressed the horizontal effect issue, concluding that "the fact that § 1982 operates upon the unofficial acts of private individuals, whether or not sanctioned by state law, presents no constitutional problem."[58] The right against slavery,

53. *Id.* at 668 (Harlan, J., dissenting).

54. *Id.* at 667 (Harlan, J., dissenting).

55. 392 U.S. 409 (1968).

56. 334 U.S. 24 (1948).

57. *Hurd* relied on § 1982 and not the Equal Protection Clause because the case arose in Washington, D.C., and the Fourteenth Amendment did not apply to Washington. The Court would later devise a workaround to this anomaly in *Bolling v. Sharpe*, 347 U.S. 497 (1954).

58. 392 U.S. at 438.

unlike other rights, had been understood from the first to be a right *erga omnes*, directly binding private and public actors alike. But how did Congress's power to enforce that right reach private real estate conveyances? The Court cited to the *Civil Rights Cases* for the proposition that the Thirteenth Amendment clothed Congress "with power to pass *all laws necessary and proper for abolishing all badges and incidents of slavery in the United States*."[59] Congress has the power "rationally to determine what are the badges and the incidents of slavery, and the authority to translate that determination into effective legislation."[60] And Congress's choice here was rational, because "whatever else they may have encompassed, the badges and incidents of slavery—its 'burdens and disabilities'— included restraints upon 'those fundamental rights which are the essence of civil freedom, namely, the same right . . . to inherit, purchase, lease, sell and convey property, as is enjoyed by white citizens.' "[61] "[W]hen racial discrimination herds men into ghettos and makes their ability to buy property turn on the color of their skin," Justice Stewart concluded, "then it too is a relic of slavery."[62]

These cases all show the Court permitting Congress to share in the task of giving content to equality rights. The Court relaxed the strict hierarchy of constitutional interpretation, just as it relaxed its adherence to the state action norm, in ways that pushed principles of racial antidiscrimination deeper into the fabric of American society. But in other cases from the same period, the Court resisted an expansive approach to Congress's enforcement powers. Notably, the Court sustained the landmark Civil Rights Act (CRA) of 1964, which barred discrimination in public accommodations, as an exercise of Congress's Commerce Clause power rather than its enforcement power under the Fourteenth Amendment.[63]

The biggest obstacle to rooting the decision in the enforcement power was the state action doctrine: the CRA banned discrimination by private parties. In a concurrence, Justice Douglas argued that the Court should have relied at least in part on Section 5 of the Fourteenth Amendment in sustaining the statute. The CRA was appropriate legislation to enforce the equal protection right because the requisite state action was present, in the availability of judicial enforcement of private discrimination, à la *Shelley v. Kraemer*. But the

59. *Id.* at 439 (quoting Civil Rights Cases, 109 U.S. 3, 20 (1883)) (emphasis added by *Jones*).

60. *Id.* at 440.

61. *Id.* at 441 (quoting Civil Rights Cases, 109 U.S. at 22).

62. *Id.* at 442–43.

63. Heart of Atlanta Motel Inc. v. United States, 379 U.S. 241 (1964).

majority opted to reach its result via an expansive approach to the Commerce Clause, rather than either granting Congress more leeway to define rights for itself (which would trench on the Court's domain) or generalizing the *Shelley* approach to state action (which would theoretically make all private discrimination constitutionally actionable). Taken together, these cases suggest that the Supreme Court permitted legislative constitutionalism only as a last resort: when no other plausible argument would sustain important antidiscrimination legislation.

The State Action Doctrine and the Civil Rights Movement

Notwithstanding Congress's legislative promotion of civil rights, there was still significant societal discrimination that was not reached by the federal statutes, especially but not exclusively in the South. And without a federal hook, these would remain matters of state law, presided over by state legislators and judges who, especially in the South, were ferociously hostile to civil rights. But the Warren Court repeatedly stepped in to measure practices in the states against federal equality norms, using the tool that unlocked federal jurisdiction: the Constitution.

Constitutionalizing issues beyond the reach of federal civil rights legislation meant finding exceptions to the strict state action requirement. And a great deal of the Court's state action doctrine—which amounts to a series of exceptions to and qualifications of the strict state action rule—was forged in the 1960s, in cases involving racial discrimination (Fee 2004, 578; Eskridge 2002, 2331–32). A sample of prominent cases gives a sense for the various workarounds the Court devised to the strict state action rule. In *Burton v. Wilmington Parking Authority*[64] (which preceded the Civil Rights Act), the Court ruled that a private restaurant could not deny service to customers on the basis of race, because it rented space in a public parking facility. In *Evans v. Newton*,[65] the Court held that a park, originally devised to a city with the proviso that it be used by white people only, retained its public character and could not discriminate on the basis of race, even after the city resigned trusteeship and the park passed into private hands. And in *Reitman v. Mulkey*,[66] the Court invalidated a California referendum that barred state interference with property owners' freedom to sell, rent, or lease their property to whomever they choose: the referendum,

64. 365 U.S. 715 (1961).

65. 382 U.S. 296 (1966).

66. 387 U.S. 369 (1967).

which voided existing antidiscrimination statutes, would "involve the State in private racial discriminations to an unconstitutional degree."[67]

The 1964 case *Bell v. Maryland* offers a revealing glimpse into the Supreme Court's strategic approach to state action issues.[68] The Court was asked to pass on the constitutionality of the criminal trespass convictions of twelve African American students who had staged a sit-in at a Baltimore restaurant in 1960. From the perspective of state action doctrine, this case posed a hard problem. The law of trespass does not itself embody a discriminatory norm: the discrimination comes entirely from the restaurant owner. This situation is not so very far afield from the classic example of private discrimination beyond the reach of constitutional scrutiny: a homeowner's use of trespass laws to permit whites but not African Americans onto his property (Tushnet 2003, 81). It would be difficult for the Court to vacate the convictions without repudiating the state action rule.

In fact, the papers of the Justices indicate that some were willing to do that. Justice Clark circulated a draft opinion that would extend constitutional scrutiny to "usages . . . which have become a kind of common law."[69] Others on the Court voted to retain the state action rule and uphold the convictions. The issue closely divided the Court, and changes of heart gave first one position and then the other a tentative 5–4 majority. Ultimately, Justice Brennan balked at rejecting the state action rule out of concern over the effect such a ruling would have on the ongoing effort in Congress to craft civil rights legislation. A sure-to-be-controversial show of judicial power at this moment might shake loose Southern senators from the coalition moving the Civil Rights Act toward passage (Ackerman 2014, 146). Instead, the Court opted to stay its hand. The Court remanded the case to Maryland with instructions to consider the convictions in light of a recently passed state antidiscrimination statute. Weeks later, Congress did pass the Civil Rights Act, which proscribed the sort of discrimination at issue in *Bell* legislatively, on a national basis. *Bell* and the cases discussed above together illustrate the pattern: the Warren Court generally turned to the Constitution to fill the normative gaps only when private discrimination tolerated by state law was beyond the reach of federal legislation.

The Court's horizontal deployment of rights, together with Congress's antidiscrimination legislation, contributed to a far-reaching transformation of American society, in which open and notorious racial discrimination was dramatically reduced. And then, the moment passed. The retirement of Earl

67. *Id.* at 378–79.

68. 378 U.S. 226 (1964).

69. Quoted in Ackerman (2014, 145).

Warren and his replacement with Warren Burger as Chief Justice in 1969 marked the end of the era in many respects. The Burger Court would prove itself far less interested than its predecessor in advancing the reach of rights. Changes on the Court mirrored, and were partially the result of, broader political changes. The last major piece of civil rights legislation was the Civil Rights Act of 1968, which banned discrimination in the housing market and was less popular among whites nationally than the 1964 Act, which had mostly affected the South. Campaigning for the presidency that year, Richard Nixon was critical of the Warren Court and promised to appoint "strict constructionists" to the Court (Engel 2011, 302–05). And once elected, Nixon appointed Justices who helped to wind down the state action innovations of previous years, including when racial discrimination was involved.[70] Rather than repudiating the new branches of state action doctrine outright, the Court more often added exceptions to the exceptions, further contributing to the subject's reputation as an unruly mess.

FREEDOM OF EXPRESSION

There are a number of areas in American law where private law rules and arrangements can implicate the freedom of expression. In contract law, individuals may be subject to legal liability for speech in violation of confidentiality agreements (Garfield 1998). The tort of invasion of privacy also can make it actionable for one private party to communicate information about another private party (Emerson 1979). The tort of libel can do the same, as can the tort of intentional infliction of emotional distress.

Ordinarily, these are all areas in which the legal relations of nonstate parties play out under the auspices of the common law, as curated by state judges. And the Supreme Court has largely permitted common law regulation to run its course, except insofar as the common law threatens to block the flow of information on matters of public concern.[71] The Court has confronted this

70. See Moose Lodge No. 107 v. Irvis, 407 U.S. 163 (1972) (holding that state's issuance of a liquor license did not render racial discrimination by private fraternal organization subject to constitutional scrutiny).

71. Largely, but not completely. For instance, in 1967 a closely divided Supreme Court overturned a damages award against *Life* magazine, in an invasion of privacy case brought by members of a family whose experience as crime victims was presented, in exaggerated form, in the pages of the magazine. Time Inc. v. Hill, 385 U.S. 374 (1967). See also Cox Broad. Corp. v. Cohn, 420 U.S. 469 (1975) (barring recovery for invasion of privacy when broadcaster obtained name of deceased rape victim from public court records).

There are other contexts in which the Supreme Court confronted state action issues and speech claims. Notably, in *Marsh v. Alabama*, 326 U.S. 501 (1946), the Supreme Court held

problem in the context of libel and (to a lesser degree) the intentional infliction of emotional distress. The Warren Court significantly constitutionalized libel law in particular. It makes sense that the Court would relax the state action norm in the context of these forms of private speech regulation more so than others. Libel cases, especially involving issues of public concern, implicated the Warren Court's push to expand civil rights and civil liberties more directly than the other classes of cases.

The Supreme Court had been alternating between periods of beefing up its protection for speech rights and backpedaling since the late 1930s (Shapiro 1966). By 1962, the high-protectionist position secured a majority on the Court (Siegel 2006, 362). From that point forward, the Court's jurisprudence consistently reflected the classic civil libertarian principle that the law could not be used to exclude views, even unpopular ones, from the public sphere (Van Alstyne 2006).[72] In the Court's typical speech cases, the threat to freedom of expression came from government actors: school boards,[73] Congress,[74] state lawmakers,[75] and so forth. Neither the enforcement of confidentiality agreements nor actions for invasion of privacy were likely to pose much of a threat to core First Amendment values, as seen from the civil libertarian perspective: the first mostly concerned matters of commerce, and the second involved disclosures with little relevance to public affairs. But libel actions, if brought by public figures, had the potential to chill debate on matters of public concern.

When this possibility presented itself, the Court did not hesitate to expand the scope of First Amendment protections to bring libel within its purview. The Supreme Court made this move in the landmark 1964 case of *New York Times Co. v. Sullivan*.[76] The Supreme Court's turn to the Constitution in *New York Times* was almost overdetermined. The case not only involved political speech but race and civil rights, issues central to the Court's rights-protecting role (Feeley 2006; Kalven 1965). The case concerned an advertisement that ran in the *New York Times* on March 29, 1960. The ad, which was raising funds

that the restriction of religious speech in a company-owned town violated the constitutional right to free speech. *Marsh* was significant in establishing a "public function" exception to the state action rule. But the case was somewhat idiosyncratic, since the facts the Court confronted were rather extreme: a company that restricted door-to-door solicitations owned an entire town.

72. For the classic articulation of the civil libertarian free speech position, see Chafee (1920).

73. W.Va. State Bd. of Educ. v. Barnette, 319 U.S. 624 (1943).

74. Yates v. United States, 354 U.S. 298 (1957).

75. Speiser v. Randall, 357 U.S. 513 (1958).

76. 376 U.S. 254.

for Martin Luther King, Jr.'s legal defense,[77] described civil rights abuses in the South, including a few specific incidents in Montgomery, Alabama. L.B. Sullivan, the police commissioner in Montgomery, brought a libel suit against the newspaper and four African American ministers, alleging that the ad contained falsehoods that damaged his reputation.[78]

Sullivan was not mentioned by name in the advertisement—indeed, no officials from Alabama were. Nonetheless, the case was tried (in a segregated courtroom), and an Alabama jury returned a $500,000 verdict against the defendants, which the Alabama Supreme Court upheld. The size and circumstances of the verdict were unprecedented. The common law defined defamatory statements as those that tend to subject a person to hatred, contempt, or ridicule (Forer 1987, 52). While this cast a very wide net in theory, in practice, libel suits generally involved expense, delay, and small recoveries, leading one authority to opine that "[n]o other formula of the law promises so much and delivers so little" (Green 1960, 907).[79]

But the Sullivan verdict was enormous, and it appeared to be the harbinger of more to come. After Sullivan filed suit against the *Times* and the ministers, so did four other Alabama officials, including the governor, for damages totaling $3 million (Lewis 1992, 13).[80] A second jury returned a $500,000 verdict for the mayor of Montgomery a few months after the Sullivan trial. These damages were so substantial as to pose an existential threat to the *New York Times*. And Sullivan's success at trial inspired a frenzy of imitators seeking to shut down news coverage of civil rights topics: by the summer of 1964, Southern officials had filed libel actions seeking more than $300 million in damages from the press (Lewis 1992, 36). Southern officials had retooled libel litigation into a very potent threat to the civil rights movement and the freedom of the press. And because libel law was state law, there was no scope for federal court oversight of these lawsuits—unless they raised a constitutional dimension.

77. King was prosecuted by the State of Alabama for felony tax evasion; this was the first felony tax evasion prosecution in the state's history. King was acquitted.

78. Sullivan claimed that the ministers, whose names appeared in the advertisement, had endorsed its message, although they offered uncontroverted evidence that they had not known about or approved of the ad. The inclusion of the ministers did serve a more practical end: their presence in the suit defeated removal of the matter from state court to federal court. In the absence of a federal issue, cases can be removed when the plaintiffs and defendants are citizens of different states. But a case can be removed only when all of the plaintiffs are from different states than all of the defendants, and the ministers were citizens of Alabama.

79. Quoted in Emerson (1970, 519).

80. The Alabama governor, John Patterson, added Martin Luther King, Jr. as a defendant as well.

The *New York Times* sought a writ of certiorari from the Supreme Court, raising the argument that the verdict violated the paper's First Amendment right to freedom of the press.[81] The Court granted review and reversed in a unanimous opinion authored by Justice Brennan. The Court acknowledged that it had never before found libel actions to raise constitutional concerns, but also noted that this case was different. Never before had the Court "sustained the use of libel laws to impose sanctions upon expression critical of the official conduct of public officials."[82] The difference matters, because "freedom of expression upon public questions is secured by the First Amendment."[83] The law of libel as applied in Alabama courts would undermine First Amendment freedoms by imposing "the pall of fear and timidity . . . upon those who would give voice to public criticisms."[84] The Constitution, therefore, bars recovery for libel by a public official unless he can prove the offending statement was made with "actual malice," which is to say, either knowledge that it was false or reckless disregard for its possible falsity.[85]

But before coming to this conclusion, the Court first had to confront the state action issue, which was one ground on which the Alabama Supreme Court rejected the defendants' constitutional claims. The state action rule was inapposite here, according to the Supreme Court:

> Although this is a civil lawsuit between private parties, the Alabama courts have applied a state rule of law which petitioners claim to impose invalid restrictions on their constitutional freedoms of speech and press. It matters not that the law has been applied in a civil action and that it is common law only, though supplemented by statute. The test is not the form in which state power has been applied but, whatever the form, whether such power has in fact been exercised.[86]

And so the Supreme Court brought libel actions within the scope of constitutional scrutiny. In reality, the case did not pose a very difficult state action problem. The Court was not facing, as in *Shelley*, a court merely standing ready to

81. The paper, represented by eminent law professor Herbert Wechsler, also argued that the Alabama court's assertion of personal jurisdiction over the paper was unconstitutional.

82. 376 U.S. at 268.

83. *Id.* at 269.

84. *Id.* at 278.

85. *Id.* at 229.

86. *Id.* at 265.

enforce agreements whose contents were dictated by private parties. The contents of Alabama libel law were the product of Alabama courts. The courts, in effect, furnished to private parties a muzzle they could use to shut up other private parties. The state's hand would be somewhat easier to see had it expressed its policy legislatively rather than in judge-made common law. But the Court noted that a rule of law is no less an instrument of the state for being embodied in common law, instead of a statute.[87] A comparison with *Flagg Brothers* is instructive. In that case, the state furnished a legal device that affected private-party legal relations—by way of a statute, no less—and yet there, the Court could see no state action. The Court is simply more likely to see state action when bringing the Constitution to bear suits its purposes.

And the *Sullivan* decision closed a potential private law loophole to its First Amendment jurisprudence that threatened to undermine core constitutional values. *Sullivan* was a landmark—"an occasion for dancing in the streets," in the words of First Amendment éminence grise Alexander Meikeljohn—and it effectively neutralized the libel suit as a weapon against the civil rights movement (Forer 1987, 17). *Sullivan* broke the state action barrier for libel actions, so that all constitutional objections to libel suits henceforth would have to be entertained on the merits. And while the Supreme Court's First Amendment libel jurisprudence grew more fragmented over time (Emerson 1970, 525), the Court by and large continued to follow the civil libertarian lodestar, protecting speech more aggressively when it implicated political debate and matters of public interest. In the absence of actual malice, speech was protected against libel claims by public officials (and soon, public figures)[88] when it addressed questions of public concern. The Court extended the mantle of First Amendment protection against claims of intentional infliction of emotional distress under

87. The Court did, perhaps, overstate the extent to which "the state rule of law" it identified really was the established law of Alabama. The Supreme Court identified several features of Alabama's rule of liability. To wit: publications are libelous per se if they impute misconduct to officials in their office; when the plaintiff is a public official, criticism of his agency is enough to find he suffered reputational harm; once libel per se is established, a defendant's only defense is that the statements were true in every respect; general damages may be presumed. In fact, pre-*Sullivan* libel precedents in Alabama were not so draconian as the Supreme Court's précis suggests. But in justifying its ruling, the Alabama Supreme Court had itself insisted that the judgment against the *Times* was amply supported by precedents. And if the Alabama Supreme Court was going to oversell its own precedents, the U.S. Supreme Court was only too happy to go along, since doing so bolstered its claim that the constitutional problem was firmly fixed in "the law" of Alabama.

88. Curtis Pub. Co. v. Butts, 388 U.S. 130 (1967).

parallel circumstances.[89] The First Amendment posed less of a bar to recovery when plaintiffs were not public figures.[90]

The *Sullivan* decision was powerful, but also surgical: it stopped libel actions from impeding the civil rights movement and from putting the brakes on other political debates. One reason that the case's impact was so tightly targeted is that the Supreme Court defined the horizontal effect of the First Amendment right in terms of an entitlement rather than a value. The Supreme Court did discuss the values that underlie the needs for First Amendment protection. But rather than leaving it there, and letting other courts balance those values against competing considerations in future cases, the Supreme Court articulated a bright-line rule. Specifically, the First Amendment grants a privilege to publish good faith criticisms of government officials (Tribe 1988, 864–65). True to form, even as it expanded the scope of constitutional protection, the Supreme Court did so by way of a tailored doctrinal formula that kept the Court in the driver's seat of constitutional development.

FAMILY LAW

A discussion of the Supreme Court's use of constitutional rights to adjust legal relations within the family will necessarily be short, because the Supreme Court has almost never used constitutional rights to adjust legal relations within the family. The explanation for the Court's inactivity on this front is not that relations within the family do not potentially implicate constitutional values; they do. Consider parental restrictions of children's speech, discriminatory terms in family trusts, and testamentary restraints on remarriage. To take one concrete example, the will of Frank Mandelbaum, which was contested in 2012, used the threat of disinheritance to attempt to coerce his gay son to marry a woman (Popoff 2014).[91] Constitutional values—of free expression, equality, freedom of choice—are at stake within the family.[92]

89. Hustler Magazine, Inc. v. Falwell, 485 U.S. 46 (1988).

90. Gertz v. Robert Welch, Inc., 418 U.S. 323 (1974).

91. The dispute was resolved by settlement.

92. A rare exception to the Court's forbearance is *Troxel v. Granville*, 530 U.S. 57 (2000), in which the Court invalidated, as applied, a state statute permitting courts to grant visitation rights to any person at any time when visitation serves the child's best interests. A court order under the statute had granted visitation rights to grandparents against the mother's wishes, and the Court held that this violated parental rights, protected by the Fourteenth Amendment, to make certain child-rearing choices for their children. The Court's decision is perhaps best understood as a one-off effort to correct what the court perceived as a serious abuse of discretion on the

The Supreme Court's choice not to intervene in this domain, like the silence of the dog that did not bark, signifies something.[93] Constitutionalizing the legal rules that govern family member interactions would not meaningfully advance a normative vision or strategic agenda that the Court has promoted. But doing so would bring the Court into conflict with state courts and legislatures, and would multiply the number of sites where constitutional law is made in ways that the Court might find difficult to control.

Moreover, rather than breaking the family open to public law values, the clear trend in the Court's jurisprudence in the past half-century has been to emphasize the *private* character of the family sphere and its consequent immunity from some forms of state intervention. This was the message of *Griswold v. Connecticut*,[94] *Roe v. Wade*,[95] and *Lawrence v. Texas*,[96] among other cases.[97] In these and similar cases, the Court had chosen to focus on threats to liberty emanating from *outside* the family, rather than those coming from within the family. Threats from outside—government efforts to dictate sexual practices, reproductive choices, or family living arrangements—are more readily identifiable as problems within the civil libertarian template and are also easier for courts to manage.

The net result of the Court's forbearance was to leave to state legislatures the project of updating family law to better comport with changing norms. This is a role that states have long occupied. State legislatures in the nineteenth century had eliminated the institution of coverture, in which women's legal personality was effectively dissolved upon marriage, and twentieth-century legislatures relaxed the legal regulation of sexual practices and liberalized divorce. William Eskridge and John Ferejohn argue that these developments amount to "small 'c' constitutional change" (2010, 238). Demographic and technological changes, social movements, administrative and legislative action, even Alfred

part of the trial judge, when the Court lacked jurisdiction to review the exercise of discretion as such (Ross et al. 2014, 614).

93. "'Is there any point to which you would wish to draw my attention?'
'To the curious incident of the dog in the night-time.'
'The dog did nothing in the night-time.'
'That was the curious incident,' remarked Sherlock Holmes." Doyle (1892, 196–97), cited in Chisom v. Roemer, 501 U.S. 380, 396 n.23.

94. 381 U.S. 479 (1965).

95. 410 U.S. 113 (1973).

96. 539 U.S. 558 (2003).

97. See, e.g., Moore v. City of East Cleveland, 431 U.S. 494 (1977) (invalidating city ordinance limiting occupancy of any dwelling to members of a family, narrowly defined).

Kinsey all contributed more to the "constitutional shift" they describe than the Supreme Court.

The clearest point of entry for the Court to constitutionalize family law, even to a limited extent, would be to recognize that individuals' rights can oblige the government to provide protection that involves interventions in familial relations. The Court roundly rejected this possibility in *DeShaney v. Winnebago County Department of Social Services*.[98] The facts of *DeShaney* are brutally sad. A divorce court had awarded custody of Joshua DeShaney to his father. State social services repeatedly received credible evidence that Joshua was being beaten by his father. Social services made visits to Joshua's home and recommendations to improve the home environment, but did not remove Joshua from his father's custody, even as the evidence suggested abuse was continuing. At age four, Joshua was beaten so severely by his father that he fell into a coma. The cumulative effects of Joshua's abuse resulted in profound permanent brain damage. Joshua's mother brought suit on her own and his behalf against the Winnebago County Department of Social Services and several employees, alleging that their failure to intervene amounted to a deprivation of substantive due process, in violation of the Fourteenth Amendment. The district court granted summary judgment for the defendants, and the court of appeals affirmed.

In their brief to the Supreme Court, the DeShaneys argued that the Fourteenth Amendment creates an affirmative duty to protect children. This would amount to indirect horizontal effect: the Constitution obligates the state to regulate the family—for instance, by terminating an abusive parent's custodial or parental rights—in ways that impact the legal relations of its members. The Supreme Court rejected the argument and affirmed the lower court. Writing for a six-Justice majority, Chief Justice Rehnquist leaned hard on the *action* part of the state action requirement:

> [N]othing in the language of the Due Process Clause itself requires the State to protect the life, liberty, and property of its citizens against invasion by private actors. The Clause is phrased as a limitation on the State's power to act, not as a guarantee of certain minimal levels of safety and security. It forbids the State itself to deprive individuals of life, liberty, or property without "due process of law," but its language cannot fairly be extended to impose an affirmative obligation on the State to ensure that those interests do not come to harm through other means. . . . Its purpose was to protect the people from the State, not to ensure that the State protected them from

98. 489 U.S. 189 (1989).

> each other. The Framers were content to leave the extent of governmental obligation in the latter area to the democratic political processes.
>
> Consistent with these principles, our cases have recognized that the Due Process Clauses generally confer no affirmative right to governmental aid, even where such aid may be necessary to secure life, liberty, or property interests of which the government itself may not deprive the individual.[99]

The Court also rejected the idea that the state had incurred affirmative obligations vis-à-vis Joshua DeShaney by undertaking to protect him. The majority also recognized the possibility of a normative gap between the accountability provided by statutory law and the justice that "natural sympathy" demands, but denied that it should be filled by the Constitution. Instead, it should be filled by lawmaking at the state level:

> The people of Wisconsin may well prefer a system of liability which would place upon the State and its officials the responsibility for failure to act in situations such as the present one. They may create such a system, if they do not have it already, by changing the tort law of the State in accordance with the regular lawmaking process. But they should not have it thrust upon them by this Court's expansion of the Due Process Clause of the Fourteenth Amendment.[100]

DeShaney illustrates the Court's antipathy to any conception of rights that might obligate the state to intervene within families. The Supreme Court has shown itself to be allergic to positive conceptions of constitutional rights in general. Even the dissenters rejected the idea that the Constitution imposes an affirmative obligation on the state to intervene within families. The Court argues that positive conceptions of rights are not part of our constitutional tradition, but as the previous chapter suggests, the reality is actually more complicated. It is true, on the other hand, that positive rights pose a significant management challenge for the Court. To the extent that constitutional rights impose affirmative duties on the state, countless thousands of legislative and executive actions and omissions take on a new constitutional salience. It is hard for a tribunal to exercise any control over such an unruly mass of actions, and since the first postwar constitutional settlement, the Supreme Court has made controlling constitutional interpretation central to its role in the American state. To the

99. *Id.* at 195–96.

100. *Id.* at 203.

extent that extending the Constitution's reach is advantageous, it is far easier for the Court to do so through ad hoc adjustments to the state action doctrine. And in the context of family law, there are simply few normative or strategic imperatives even to do this.[101]

ASSESSMENT

This chapter has argued that state action doctrine has proved an effective tool for the Supreme Court's management of (potentially unruly) constitutional rights. The stark formulation of the general state action rule allowed the Court to keep a lid on constitutional pluralism, while the Court has licensed deviations from the rule to avoid unpalatable results and keep states in line. The Court has never articulated a theory of when, exactly, constitutional rights require states to curb private behavior, but this vagueness has its use as well, in securing to the Supreme Court the role of sole authoritative state action gatekeeper.

The state action rule was born out of the Supreme Court's denial of horizontal effect in the years after Reconstruction. Then for a generation after the end of World War II, the Court applied rights horizontally in a number of high-profile contexts, all while maintaining the rhetorical insistence on a state action requirement. Extending the reach of rights into private orderings served the Court's interests in the second period in a way that it had not in the first. Crucially, there was much broader political and institutional support for the nationalization of rights protection in the years after the Second World War than in the years after construction. After retiring from its (self-appointed) pre-New Deal role as council of revision for economic legislation, the Court found a new role for itself in the American political economy, one in which the promotion of civil rights and civil liberties was central to its raison d'être. As the preceding sections have argued, the Court relaxed the state action rule where doing so furthered this agenda.

At times, the Supreme Court permitted rights to disrupt private-party relationships forcefully—for instance, by generating causes of action against private parties for legal and injunctive relief. Most of the time, though, constitutional rights had no effect on private parties. State action doctrine itself did not offer an adequate explanation for when rights would and would not be permitted to matter and, as a result, has justly received low marks for coherence. Rights

101. There is, of course, a hugely important constitutional family law issue that has engaged the Court: the constitutionality of same-sex marriage restrictions. But since the question concerns governmental definitions of marriage, the same-sex marriage cases do not implicate the state action rule. Matters are different in Canada, as Chapter Seven explains.

apply to private-party relations when the Supreme Court says they do. In a sense, the decisionism of the state action jurisprudence is the obverse face of the judicial supremacy narrative that the Court continues to cultivate. If the Court is the oracle of the Constitution, whose rulings are supreme just because they are the Court's, it has no need to hem itself in with an intelligible theory of horizontal effect. State action doctrine continues to function as a constitutional containment device even while the Supreme Court licenses departures from it.[102] Although the Court allowed Congress some room to share in the work of defining rights to a limited extent, this did not unleash a more general constitutional cascade that fundamentally blurred the categories of ordinary and constitutional law, or the roles of court and legislature.

In recent years, prominent scholars have argued that the lines between ordinary and constitutional law *are* blurred in the United States as a practical matter, and that statutes have a constitutional character. There are different aspects to, and variants of, the argument.[103] William Eskridge and John Ferejohn coined the term "super-statutes" to describe a class of legislative enactments that enjoy a kind of quasi-constitutional stature (Eskridge and Ferejohn 2001). There are two chief respects in which these statutes (which by Eskridge and Ferejohn's lights include the Sherman Antitrust Act, the National Labor Relations Act, the Civil Rights Act of 1964, and many more) resemble constitutional commitments. First, like the Constitution, they are deeply entrenched in our law, and therefore hard to change.[104] Second, they are distinguished from ordinary statutes by their substantive importance. In Eskridge and Ferejohn's words, "[i]n America's republic of statutes, republican deliberation over fundamental national commitments has migrated, relatively speaking, away from Constitutionalism and towards legislative and administrative constitutionalism" (Eskridge and Ferejohn 2010, 16). Eskridge and Ferejohn claim that these statutes exercise a

102. One context in which the Supreme Court has applied rights horizontally in recent years is in reviewing punitive damages awards. The Court has held that excessive punitive damage awards amount to a violation of due process and struck down the awards recovered by private parties. See State Farm Mut. Auto. Ins. Co. v. Campbell, 538 U.S. 408 (2003); BMW of N. Am., Inc. v. Gore, 517 U.S. 559 (1996). This line of cases has been viewed by some popular and academic observers as part of the broader efforts by the Rehnquist and Roberts Courts to create a more favorable legal climate for business (Rosen 2008).

103. These claims are also related to a broader body of work on popular constitutionalism, which denies the starring role in American constitutional development to courts, in favor of democratic institutions. Leading voices in this direction include Balkin (2011), Kramer (2004), Tushnet (2000), and West (2003).

104. They are entrenched not least because they have been institutionalized in agencies dedicated to maintaining the regimes that they establish.

gravitational force on other law and argue that their special stature justifies a special solicitude from courts, which includes liberal, purposive construction and ample deference to administrative interpretations.[105]

In a similar vein, Bruce Ackerman argues that "Our Living Constitution" lives on through statutory law, which changes over time to meet the fundamental challenges the polity faces even as the formal Constitution remains frozen (2007). Ackerman, like Eskridge and Ferejohn, believes that "[t]he Supreme Court has an institutional obligation to recognize that superprecedents crystallize fixed points in our constitutional tradition, and should not be overruled or ignored in the course of doctrinal development" (2007, 1752). But while Eskridge and Ferejohn treat legislative constitutionalism as a fait accompli, Ackerman is less sanguine. Notwithstanding their institutional entrenchment, super-statutes in Ackerman's treatment come off as more vulnerable to judicial undermining, and Ackerman is more critical of the Court's handling of them, especially in recent years (2014, 328–37).

It is useful to consider these claims in a comparative context, and this project helps us to do that. Eskridge and Ferejohn are certainly correct that many of the most fundamental collective choices of the American people are expressed in statutes. In that sense, and because their institutionalization makes them "sticky," it is reasonable to consider landmark statutes to have a small-c constitutional character. But what comparison with Germany points up is how these policy processes are cut off from the conceptual and institutional resources of constitutionalism proper. In Germany, the high courts' constitutional jurisprudence has treated rights as the embodiments of values that pervade the whole legal system. This turns important legislative choices into the site for multi-branch "constitutional dialogues." This means, on the one hand, that legislatures self-consciously engage in constitutional deliberation, and on the other, that when courts are called to intervene, they do so with some deference to the choices legislatures have made. Consider, for instance, how civil courts, the national legislature, and the Federal Constitutional Court collectively dragged German family law into compliance with the Basic Law's gender equality mandate over a period of years. By comparison, the United States experiences a much more limited form of legislative constitutionalism.

Also, super-statutes enjoy their superpowers at the sufferance of courts. As a descriptive matter, Eskridge and Ferejohn have argued that courts—including the Supreme Court—by and large do treat super-statutes with extra deference, owing to their "quasi-constitutional" stature (Eskridge and Ferejohn 2001, 1217,

105. See also Lupu (1993) (arguing that certain statutes "revolve in constitutional law orbits" and should be interpreted accordingly).

1246–63). Ackerman is more skeptical, and his skepticism seems increasingly warranted. While the Supreme Court may in the past have shown compunction about sweeping aside the "quasi-constitutional" conclusions of the legislative branch, it shows little now.

The Court's 2013 decision regarding Congress's enforcement powers, *Shelby County v. Holder*, illustrates the point and offers a bookend to our discussion of earlier Voting Rights Act cases.[106] When Congress reauthorized the Voting Rights Act in 2006, leaving in place the existing preclearance formula, Shelby County, a covered jurisdiction in Alabama, cried foul, arguing that Justice Department review of its voting practices could no longer be justified as a measure to enforce the right to be free from race-based voting discrimination.

The Supreme Court agreed. While the VRA's coverage formula may have originally tracked voting discrimination, the country had changed dramatically since 1965, but the formula had not changed at all. The Warren Court's permissive approval of legislation with a rational relation to the rights in question was replaced with a newfound parsimony. If Congress was to subject the voting practices of states to extra oversight, Chief Justice Roberts wrote for the 5–4 majority, it must do so on the basis of "current data reflecting current needs." In other words, legislation that was at one time a valid exercise of Congress's enforcement power will cease to be if Congress fails to update its statute to mirror the changing shape of the problem.

In the United States, the formal hierarchies of constitutional law over ordinary law, and court over legislature as steward of constitutional meaning, functionally dictate how policy-relevant decisions are made to a greater degree than in Germany or Canada. In the domain of ordinary law, the courts are assigned the role of legislative amanuensis, discerning and applying congressional intent. But when the Constitution is "switched on," judicial construction displaces congressional deliberation entirely. The ordinary law discourse and the constitutional law discourse are largely separate conversations.

And yet the relationship between constitutional and ordinary law can be dynamic and interactive, notwithstanding the fact that they have a strictly hierarchical relationship as a formal matter. Indeed, the common law tail can even sometimes wag the constitutional law dog. When ordinary law fails to meet potent demands for the protection of individuals' interests, pressure can build

106. *Shelby County* was a Fifteenth Amendment case; the Court had already revisited its Fourteenth Amendment enforcement jurisprudence in the 1997 case of *City of Boerne v. Flores*. In *City of Boerne*, the Supreme Court declared that there must be "a congruence and proportionality" between measures adopted by Congress pursuant to its Fourteenth Amendment rights enforcement power and the rights themselves—as defined by the Court. 521 U.S. 507, 520 (1997).

on courts to turn to the Constitution, even when the threats to those interests come from other individuals. In this way, and in an inversion of the official hierarchy in which constitutional law reigns supreme, ordinary law can shape what constitutional law becomes. So, for instance, in *New York Times v. Sullivan*, the deficiencies of the law of defamation draw the First Amendment into tort law. So functionally, constitutional law can have a supplementary relationship to ordinary law, even if constitutional doctrine has no way to account for this. The Constitution is pressed into this role of private law gap-filler only on occasion, notably to bring regional outliers back into line with national norms.

The gap between doctrine and reality is the cost of preserving the Court's two postwar constitutional settlements. Since the late nineteenth century, the Supreme Court has articulated a narrative for itself that fused constitutional supremacy and judicial supremacy. In the mid-twentieth century, it added to this narrative a role for itself as defender of civil liberties. Maintaining its role in the driver's seat required that the Court exercise tight control over how constitutional rights could be deployed, even as the Court itself sometimes applied rights horizontally in furtherance of its agenda. Whatever else can be said about the state action doctrine, over the long haul, it has performed as an effective constitutional containment device.

6

Canada's Constitution and Courts

INTRODUCTION: OLD COURT, NEW RIGHTS

At the bottom of the official edition of Canada's Charter of Rights and Freedoms appear these words from Prime Minister Pierre Trudeau, the Charter's indefatigable and ultimately successful champion:

> We must now establish the basic principles, the basic values and beliefs which hold us together as Canadians, so that beyond our regional loyalties there is a way of life and a system of values which makes us proud of the country that has given us such freedom and such immeasurable joy (Waluchow 2009, 2).

The enactment of the Charter in 1982 was a watershed event in Canada. Canada's Parliament had enacted a statutory bill of rights in 1960, but this had proved ineffectual. The Charter marked the culmination of almost fifteen years of effort to introduce a roster of legally enforceable rights of constitutional stature. But the true import of the Charter for Canada was by no means clear in 1982.

The quotation from Prime Minister Trudeau speaks to some of the tensions and ambiguities of the Charter project and of political life in Canada more generally. The Charter purports to "establish" basic principles, but it is also asserts that these principles are already present—indeed, they "hold us together as Canadians." This ambiguity about just what the Charter claims to be goes to the central question surrounding the entire project: Just how much is the Charter going to change things in Canada?

Trudeau also acknowledges federalism, the key constitutional fact about Canada, along with the hope that the Charter will transcend "our regional loyalties." The Charter, in other words, will foreground Canadians' national identity, which is rooted in the shared values to which the Charter gives expression. But mediating between competing claims of national and provincial primacy is

Extending Rights' Reach. Jud Mathews.

a tricky business in Canada. And in the post-Charter era, just as in the pre-Charter era, sorting out these claims would fall in large measure to the courts, and to the Supreme Court of Canada (SCC) in particular.

This chapter and the next focus on one particular aspect of the Charter's impact in Canada: the impact of constitutional rights on relationships between private parties. In its approach to the horizontal effect of rights, the SCC in some respects resembles Germany, and in others the United States.

When first presented with the opportunity to give horizontal effect to Charter rights, the SCC declined. The Court's decision in the *Dolphin Delivery* case formally demarcated a substantial portion of Canadian law as a Charter-free zone.[1] In *Dolphin Delivery*, the Court declared that the Charter does not apply to the common law, except insofar as it is the basis for executive or administrative action; that the Charter does not apply to private litigation; and that the Charter does not apply to courts. The SCC seemed to take a strong stance in favor of the exclusive vertical effect of rights.

As a strategic matter, the SCC's position made considerable sense. The SCC is not a constitutional court but a supreme court, and a supreme court with general subject matter jurisdiction. In other words, it is the final authority on cases raising any kind of legal questions: questions of constitutional law, of common law, of federal or provincial statutory law. The practical implication is that invoking the Charter does little to expand the SCC's reach: it does not provide a basis for jurisdiction over any cases not otherwise subject to review. The contrast with Germany is instructive. Constitutionalizing private law potentially made the GFCC into a court of last resort for a dispute in that area of law. The SCC was already the court of last resort for disputes in every area of law. This is not to say that giving horizontal effect to rights would change nothing for the SCC. Doing so would make available to the Court additional grounds on which to decide the cases before it, and recognizing a constitutional cause of action in private litigation could spawn additional litigation. But the breadth of the Court's existing jurisdiction meant that any impact on its docket would be limited.

Furthermore, other features of Canada's situation counseled against a far-reaching constitutionalization of private law. One of these, I argue, is a deep-rooted ambivalence about judicial power in Canada, linked to issues of federalism. The balance between provincial and national power is a "megaconstitutional" issue in Canada and has been a politically explosive one throughout Canadian history. The exercise of judicial power by national courts has a complex relationship to this balance. Structurally, expanding the role of national

1. Retail, Wholesale & Dep't Store Union, Local 580 v. Dolphin Delivery Ltd. [1986] 2 S.C.R. 573.

courts in governance means concentrating power in the organs of the central government. But the SCC has allayed provincial hostility and suspicion, at least to some extent, through decisions that take the provinces' part in disputes with the central government. Constitutionalizing *private law* raises federalism concerns to an especial degree in Canada, since private law is largely made by provincial courts. While the SCC's Charter jurisprudence has actively pushed a rights agenda in many areas of law, it makes sense that the Court would proceed with some delicacy when it comes to the Charter's impact on private law.

Moreover, Canada's constitutional moment came late. The Charter was enacted after the rapid social and political changes of the 1960s and 1970s, and by the time it took effect, many of the normative demands that had emerged during those years had been met by legislation.[2] This is not to say that by 1982 there were no normative gaps in the private law that could be filled by constitutional norms, but that some of the low-hanging fruit had been already picked from the trees by the legislatures or common law courts.

Crucially, though, the SCC only *appeared* to shut the door on the horizontal effect of Charter rights. The Court's doctrine, as framed in *Dolphin Delivery* and developed in subsequent cases, trumpets a narrative of judicial restraint, declaring huge swaths of Canadian law off limits to Charter rights. At the same time, the doctrine established a loophole that does permit Charter *values* to shape the legal relations of private parties in Canada. The Court in *Dolphin Delivery* noted, almost in passing, that courts ought to "apply and develop the principles of the common law in a manner consistent with the fundamental values enshrined in the Constitution." As a practical matter, the development of the common law in accordance with Charter values can look an awful lot like the Charter applying to the common law, but with two important differences: the Court maintains the useful fiction that it is not conducting Charter review, and the Court enjoys broad discretion to apply Charter principles when and how it chooses.[3]

The SCC's approach in some respects resembles that of Germany's Federal Constitutional Court. Charter rights, like Basic Law rights, have a double existence: they are not only entitlements that apply in public law contexts but also values that can shape the interpretation of private law. As values, they place courts—and other actors—in a position to balance rights against competing considerations in concrete situations. The SCC's doctrine does not go so far as

2. This is particularly so in the area of gender equality (Epp 1998, 164–66).

3. A third difference is that, in a proper Charter challenge, the government bears the burden of persuading the court that an infringement of a right is justified, once the claimant has established that a right has been infringed (Hogg 2015, 38-7–38-9). Whether this changes matters as a practical matter in concrete cases is not clear.

Germany's: the Court has not, for instance, created new Charter-based causes of action in private litigation. But the disruptive effect of Charter values on the private law has edged up some over time. For instance, the Court has gone from declaring that the Charter licenses only "incremental revisions to the common law"[4] to invalidating common law rules on the basis of the Charter.[5] The SCC's approach differs from that taken in Germany in other important respects. The SCC frames the horizontal application of rights as one aspect of courts' role as stewards of the common law. Because of this framing, and because the Court has limited rights' potential to disrupt ordinary law, the SCC has remained in the driver's seat of constitutional change to a greater extent than its German counterpart. But even so, litigants in Canada have successfully used horizontal rights claims to advance agendas not anticipated by the Court, in ways largely unknown in the United States.

The SCC's approach to the horizontal effect of rights has had some broader impacts on lawmaking in Canada, though without touching off a general constitutional cascade as in Germany. Here as well, the Court has emphasized the limited reach of constitutional rights, declaring that the Charter does not apply to private choices permitted within, but not required by, a statutory scheme.[6] But here as well, the reality has been more complex. While the SCC generally has been reluctant to impose on the legislatures a duty to provide protection for Charter rights in statutes, there is an interesting twist. Once a legislature introduces some Charter values into a domain of private-party relationships, the SCC may apply Charter scrutiny, eliminating gaps in the legislature's promotion of Charter norms. The Court's doctrine of "reading in" to statutes to eliminate Charter problems permits the SCC to hang back and wait for a legislature to make the first move before advancing the Charter agenda in a new domain. This kind of "caboose constitutionalism" thus permits the Court to expand the Charter's reach into private-party relationships, but in a manner that also permits some legislative agenda-setting.

The SCC's willingness to take some cues from the provincial and national legislatures when it comes to extending rights is consistent with its measured acceptance of legislative constitutionalism more generally. The Charter was not meant to be given meaning by the courts alone. Rather, it was part of the design that legislatures would engage in their own constitutional deliberations and that their considered conclusions about what the Charter required, as reflected in

4. Hill v. Church of Scientology of Toronto [1995] 2. S.C.R. 1130.

5. RWDSU Pepsi-Cola Canada Beverages (West) Ltd., [2002] 1 S.C.R. 156; Grant v. Torstar Corp., [2009] 3 S.C.R. 640.

6. Stoffman v. Vancouver Gen. Hosp., [1990] 3 S.C.R. 483.

the statutes they passed, would be entitled to some respect from courts (Hiebert 2013, 304; Erdos 2010). While the legislatures are by no means treated as independent and coequal interpreters of the Charter, it is still meaningful to speak of constitutional "dialogues" between the SCC and Parliament, as many scholars do.[7] The horizontal application of rights is not the root cause of legislative constitutionalism in Canada, but both developments are of a piece and reflect the conception of rights as values that the SCC has endorsed.

This chapter and the next are organized as follows. The next section describes the Canadian Constitution, both before and after the advent of the Charter. The burning constitutional questions for most of Canada's history have been about federalism, not rights; the rights issues brought to the fore by the Charter did not displace federalism concerns, and many of the rights dispute themselves have a federalism dimension. The following section analyzes the jurisdiction of the Supreme Court and the structure of the judiciary. Historically an underpowered court, the SCC found itself with formidable formal powers owing to changes to its jurisdiction and the advent of the Charter. The final section gives context for the SCC's horizontal effect doctrine by describing the Court's emerging rights jurisprudence in the years following enactment of the Charter.

The first section of Chapter Seven analyzes in detail the *Dolphin Delivery* decision, in which the Court appeared to exercise more forbearance than it actually did. The following three sections explore how constitutional rights in Canada have shaped the law, and lawmaking processes, with respect to private law restrictions on the freedom of expression, discrimination, and family law, respectively. The final section concludes.

THE CANADIAN CONSTITUTION

"The Constitution of Canada" is a phrase without a clear referent. Canada's Constitution consists of more than one foundational legal document, as well as, perhaps, conventional understandings about the operation of government that are not committed to an authoritative text (Courtney and Smith 2010, 11; Hogg 2015, 1-3).[8] The first of these foundational documents is the British

7. The "dialogue" metaphor is not original to Canada: Louis Fisher used it to describe legislative-judicial interactions in the United States (1988), and Alec Stone Sweet used it with reference to France (1992) and Europe (2000). But the metaphor seems to have particularly caught the imagination of Canadian constitutional law scholars, who have debated its use in a long-running scholarly exchange—a dialogue, if you will.

8. These nontextual constitutional ideas would surely include the principle of responsible government: that the members of the cabinet are responsible to the House of Commons and must resign if the government loses the confidence of that chamber.

North America (BNA) Act of 1867 (renamed the Constitution Act, 1867 in 1982).[9] The BNA Act was a statute of the British Parliament that established the Dominion of Canada, consisting of Britain's three North American provinces. As a Dominion of the Crown, Canada was not a sovereign state, but the BNA Act set up freestanding, national legislative institutions in Canada for the first time.

For more than a century, the key constitutional controversies in Canada concerned not rights—the BNA Act did not contain individual rights provisions—but structural issues and, specifically, the allocation of power between the national government and the provinces. The BNA Act enumerated the subjects of both national and provincial legislative competence and also included a residual clause (the so-called "Peace, Order, and good Government" clause) reserving to Parliament legislative powers not granted to the provinces.[10] It fell to the courts to draw the lines demarcating provincial and national authority. And although the Supreme Court of Canada was established in 1875, it was not the tribunal with the final word on federalism questions for many years. That would be the Judicial Committee of the Privy Council (JCPC) in London, which decided cases from Commonwealth countries on behalf of the British monarch. The JCPC generally used its interpretive authority to enhance provincial authority, in many cases overruling the SCC (Jackson 2013, 93; Kelly and Manfredi 2010, 49). After legislation abolished appeals to the JCPC in 1949, the SCC generally tilted the balance back more in the direction of national power (Bernier and Lajoie 1986).

If the SCC had long experience deciding federalism questions, the first attempt to get it into the constitutional rights arena was a bust. Parliament had passed a statutory Bill of Rights, which contained a familiar roster of liberal rights, in 1960. But the SCC's approach to rights-based judicial review was tepid at best, and the Court invalidated only one federal law for violating a protected right (Macfarlane 2013, 41).[11]

The adoption of the landmark constitutional reform of 1982, which included the Charter of Rights and Freedoms, was responsive to two perceived problems. One was structural: as an act of the British Parliament, the BNA Act contained

9. I refer to the BNA Act when focusing on historical developments in Canada and the Constitution Act, 1867 when focusing on the legal effects of the document.

10. The clause reads: "It shall be lawful for the Queen, by and with the Advice and Consent of the Senate and House of Commons, to make Laws for the Peace, Order, and good Government of Canada, in relation to all Matters not coming within the Classes of Subjects by this Act assigned exclusively to the Legislatures of the Provinces." Constitution Act, 1867, 30 & 31 Vict., c. 3, 91 (U.K.), reprinted in R.S.C. 1985, app. II, no. 5.

11. R. v. Drybones, [1970] S.C.R. 282.

no provisions whereby it could be amended in Canada. The idea of petitioning the British Parliament for amendments to Canada's constitution became steadily more incongruous as Canada increased its independence from Britain through the twentieth century. The second problem was the lack of effective rights protection, in the wake of the failure of the statutory Bill of Rights. Incorporating a new roster of rights into the constitutional reform agenda was the project of Pierre Trudeau, first as Justice Minister, and later as Prime Minister, more than any other official (Hiebert 2010, 56). But the campaign for rights protection found vigorous support in civil libertarian activists and other organized interest groups representing women, minorities, and others (Epp 1998, 190–94; Erdos 2010, 77–83). Trudeau argued that a charter of rights should be included in Canada's "patriated" constitution, because protecting fundamental rights was one of the defining responsibilities of government.

The effort to get provincial agreement on a constitutional reform package was protracted and need not be recounted here.[12] A key ground for resistance to the Charter reforms—although not the only one—was concern among the provincial premiers that the inclusion of justiciable constitutional rights would override provincial parliamentary sovereignty and further centralize governance in Canada by taking certain policy options off the table (Kelly and Manfredi 2010, 50; Russell 2010, 31).[13] Following many false starts and near misses—and a ruling from the SCC that disfavored Trudeau's plan to ignore the recalcitrant provinces and pursue patriation with the support of only two[14]—Parliament approved the Constitution Act, 1982, which took effect in April of that year.[15]

The Constitution Act, 1982 did set out procedures for amending the Constitution and also tweaked some provincial powers and the financing of federal programs (Russell 2010, 31). But the part of the Act most relevant for present purposes, not to mention the part with the most transformative effect, was the Charter of Rights and Freedoms.

Substantively, the Charter mostly contains a conventional assortment of negative liberties and criminal trial protections, with some rights that speak to the particularities of Canada's experience as a bilingual and multicultural federation. The Charter protects rights to freedom of conscience, expression, assembly, and association (s. 2); the right to vote (s. 3); and the right to move within

12. The process is chronicled in some depth, from the perspective of a key participant, in Strayer (2013).

13. For more on the concerns of the provinces, see Monahan (1987) and Smiley (1980).

14. Reference re Resolution to Amend the Constitution, [1981] 1 S.C.R. 753.

15. The patriation of Canada's constitution also required the approval of the British Parliament, and this was granted through passage of the Canada Act (Strayer 2013, 214–15).

Canada and pursue a livelihood (s. 6). The Charter also bars deprivation of life, liberty, and security of the person "except in accordance with the principles of fundamental justice" (s. 7) and creates rights against arbitrary detention (s. 9) and cruel and unusual treatment or punishment (s. 12). The Charter grants a right to "equal protection and equal benefit of the law," but stipulates that affirmative action programs are constitutional (s. 15). And a number of provisions concern language rights in Canada.

At least as significant as the rights guaranteed by the Charter are the two built-in escape hatches from them that bookend the Charter. The Charter opens with a limitations clause: "The Canadian Charter of Rights and Freedoms guarantees the rights and freedom set out in it *subject only to such reasonable limits prescribed by law as can be demonstrably justified in a free and democratic society*" (s. 1; emphasis added). The limitations clause was an innovation of the provincial premiers, and as originally proposed in 1980, it read: "The Canadian Charter of Rights and Freedoms recognizes the following rights and freedoms subject only to such reasonable limits as are generally accepted in a free society living under a parliamentary democracy" (Kelly 2006, 56). The reference to "parliamentary democracy" was included to subordinate judicial review to parliamentary supremacy: in effect, to inoculate "reasonable" legislation against judicial invalidation. Trudeau's government acceded to a limitations clause, but ultimately reworded it to narrow its scope in response to concerns expressed in public hearings that it gave Parliament a blank check to erode Charter rights (Kelly 2006, 67).[16]

The limitations clause at the start of the Charter offers courts a means to avoid invalidating legislation on Charter grounds. The end of the Charter offers legislatures, both federal and provincial, a way to evade unfavorable judicial rulings on Charter claims. Section 33 contains a *non obstante* clause: Parliament or provincial legislatures may enact laws, notwithstanding their violation of Charter rights, for a fixed but renewable period of five years. This provision was also adopted at the urging of the provinces. Drafted only days before federal-provincial negotiations concluded, the notwithstanding clause was one of the final prizes that the premiers extracted in exchange for their agreement to patriation (Strayer 2013, 195–96).

The Charter gave Canada a roster of constitutionally entrenched and judicially enforceable rights for the first time, but it did more. The limitations clause and notwithstanding clause implied a rights jurisprudence with certain features. The former meant that rights would not be absolute but subject to

16. Walter Tarnopolsky, a longtime advocate for constitutional rights, argued that "section 1 permits Parliament to take away everything that Parliament gives by the rest of the Charter" (Kelly 2006, 67).

balancing against other considerations. The latter meant that the legislatures, rather than the SCC, could have the last word in a constitutional controversy. The Charter thus implicitly rejected both rights absolutism and strong-form judicial supremacy. The Charter did not contain rights that implied duties on other citizens, such as the rights of mothers and children in the Basic Law, but neither did it exclude the possibility of horizontal effect. Whether and how the Charter would affect private-party relations would be up to the Court.

JUDICIAL POWER AND FEDERALISM

Section 24(1) of the Charter granted anyone whose rights were infringed or denied the power to bring a claim in "any court of competent jurisdiction." As with legislative powers, judicial powers in Canada are divided between provincial and national institutions. And much like legislative federalism, judicial federalism in Canada is complicated. Some of the finer points are described below.

For present purposes, there are two important points to emphasize about the organization of the judiciary in Canada and the powers of Canada's Supreme Court. The first is that the SCC is the court of final appeal in Canada, not just on Charter matters but on all matters. I will argue later that the breadth of the Court's subject matter jurisdiction shaped its restrained approach to the horizontal effect of Charter rights.

Second, the SCC's Charter jurisprudence helped complete its transformation from a "second-rate institution" (Hausegger et al. 2008, 57) to a powerful and influential one. A series of changes over the years had amplified the Court's powers, and an uptick in the quality of appointments had increased the Court's prestige, even before the Charter took effect. When the Charter was passed, the Court had the tools at its disposal to craft a robust rights jurisprudence. At the same time, the SCC operated against a backdrop of significant anxiety about judicial power, as demonstrated both by provincial opposition to the idea of a rights charter and by the limitation and notwithstanding clauses added to the Charter to mollify the premiers. I will argue later that these misgivings about judicial power also contributed to the Court's restraint with respect to horizontal effect.

Canada has what some political scientists have termed a "federal but unified court system" (Hausegger et al. 2008, 29). Canada has provincial courts, federal courts, and courts that blend provincial and federal features. Jurisdictional issues are complex and sometimes the subject of intrajudicial conflict. Some provincial courts can decide issues of both provincial and federal law, but except for the SCC, the federal courts can decide issues of federal law only.

Canada's judiciary contains three kinds of courts, named after the provisions of the Constitution Act, 1867 that establish them: Section 92 courts, Section 96 courts, and Section 101 courts. Section 92 trial courts are established and administered by provincial governments, which also select the judges and establish their salaries (Kelly and Manfredi 2010, 40). They have jurisdiction over provincial criminal cases and relatively minor federal criminal cases, civil suits involving small claims, certain family law issues, and cases involving youthful offenders (Hausegger et al. 2008, 34–37). Most of the Section 92 courts are courts of general jurisdiction, but some provinces have developed specialized courts for youthful offenders.

The Section 96 courts blend provincial and federal elements in a manner utterly unique to Canada (Hausegger et al. 2008, 31). The courts are organized and administered by the provinces, but the judges are selected by the governor general and paid out of federal funds. Every province but Ontario has two levels of Section 96 courts: a trial court (which also handles appeals from Section 92 courts) and an appeals court, which is the highest court in the province (Hausegger et al. 2008, 51). The Constitution Act, 1867 imposes no limit on the subject matter jurisdiction of Section 96 courts, meaning that Parliament could assign them to hear any class of case, whether arising under federal or provincial law. In practice, they handle more serious criminal trials, criminal appeals from Section 92 courts, high-stakes civil matters, and family law issues concerning divorce.

Section 101 of the Constitution Act, 1867 authorizes the creation of the Supreme Court, as well as "any additional Courts for the better Administration of the Laws of Canada." Under this latter grant of power, Parliament has established several courts since the 1970s, including the Tax Court of Canada, the Court Martial Appeal Court, the Federal Court (for trials), and the Federal Court of Appeal (Greene 2007, 8). These are fully federal courts, in that the judges are selected and compensated by the national government. Their subject matter jurisdiction is also confined to federal law. Although Section 101 courts (apart from the SCC) are barred from hearing provincial law issues, their decisions are binding through the whole of Canada. Decisions by provincial courts, even as to issues of federal law, are binding within the province only (Hausegger et al. 2008, 59).

Different Charter claims can originate in different kinds of courts in Canada. For instance, a Section 92 court cannot entertain a civil suit claiming that a federal statute violated the Charter, but it can hear a Charter-based defense to a criminal case that fell within the court's jurisdiction. What is important is that claims brought in whatever court can ultimately be funneled to the Supreme Court. As a court of general jurisdiction, the SCC can hear—and is the final authority on—issues of both provincial and federal law. This distinguishes it not only from specialized constitutional courts but also from the U.S. Supreme

Court, which can decide questions both of constitutional law and ordinary law, but not state law. More generally, when it comes to the precedential effect of rulings in the Canadian judiciary, the hierarchical principle trumps the federal principle: rulings of courts higher in the pyramid of authority are controlling over courts below them in the hierarchy (Hausegger et al. 2008, 29).

The breadth of the SCC's subject matter jurisdiction, particularly with respect to provincial law, may seem surprising in a federal system. It's important to remember, however, that when the SCC was established, in 1875, it was not the final court of appeal for Canada: the JCPC was. And while the JCPC was the court of last resort, it functioned as a strong counterweight to any centralizing or nationalizing tendencies of the SCC. The elimination of appeal to the JCPC instantly converted the SCC from a weak court to one that was potentially much stronger.

Two other pre-Charter developments also enhanced the Court's ability to pursue an agenda of its own, by increasing its control over case selection and expanding its potential docket. In 1975, Parliament eliminated an appeal of right in civil cases worth more than $10,000 Canadian (Kelly and Manfredi 2010, 47). As a result, since that time, the SCC has been permitted to decide for itself which cases to decide, apart from references (discussed below) and criminal appeals. The lion's share of the SCC's docket is composed of discretionary cases, in which the parties must obtain leave to appeal from the Court before proceeding.[17]

Also, in a series of pre-Charter cases starting in the 1970s—the so-called "Standing Trilogy"—the SCC progressively relaxed its own standing requirements. These cases held that, in order to challenge legislation, "a person need only to show that he is affected by it directly or that he has a genuine interest as a citizen in the validity of the legislation and that there is no other reasonable and effective manner in which the issue may be brought before the Court."[18] These cases "gave Canada one of the common law world's most lax laws of standing" (Macfarlane 2013, 44).[19] Furthermore, a 1977 statute enhanced the

17. Still, because the total volume of litigation in Canada is relatively small, the SCC agrees to accept around 12 percent of all the discretionary appeals a year, more than ten times the percentage of petitions that the U.S. Supreme Court typically grants (Supreme Court of Canada 2012, 4).

18. Minister of Justice v. Borowski, [1981] 2 S.C.R. 575–76.

19. Canada's law of standing became more lax still in 2012, when the SCC loosened the third requirement for public interest standing in the *Downtown Eastside* case. Now a party need only show that the proposed suit is a reasonable and effective means of bringing the case to court. Canada (Attorney General) v. Downtown Eastside Sex Workers United Against Violence Society, [2012] 2 S.C.R. 524.

SCC's administrative independence, establishing it as a separate institution of government (Greene 2007, 84).

In addition to deciding concrete legal disputes, the SCC also hears constitutional references from the federal government. The references seek an advisory opinion from the Court on a question of constitutional law, and as such, they are considered part of the Court's executive (as opposed to strictly judicial) function (Flemming 2005, 9). Numerically, the references make up a small part of the SCC's docket—in a typical year, there will be one or two—but the questions they raise are often very important, and with high political salience (Flemming 2005, 9). For instance, in 1998 the SCC was asked whether and through what process Quebec might secede from Canada. The Court's references resemble the power of abstract review that many constitutional courts possess (Comella 2009, 66–70).

THE SCC'S EMERGENCE AS A RIGHTS-PROTECTING COURT

Almost overnight, it appeared that what scholars have variously termed "the new constitutionalism" or the "postwar model" of constitutionalism had come to Canada: the nation's fundamental legal commitments were committed to paper, and a justiciable catalog of fundamental rights displaced parliamentary supremacy (Stone Sweet 2008; Weinrib 2002, 125–26). What would the SCC make of its newfound role in the governance of Canada? The first years of the Charter era saw the Court embracing its expanded role, but also showing some ambivalence about it. On the one hand, the SCC borrowed some moves from the playbook of a strong constitutional court. In particular, it inaugurated a proportionality approach to determining whether limitations on rights were justifiable under Section 1, which meant both that rights would be defined expansively and that the Court would be at the center of the value conflicts at issue in rights claims. At other times, however, the Court seemed to shrink from that role.

This section describes the foundations of the SCC's rights jurisprudence, as background to a discussion of its horizontal rights jurisprudence specifically, which is covered in the following chapter. I argue that the SCC's approach to rights in general reflects both an ambitious rights-protective agenda and caution about pushing that agenda too aggressively. In particular, the SCC took steps to limit how far in advance of the legislatures its own development of rights doctrines could race. And I will argue later that this tension also informs the SCC's ostensibly restrictive approach to the horizontal effect of rights.

The SCC began defining its role with respect to Charter rights in a series of important decisions handed down starting in the mid-1980s. These rulings not only affirmed that the Court would accept its rights-protecting role under the Charter as it never really had under the 1960 Bill of Rights, they framed rights adjudication in ways that placed the Court in the position of reviewing sensitive policy judgments. The SCC's early Charter jurisprudence cast the Court very much in the mold of a strong constitutional court.

In the 1985 *Big M Drug Mart* case, the SCC explained how its responsibilities under the Charter dictated a new approach to rights claims.[20] The case concerned a challenge to a national Sunday closing law on the grounds that it violated the Section 2 right to freedom of conscience and religion. The Court explained that it was obligated under the Charter to scrutinize challenged legislation both for an unconstitutional purpose and an unconstitutional effect. The Charter, in other words, creates a right to be free from either. This searching review contrasts sharply with the characteristic inquiry of the pre-Charter era, the "pith and substance" test applied in federalism cases. This approach directs courts to determine the "essential character" of a challenged law and to decide whether it is more properly in the province of the federal government or the provinces.[21] Pith and substance permits courts to decide cases without probing legislative purpose or evaluating policy impacts, while the SCC's new approach required them to do both.

Also in 1985, the SCC ruled that the Section 7 right against deprivations of life, liberty, and security of the person that do not accord with "principles of fundamental justice" guaranteed substantive fairness, not merely procedural due process.[22] In reaching this conclusion, the Court brushed past legislative history indicating that the framers of the Charter intended Section 7 to license judicial review of procedural fairness only. This interpretive move brought forth some criticism and accusations of bad faith from participants in the Charter process, who feared it would open the door to American-style substantive due process review in Canada (Strayer 2013, 256–60).

And the following year, the Court adopted a proportionality approach to the Section 1 limitations analysis. In *Oakes*, the Court faced the question whether the presumption of innocence, guaranteed in Section 11(d) of the Charter, was violated by a rebuttable presumption (or "reverse onus") that a person in possession of drugs possesses them for the purpose of trafficking.[23] The SCC recognized that such a presumption did constitute a prima facie infringement of the presumption of innocence. The question then became whether such a restriction on the right constitutes a "reasonable limit[] prescribed by law as can be demonstrably justified in a free society," under Section 1.

20. R. v. Big M Drug Mart, Ltd., [1985] 1 S.C.R. 295.

21. Union Colliery Co. of B.C. v. Bryden, [1899] A.C. 580 (P.C.), 589.

22. B.C. Motor Vehicle Reference [1985] 2 S.C.R. 486.

23. R. v. Oakes, [1986] 1 S.C.R. 103.

For a limit on a right to qualify as reasonable and demonstrably justified in a free society, according to the SCC, it must satisfy two tests. First, the rights-limiting measure must serve an important objective. And second, the limits must be proportional. The Court outlined a three-part proportionality test that closely tracks the analysis pioneered in German law (without acknowledging the debt): the challenged measure must be rationally connected to the objective; it should impair rights "as little as possible"; and the benefits of the measure must be proportional to its effects on the right (Stone Sweet and Mathews 2008, 114). The advent of proportionality analysis in *Oakes* drew the SCC deeper into the realm of policy judgments about the effects of statutes on protected interests and the proper balance between rights and policy objectives. Some Canadian commentators regarded *Oakes* as a license for judicial lawmaking, on the grounds that its criteria are too indeterminate to impose real constraint on judicial decision making (Bakan 1997, 27–29).

By the late 1980s, the SCC appeared to be operating as a strong constitutional court. Charter cases soon made up a substantial, though not overwhelming, share of the Court's docket, averaging 18 percent per year in the first decade of the Charter (Vaughan 2001, 15). The size of the Court's docket increased too, from around 120 cases a year in the 1960s and 1970s, to an average of around 200 a year in the first few years under the Charter (Monahan 1987, 13, 16).

In striking contrast to its exercise of judicial review under the 1960 Bill of Rights, the SCC did not shrink from striking down legislation when it perceived a conflict with Charter rights. Between 1982 and 2007, the SCC upheld Charter claims in 34.6 percent of the 489 Charter cases it heard, in the process striking down 84 federal or provincial statutes (Kelly and Manfredi 2010, 48). The character of the Court's reasoning has also changed in the Charter era, in ways that can be captured empirically. A study by Daved Muttart documents a sharp rise in the Court's references to policy considerations, relative to law and fact, in its decisions during the Charter era (Muttart 2007, 42–44). Muttart's results suggest that the Court has ventured beyond legalism to more openly play a role resolving politically charged value conflicts on their own terms.

But the SCC did not always charge boldly ahead. Rather than defining the content of Charter rights unilaterally, the Court often gave deference to the considered views of the legislatures on these issues. It is not unusual even for powerful constitutional courts to give some deference to legislative judgments, allowing a degree of legislative constitutionalism. But the SCC has taken particular pains to emphasize its regard for the policy judgments of legislatures and the limited scope of its review of these.[24] Indeed, some critics of the Court have

24. See, for instance, R. v. Edwards Books and Art Ltd., [1986] 2 S.C.R. 713, and Irwin Toy Ltd. v. Quebec, [1989] 1.S.C.R. 927.

argued that it too often carries deference too far, watering down its Section 1 proportionality analysis to a weak "reasonableness" test (Weinrib and Weinrib 2001, 739–42). In not merely considering legislative judgments, but capitulating to them, the argument goes, the Court abdicates its responsibility to protect rights.[25]

It makes sense that the SCC would sometimes act with conspicuous restraint, since the Court's Charter jurisprudence has been a source of controversy since the 1980s (James 2011, 3). Charges of "judicial activism" have been hotly debated, in exchanges that display varying ratios of heat to light. Alongside the scholarly engagement over whether the Court has overstepped its proper bounds (Choudhry and Hunter 2003; Howe and Russell 2001; Kelly 2006), the Court's role has been the subject of popular attention and political debate. The Canadian reading public has been made acquainted with books featuring sky-is-falling titles such as *Against Judicial Activism: The Decline of Freedom and Democracy in Canada* (Leishman 2006) and *The Most Dangerous Branch: How the Supreme Court of Canada Has Undermined Our Law and Our Democracy* (Martin 2005).

Charges that the SCC is overreaching have a potency in Canada in part because they are connected to issues of federalism, the most explosive issues in Canadian political life. Judicial rulings that uphold rights claims redistribute decision-making power not only from other branches of government to the judiciary but from the provinces to the national government. The fact that

25. Another feature of the SCC's Section 1 jurisprudence is worth mentioning in this regard. While the final step of the *Oakes* framework contemplates a proportionality *stricto sensu* analysis—that is, a judgment as to whether a challenged measure is "worth it," comparing its benefits against the costs in terms of rights infringement—the SCC has never found against the government on this stage of analysis (Grimm 2007, 394). Although the SCC has insisted that this step is a crucial component of the analysis, see *Attorney General of Canada v. JTI-MacDonald Corp.*, [2007] 2 S.C.R. 610, it has never directly substituted its own judgment for the legislature's on whether the gain to some interests justifies the detriment to others. And although the SCC's Section 1 limitations analysis contemplates a judicial balancing of the benefits and costs of government action—the most naked intervention into value judgments—the SCC tellingly avoids invalidating legislation on this basis (Bakan 1997, 28). Arguably, the Court has avoided reaching the final stage of the analysis in some cases by characterizing the purpose of statutes in ways unfavorable to the government's case. For instance, in *Ford v. Quebec*, [1988] 2 S.C.R. 712, the SCC invalidated a Quebec law forbidding the use of languages other than French in public signs and advertisements. The court concluded that measures infringing less on the Charter right to free expression could equally well achieve the statute's purpose, which the SCC identified as assuring that the "visage linguistique"—the linguistic face—of Quebec reflects the predominance of French. Arguably, the real purpose of the statute was to force the Quebec's sizable and obdurate population of English-only speakers to finally learn French. But if the SCC were to identify this as the purpose, it would likely need to engage in proportionality *stricto sensu* analysis, because less restrictive means to this end are harder to identify.

provincial statutes found to violate Charter rights can be re-enacted under the notwithstanding clause does not obviate the concern, any more than the availability of workarounds to limits on provincial power does in federalism cases.[26] The existence of a rights charter only created a new source for provincial anxieties about the Supreme Court of Canada, which date back to its establishment (Bushnell 1992).[27] So debates in Canada about judicial review always implicate federalism, Canada's most contentious constitutional issue, as they did in the days of the Judicial Committee of the Privy Council. And the SCC was finding its footing as a constitutional court in a period when the stakes of federalism issues in Canada were becoming even higher, with Quebec again making noises about secession.[28]

Skepticism over the Charter in Quebec has run high ever since the Constitution Act, 1982 was enacted without Quebec's consent, unleashing a furious response within the province, which included its premier ordering flags flown at half-mast (Sauvageau et al. 2005, 24). And reaction in the province to some of the Court's early rights jurisprudence, particularly with respect to Quebec's language laws, was scathing. But importantly, opposition to the muscular use of judicial power was not confined to Quebec. Populists in the Western provinces have seized on "the Supreme Court . . . [as] a symbol of the entrenched power of the East," and limiting judicial power has found its way into the platforms of political parties with support bases in the West (Sauvageau et al. 2005, 25). The SCC has operated

26. The SCC's federalism jurisprudence had long since dispensed with the idea that federal and provincial competences were "watertight compartments" and permitted federal transfer payments to provinces, and what amounted to the trading of legislative powers, as workarounds to federalism restrictions (Monahan 1987, 145, 160–61). The "central law of the federalism equation" was "it is always possible to do indirectly what you cannot do directly" (Monahan 1987, 161).

27. In fact, the Court was established only in 1875, eight years after it was authorized by the BNA Act, owing to opposition from Conservative members of Parliament from Quebec. Ultimately, their concerns were mollified by special concessions to Quebec in the design of the SCC. The bill creating the court set a $2,000 Canadian amount-in-controversy threshold requirement for SCC jurisdiction over cases from Quebec—and only from Quebec. Also, the bill specified that two of the six Justices on the Court would be selected from the Quebec bar (Bushnell 1992, 14–15). When the membership of the SCC was increased from six to nine, the number of Justices from Quebec was increased to three.

28. For a discussion of the SCC's federalism jurisprudence specifically during the Charter era, see Saywell (2004, 274–307). The general tendency over the first two decades of the Charter, in Saywell's opinion, was to expand federal power at the expense of the provinces. And Saywell believes the SCC's role in applying the Charter is at least partly responsible: "there was an inevitable spillover from the necessarily innovative approach to Charter interpretation to the more traditional federalism jurisprudence" (Saywell 2004, 276).

in this challenging political environment by adopting what amounts to a mixed strategy, sometimes acting boldly and other times acting with restraint.

The idea of Charter "dialogues" between court and legislature is both symptomatic of the Court's problem and emblematic of the Court's solution to it. Peter Hogg and Allison Bushnell famously characterized the communication between the SCC and the legislatures over the course of successive rounds of rights litigation as a "Charter dialogue between courts and legislatures," and the concept has been much discussed and debated (Hogg and Bushell 1997; Hogg and Thornton 1999; Manfredi and Kelly 1999; Roach 2001). Hogg and Bushnell observed that a judicial invalidation of a statute on Charter grounds rarely ends the matter, because the legislature frequently re-enacts the measure with greater attention to Charter values. And in many instances, the Court permits the re-enacted legislation to stand, in effect deferring to the legislature's newly explicit weighing of the interests at stake. To take one prominent example: the Supreme Court struck down a federal ban on the advertisement of tobacco products in 1995,[29] but upheld a substantially similar ban twelve years later,[30] in part because the Parliament demonstrated more convincingly that it had considered the interests at stake and carefully tailored the law to be no more restrictive of speech than necessary.

Engaging in dialogue makes sense for a court in the SCC's position. In the Charter dialogue, the SCC found a mechanism that protects the Court against permanently getting too far out in front of the elected bodies in pursuit of its Charter agenda. Institutionalizing solicitude for the views of the legislatures, as the Charter dialogue does, tightens the link between the Court and the political branches in a way that can blunt concerns about judicial activism.

The early years of the SCC's Charter jurisprudence show a court simultaneously engaged in the rights-protecting business of a postwar constitutional court and sensitive to overstepping its bounds in the Canadian political order. In the following chapter, I argue that some of this same sensitivity animates the SCC's careful approach to the horizontal effect of rights.

29. RJR-MacDonald Inc. v. Canada (Att'y Gen.), [1995] 3 S.C.R. 199.

30. Canada (Att'y Gen.) v. JTI-MacDonald Corp., [2007] 2 S.C.R. 610.

7

Horizontal Effect and Caboose Constitutionalism

CHARTER RIGHTS AND PRIVATE LITIGATION: THE SCC'S APPROACH

Before long, the Supreme Court of Canada (SCC) was asked to decide whether and when Charter rights had horizontal effect. Picking its way through this unfamiliar (and potentially treacherous) terrain with great care, the Court outlined an approach that conveyed judicial restraint above all. The Court emphasized what Charter rights *didn't* apply to: the common law (insofar as it governed legal affairs of private parties), private litigation, and courts (at least initially).

It is not surprising that the SCC would ostensibly hold back from giving rights horizontal effect. Canada's Charter revolution had come late enough that ordinary law had already proscribed many of the most glaringly antiliberal practices, especially with respect to discrimination, by the time the new rights came online. Notably, the enactment of human rights statutes and the creation of commissions to enforce them in the 1960s and 1970s meant that equality in Canada would largely be given content legislatively and administratively. Plus, as noted in Chapter Six, the SCC could hear any case parties wished to appeal even without invoking constitutional rights. And in light of the misgivings some of the Court's expansive rulings of the mid-1980s had already unleashed, there was no percentage for the Court in launching a patently disruptive horizontal effect doctrine on the *Lüth* model.

But in actuality, the Court did not commit to the position that Charter rights had vertical effect exclusively. Indeed, the Court's doctrine more or less put it in the position of being able to give rights horizontal effect when it wished to, and not otherwise. This section describes the cornerstones of the SCC's horizontal effect doctrine, and the following three sections explore its impact in three

Extending Rights' Reach. Jud Mathews.

areas of law, both with respect to the Court's decision making and its relations to lower courts and the legislatures.

The Charter and the Common Law: *Dolphin Delivery*

The Court first faced the question of Charter rights' horizontal effect in *Retail, Wholesale, and Department Store Union, Local 580 v. Dolphin Delivery Ltd.* in 1986.[1] The case grew out of a labor dispute that implicated, on the one side, commercial interests protected by the common law, and on the other, expressive freedom protected by the Charter. In June 1981, an Ontario-based courier company, Purolator, locked out its employees after failing to reach an agreement with the union that represents them, the Retail, Wholesale, and Department Store Union (RWDSU). The union responded with a boycott of Purolator. More controversially, the union also announced its intention to picket Dolphin Delivery, a courier company based in Vancouver, on the grounds that Dolphin Delivery was an ally of Purolator.[2] Secondary picketing—picketing against third parties—had long been considered unlawful under the common law, which, owing to the peculiarities of Canadian federalism, governed this dispute.[3]

Dolphin Delivery sought and received an injunction against the picketing from the Superior Court, and the union appealed to the Court of Appeal for British Columbia, arguing that the common law rule against secondary picketing violated its Charter rights to free expression and free association. The appeals court panel rejected the claim, and the union appealed on the basis of its free expression claim alone.

1. RWDSU v. Dolphin Delivery Ltd. [1986] 2 S.C.R. 573.

2. Dolphin Delivery denied that it was an ally, insisting instead that it was a third party to the labor dispute. Prior to the labor dispute, Dolphin Delivery had been in a business relationship with Purolator, making deliveries for Purolator in the Vancouver area. After the lockout, Dolphin Delivery stopped making deliveries for Purolator, but began doing so for Supercourier, another Ontario-based company that was itself somehow allied with Purolator.

3. British Columbia did have a labor relations statute, which also proscribed secondary picketing, but the statute did not apply to this case. Labor relations in Canada are matters of either provincial or federal law, depending on whether the industry at issue is subject to regulation at the provincial or national level. Most industries are regulated by provinces, but some industries are designated for federal regulation, including transportation. As a courier service, Dolphin Delivery was governed by federal law. But the Canada Labor Code is silent on the issue of whether secondary pickets are lawful. And in Canada, the common law acts as a gap-filler for issues not addressed by federal statutory law. As noted above, under the common law, secondary picketing is considered tortious. [1986] 2 S.C.R. at 589.

Justice McIntyre wrote the decision for the Supreme Court. A number of features of the decision are curious, including the threshold resolution of contested factual questions and the sequencing of the analysis.

With respect to the factual questions, Justice McIntyre noted that, since the injunction was granted, no picketing had taken place, making it difficult to assess the expressive and commercial interests at stake in the picketing. However, that did not stop the Court from concluding, on the basis of the trial court's somewhat ambiguous decision, that Dolphin Delivery was just a third party to the labor dispute and not an ally of Purolator, as the union had argued. Moreover, the SCC also accepted the trial court's conclusion that "the dominant purpose [of the proposed picketing] was to injure the plaintiff rather than the dissemination of information and protection of the defendant's interest."[4] At the outset, then, the Court downplayed the relevance of Dolphin Delivery to the union's collective bargaining objectives and downgraded the expressive content of the union's activity. In other words, the Court signaled that Charter values were not flagrantly disserved in this case by the common law rule against secondary picketing.

The Court then sequenced the issues to be addressed as follows:

1. Does the injunction complained of in this case restrict the freedom of expression secured under s. 2(b) of the Canadian Charter of Rights and Freedoms?
2. Does the Charter apply to the common law?
3. Does the Charter apply in private litigation?
4. If it is found that the injunction does restrict freedom of information, is the limit imposed by the injunction a reasonable limit in accordance with s. 1 of the Charter?[5]

The first question asked whether there is even an expressive interest at stake that triggers constitutional protection, and so it is necessary to everything that follows. After an extended paean to the value of free speech, the Court concluded that Charter-protected free expression is implicated by the injunction. What happened next, though, is peculiar: the Court jumped ahead to the fourth question in the list it had just established and asked whether this ban on secondary picketing would represent a reasonable limit on free expression rights and therefore be constitutional. The Court acknowledged that "it is not necessary, in view of the disposition of this appeal that I propose, to deal with the application

4. *Id.* at 582.

5. *Id.*

of s. 1 of the Charter,"[6] but went ahead and did so anyway, because the appeals court had addressed the issue. Following a weighing of the interests at stake, the Court concluded that "a limitation on secondary picketing against a third party, that is, a non-ally, would be a reasonable [and hence, constitutional] limit in the facts of this case."[7]

The Court offered no reason for jumping the queue of questions it had established and deciding a constitutional issue that, because of its ruling on the scope of constitutional rights, ultimately is not necessary to the disposition of the case. If the ground for the decision is that the Charter does not apply in the circumstances of this litigation, as the Court went on to hold, its ruling that the limitation on secondary picketing is constitutional has the status of dicta. Whatever the reason the Court addressed this issue, it has the effect of lowering the stakes for the Court's subsequent holding that the Charter does not apply, as does the Court's devaluing of the expressive interests at stake right at the outset of its opinion. The heart of this decision is the Court's conclusion that the Charter does not apply, but the opinion is set up in such a way as to soften that blow.

The Court next addressed the question whether the Charter applies to the common law. The Court answered in the affirmative, pointing to the Section 52 supremacy clause: "The Constitution of Canada is the supreme law of Canada, and any law that is inconsistent with the provisions of the Constitution is, to the extent of the inconsistency, of no force or effect." Working from the plain text of the Charter, the Court reasoned that "any law" meant "any law," including the common law.

The next question for the Court was whether the Charter applies to private litigation, and here its answer was more complicated. In its discussion, the Court toggles back and forth between two different, but related, questions: whether the Charter applies to private litigation, and whether it applies to private parties. As German scholars could have explained,[8] the questions are different, because a Charter right could apply to a legal rule that decides the outcome of private litigation, even if private parties themselves are not subject to obligations under the Charter. The Court's conflation of the Charter's applicability to private litigation and to private parties blurs the issues at stake and renders its analysis more confusing than it otherwise might be.

Justice McIntyre began by canvassing legal scholars to the effect that the Charter is intended to regulate the relationship between the individuals and the

6. *Id.* at 588.

7. *Id.* at 592.

8. See Chapter Three.

government and to restrict the powers of government only. He then concluded with the broad statement that "I am in agreement with the view that the Charter does not apply to private litigation."[9] He then proceeded almost immediately to undercut it. Switching from the *proceedings* in which the Charter applies to the *actors* to whom it applies, the decision cited Section 32 of the Charter for the proposition that the Charter applies to the legislative, executive, and administrative branches of government. And "[i]t will apply to those branches of government whether or not their action is invoked in public or private litigation."[10]

The Charter did not, however, apply here. Although the injunction against the RWDSU is based on the common law rule against secondary picketing, the case lacks "[t]he element of governmental intervention necessary to make the Charter applicable."[11] This is so because the Court does not regard a court order as government action. Although courts are bound by the Charter, they are acting only as "neutral arbiters, not as contending parties involved in a dispute."[12] If the content of court orders were attributed to the courts, and counted as governmental action that triggered the Charter, "the scope of Charter application" would widen "to virtually all private litigation."[13] Before applying the Charter, the Court requires "[a] more direct and a more precisely-defined connection between the element of government action and the claim advanced."[14] But where "private party 'A' sues private party 'B' relying on the common law and where no act of government is relied upon to support the action, the Charter will not apply."[15]

Significantly though, if the common law flies beneath the radar of full Charter scrutiny in ordinary private litigation, that does not mean it is "irrelevant to private litigants whose disputes fall to be decided at common law." Rather, the Court makes clear that "the judiciary ought to apply and develop the principles of the common law in a manner consistent with the fundamental values enshrined in the Constitution."[16]

9. *Id.* at 597.

10. *Id.* at 598–99.

11. *Id.* at 599.

12. *Id.* at 600.

13. *Id.*

14. *Id.* at 601.

15. *Id.* at 603.

16. *Id.* at 603.

Assessing the Court's Approach

The SCC would later tweak the approach to the scope of rights it announced in *Dolphin Delivery*, but within the broad contours of the doctrine established by that case. The decision very much has the feel of a court groping its way through unfamiliar territory. The set of questions the Court announces at the outset to guide its analysis ends up being a distraction, because the applicability of the Charter turns out not to turn on whether the common law or a statute is at issue, or whether litigation is public or private. The Court first holds that the Charter applies to the common law, before later admitting it does not some of the time, and first holds that the Charter does not apply to private litigation, before conceding that it may. Understanding the rule of law to emerge from *Dolphin Delivery* requires some reconstruction of the Court's analysis.

The critical question for understanding the SCC's approach is, whose conduct must be justified in terms of the Charter? The court's answer is: the conduct of the legislative, executive, and administrative branches of government. Not the conduct of private actors, and not the conduct of courts. Courts should develop the common law to be consistent with Charter values, but their application of common law norms does not trigger Charter scrutiny.

Asking whose conduct must be justified helps to make sense of the Court's confusing answers to the questions about whether the Charter applies to the common law or to private litigation. The Charter applies to the common law when the common law provides the basis for an action by a government actor other than a court: so, for instance, when the executive acts on the basis of common law prerogative powers. The Charter would also apply against government actors bringing a common law action in their official capacity.[17] The Charter also applies to private litigation to the extent that it implicates the conduct of government actors besides courts. For instance, the Charter may apply to litigation between private parties that is governed by legal norms derived from a statute, although the Court does not explain exactly what the Charter requires of the legislature with respect to the regulation of private parties.[18] The honest answer to the question of whether the Charter applies in litigation arising under the common law or between private parties is therefore "it depends," and what it depends on is whether the conduct of a government actor other than the courts is being challenged as violative of the Charter. The categories

17. Owing to sovereign immunity, the government in Canada may be sued only with statutory authorization, so the common law does not apply to suits against the government.

18. The Court does give one example in its decision, drawn from *Blainey and Ontario Hockey Association*, which is described below.

of "common law" and "private litigation" are themselves doing no work in the analysis.

One thing that is noteworthy about the Court's approach is that a given statutory rule governing private parties would be subject to Charter scrutiny, while an identical common law rule would not be. Under *Dolphin Delivery*, the standard response is that the common law rule, unlike its statutory counterpart, does not represent a policy choice made by one of the branches of government expressly subjected to the Charter (Hogg 2015, 37-24). But this response ignores the fact that the common law itself governs in Canada as the result of a legislative choice: the Reception Acts, which adopted English common law in Canada (Slattery 1986, 910–11). It is less satisfactory still with respect to Quebec, where the equivalent to the common law is the Civil Code, which is not judge-made law at all but legislation—but still escapes Charter review (Slattery 1986, 915–16). Traditionally, of course, the common law—especially as systematized by Blackstone—was venerated as the last word in fairness and reasonableness, which defined the rights Englishmen enjoyed (Holdsworth 1938, 729–30). To the extent that the common law still retained these positive associations, giving it a pass on Charter scrutiny may have seemed less anomalous.

Moreover, *Dolphin Delivery*'s ostensible limitations on Charter scrutiny did important rhetorical work. The decision announced to the world that the Charter does not apply to private litigation and also that the Charter does not apply to courts. The case also advanced the useful idea that courts are not agents in their own right, with policies or agendas of their own, but merely "neutral arbiters."

The SCC's framing of *Dolphin Delivery* spared it the charges of judicial overreach that would have followed had the Court instead declared that the Charter *did* apply in private litigation governed by the common law. As discussed in Chapter Six, anxiety about judicial power in Canada is entangled with federalism concerns, and *Dolphin Delivery* has an unstated federalism dimension. *Dolphin Delivery* seems to wall off private litigation from Charter scrutiny. Most private litigation occurs under the auspices of provincial courts, so the decision reinforces the provinces' autonomy when it comes to regulating private interactions. Of course, the decision really only exempts from Charter review private litigation that arises under the common law, so provincial lawmakers are bound by the Charter, even when they make rules for private interactions. But language in the decision appears to promise the crown jewels of the common law—ordinary contract and tort actions—immunity against frontal challenges under the Charter.

Nor did the SCC give up much by declaring a big chunk of private litigation off limits to Charter scrutiny. *Dolphin Delivery* acknowledged legislative, executive, and administrative action as triggers for Charter scrutiny. So after *Dolphin Delivery*, as before, the Court retains the power to review policy choices made by legislatures, whether federal or provincial, including policy choices relating to relations among private parties. Likewise, the Court retains full authority to review administrative or executive decisions relating to those policies. *Dolphin Delivery* just carved out an exception to Charter scrutiny for common law rules as applied by judges. But the SCC already *had* the authority to review judges' applications of the common law, and the decision did not change that. As emphasized in Chapter Six, the Supreme Court of Canada is importantly different from the U.S. Supreme Court in that it is a court of general jurisdiction with the authority to review applications of provincial law as well as federal law. Ruling that the Charter applies to the common law in private litigation would not expand the SCC's reviewing power to encompass more cases, because the SCC is already the court of final appeal for all cases in Canada. And while applying the Charter would give the Court extra normative resources for sculpting the common law, the Court was already its steward. To put the point concretely, the SCC had the power to set aside the common law rule against secondary picketing even without the Charter (although abolishing a common law rule outright might generate controversy).

And—crucially—*Dolphin Delivery* quietly left open the possibility that the Charter *could* change the common law. As mentioned above, the SCC noted, almost in passing, that courts should apply and develop the principles of the common law in a manner consistent with constitutional values. This would come to be an important channel for what amounts to the horizontal application of constitutional rights. Indeed, Professor Hogg has concluded that the SCC's cases have rendered "the exclusion of the common law from Charter review . . . not particularly significant" (Hogg 2015, 37-29).

On its face, the SCC's approach is less disruptive than the German Federal Constitutional Court's (GFCC's) approach. It offers no basis for new Charter-based causes of action in private-party matters governed by the common law. And the Court would later explain that the Charter licensed only "incremental" changes to the common law[19]—although this precept was not infrequently honored in the breach. But the SCC's approach also resembled the GFCC's in that it conceptualized rights as values that had purchase on nonconstitutional law. And treating rights as values to be considered alongside others invites courts into a deeper engagement with the policy choices underlying the ordinary law.

19. R. v. Salituro, [1991] 3 S.C.R. 654, 670.

The SCC's approach also differs from the GFCC's in how it is justified. The GFCC presents the judicial interpolation of rights into private law as a constitutional command. The SCC frames it as an aspect of the business of judging. As the SCC later explained, the obligation to interpret the common law in a manner consistent with the Charter "is simply a manifestation of the inherent jurisdiction of the courts to modify or extend the common law in order to comply with prevailing social conditions and values."[20] The failure of a judge to apply constitutional values "correctly" is not the basis for a constitutional complaint, as it would be in Germany. The SCC framed its doctrine in a way that favored judicial discretion.

Nor was this the only respect in which the *Dolphin Delivery* approach served the interests of the judiciary more broadly. The common law's qualified exemption from Charter scrutiny amounted to a special dispensation to courts: while they received power from the Charter to review the conduct of other branches of government, they were not obliged to apply the same scrutiny to judge-made rules of private law. The courts, with the SCC at their head, were made the masters of their domain in a way that no other government actors were after the Charter. Again, the contrast with Germany is instructive: the GFCC had to make constitutional rights applicable to private law disputes in order to assert control over the other courts, owing to its limited jurisdiction. The SCC could review lower courts' rulings regardless. And it opted not to impose new duties on lower courts but to empower the judicial branch as a whole to develop the common law in light of Charter values.

That said, when the SCC did find a need to bring a lower court to heel, it did use the Charter to that effect. In *R. v. Rahey*, the Court qualified its earlier holding that judicial orders do not trigger Charter scrutiny.[21] *Rahey* concerned a challenge to a court's nearly year-long delay in ruling on a defendant's directed verdict motion in a criminal case. The SCC agreed with the defendant that the lower court's delayed ruling had violated his Section 11(b) right to trial within a reasonable time. Also, in *British Columbia Government Employees' Union v. British Columbia*,[22] the Court held that a judge's *sua sponte* order enjoining picketing of his courthouse was subject to Charter review. These two cases helped to clarify the real rule of law emerging from *Dolphin Delivery*: that a court order is not governmental action to which the Charter applies when it resolves a dispute between private parties on the basis of the common law (Hogg 2015, 37-22).

20. Hill v. Church of Scientology of Toronto, [1995] 2 S.C.R. 1130, 1169.

21. [1987] 1 S.C.R. 588.

22. [1988] 2 S.C.R. 214.

Legislation and Horizontal Effect of Charter Rights

As *Dolphin Delivery* affirmed, the Charter *does* apply to legislatures. But what exactly does the Charter require of the legislatures when it comes to statutes that govern the interactions of private parties? Are actions taken by private parties under the auspices of a statute subject to Charter scrutiny? Might the Charter in some circumstances *require* legislation to protect rights-holders against the actions of private parties?

The SCC has not given clear or consistent answers to these questions. First, while the Charter makes clear that government entities must observe the Charter, it is not clear what quantum or quality of legislative involvement in creating or directing an institution makes it a government entity. The Court has found that even some bodies established by federal legislation, such as the hospital in *Stoffman v. Vancouver General Hospital*,[23] do not count as government entities and are therefore not automatically bound by the Charter. Even private (i.e., nongovernmental) bodies must respect the Charter insofar as they implement a government policy or practice. The activities of many nongovernmental institutions are significantly shaped by law, but it is not clear from the Court's rulings just what kind of government connection is required to trigger Charter scrutiny. So, for instance, in *Lavigne v. OPSEU*,[24] the SCC suggested the Charter may not apply to the terms of a collective bargaining agreement given binding force by the British Columbia Labour Code, but in *Eldridge v. British Columbia*,[25] the Court found a hospital's failure to provide sign language interpreters to be subject to Charter scrutiny even though the Hospital Insurance Act said nothing about the issue and conferred no special powers on the hospital.[26]

From a strategic perspective, the SCC's lack of clarity on these issues amplifies its discretion to make ad hoc decisions as it sees fit. But the context in which the Charter was adopted arguably reduced the need for comprehensive answers. By the time the Charter was adopted in 1982, Canada already had in place an extensive legislative and administrative regime for protecting many of the liberal values that the Charter enshrined, particularly with respect to equality. Notably, following vigorous social mobilization, by 1977 every province and the federal government had adopted human rights statutes that were administered by commissions (Howe and Johnson 2000, 25–36). The federal

23. [1990] 3 S.C.R. 483.

24. [1991] 2 S.C.R. 211.

25. [1997] 3 S.C.R. 624.

26. In the latter case, the Court found it significant that the hospital was implementing a specific government policy or program.

government also enacted an Employment Equity Act, which promoted minority employment, in 1986, just as the SCC's rights jurisprudence was beginning to take shape (Jain et al. 2012, 2).

The SCC entertained Charter challenges against this backdrop of legislative and administrative rights promotion, and it self-consciously made space for these other institutions to operate. The Court explained as much in *McKinney v. University of Guelph*,[27] in which the Court was asked to invalidate on Charter grounds age discrimination by a university, which was regulated by the state but not itself a state institution. In declining to apply the Charter, the Court argued that "[o]pening up private activities to judicial review could impose an impossible burden on the courts." What is more, according to the Court, "government may, in many cases, establish more flexible means to deal with individual rights. Thus Human Rights Commissions have more flexible techniques for dealing with discriminatory practices without unduly constraining the exercise of other democratic rights that are extremely hard to balance."[28] Thus, the SCC recognized the legitimacy of legislative and administrative constitutionalism in Canada and defined its own (limited) role in injecting Charter values into private activity in light of it.

This does not translate into total judicial passivity, though. Below, I describe the characteristic Canadian mode of interaction between court and parliament over private law legislation as "caboose constitutionalism." Unlike the GFCC, the SCC does not hold that the Charter requires legislation to protect Charter values in an area of private law. More typically, the SCC will let legislators be the first movers who bring Charter values into play in a field through statutes. Once legislation has established a Charter beachhead, however, the Court may then become more active, eliminating gaps in the protection provided by legislation. As with the Charter dialogues, this mode of constitutional change tempers judicial initiative with deference in ways that limit the distance between court and legislature and reduce "judicial activism" backlash.

The rest of this chapter explores the SCC's horizontal effect jurisprudence and how it has shaped lawmaking processes in Canada. The next section, on the freedom of expression, illustrates how the SCC has been able to use the Charter to reshape the common law, despite its insistence in *Dolphin Delivery* that the Charter did not apply. The subsequent discussions of antidiscrimination law and family law illustrate how the Charter shapes the interactions between the courts and other institutions in the lawmaking process.

27. [1990] 3 S.C.R. 229.

28. *Id.* at 263.

FREEDOM OF EXPRESSION

Dolphin Delivery had pronounced that the Charter has an indirect effect on the development of the common law, even when it is not directly applicable to the common law in private litigation. But what, exactly, does this mean? Cases decided in the nearly three decades after *Dolphin Delivery* suggest that it means almost whatever the SCC wants it to mean at that moment. The rulings show that the Court can deploy Charter rights flexibly, to give them more or less play in common law cases. But they also suggest a secular trend toward rights having a greater impact on the common law over time. The evidence for this in particular comes from cases where the SCC has revisited earlier decisions and come to more rights-favoring results. The changes in jurisprudence are not all emanating solely from on high: litigants and lower courts are presenting the SCC with the legal arguments and conclusions to which it responds, and which in many cases it adopts. This process shows that the strategic logic of making rights claims is having an impact on private law litigation in Canada, even if the impact is not as extensive as in Germany.

The rest of this section illustrates this point with reference to a number of cases concerning the freedom of expression. It describes one case that liberalized somewhat the Court's approach to rights and the common law, and then compares two pairs of cases to show how outcomes have changed over time.

In *Dagenais v. Canadian Broadcasting Corporation* (CBC),[29] as in *Dolphin Delivery* before, the SCC was again faced with a collision between a common law rule and the Section 2 free expression right. But this time—for the first time—the Court deployed the Charter right horizontally to upgrade the protection otherwise available for expressive interests. Four members of a Catholic religious order were charged with the alleged physical and sexual abuse of boys in their care. The CBC (which counts as a private actor for purposes of the Charter) was scheduled to broadcast nationally a fictional four-hour miniseries about the sexual abuse of boys in a Catholic institution at a time when the four defendants were either on trial or awaiting trial. On the defendants' motion, the judge in the criminal case filed an injunction banning the broadcast of the miniseries anywhere in Canada during the pendency of the trials. The injunction was authorized by the common law and justified, in the trial court's view, by the miniseries' potential to influence the juries. The CBC and other media outlets that joined as appellants challenged the court's order to the Court of Appeal for Ontario. The Court of Appeal recognized the free press interests implicated by the broadcast ban, but ruled that they were outweighed by the defendants' fair trial rights.

29. [1994] 3 S.C.R. 835.

The case was appealed to the SCC. The SCC began by revisiting the Charter's applicability to the common law, and qualified the *Dolphin Delivery* position that common law rules in private litigation evade Charter scrutiny:[30]

> Challenges to publication bans may be framed in several different ways, depending on the nature of the objection to the ban. If legislation *requires* a judge to order a publication ban, then any objection to that ban should be framed as a Charter challenge to the legislation itself. Similarly, if a common law rule *requires* a judge to order a publication ban or authorizes a judge to order a publication ban that infringes Charter rights in a manner not reasonable and demonstrably justified in a free and democratic society, then any objection to that ban should be framed as a Charter challenge to the common law rule.
>
> In the case at bar, we are dealing with a common law rule which provides judges with the *discretion* to order a publication ban in certain circumstances. Discretion cannot be open-ended. It cannot be exercised arbitrarily. . . . I would extend this reasoning, and hold that a common law rule conferring discretion cannot confer the power to infringe the Charter. Discretion must be exercised within the boundaries set by the principles of the Charter; exceeding these boundaries results in a reversible error of law. In this case, then, we are dealing with an error of law challenge to a publication ban imposed under a common law discretionary rule.[31]

This passage does two things. First, it asserts, pace *Dolphin Delivery*, that mandatory common law rules—those that require a given result—can be subject to *direct* Charter challenge. More relevant to the instant case, however, was the Court's statement about discretionary common law rules. The scope of discretion available to a court is limited by the Charter. And the failure to observe those limits constitutes reversible legal error. Even though, with respect to discretionary common law rules, the Court did not disturb *Dolphin Delivery*'s holding that direct Charter challenge is unavailable, the Court's framing here suggests more serious Charter scrutiny than *Dolphin Delivery* did. Developing common law principles in a manner consistent with constitutional values is not left to judicial discretion: it is an enforceable legal obligation.

Here, the Court went on to determine that the common law rule permitting publication bans must give ground to the freedom of expression right

30. Although the publication ban was issued incident to a criminal trial, the litigation over it was between private parties: the criminal defendants on one side versus the media outlets on the other.

31. [1994] 3 S.C.R. at 874–75.

recognized in the Charter. This is so, the SCC finds, even though the publication ban itself promotes a constitutional right: the right to a fair trial. Ultimately, the court rules that publication bans are permissible only if proportional: that is, only when necessary to prevent a risk of unfairness and when the benefits from the publication ban (in terms of ensuring fair trials) outweigh their harms (in terms of curtailing free speech).[32] Following a detailed analysis, the Court concluded that a publication ban was not proportional in this case, and therefore was not permissible.

Ostensibly, the Court in *Dagenais* was not directly applying the Charter to the common law rule permitting publication bans but only "develop[ing] the principles of the common law in a manner consistent with the fundamental values of the Constitution." Yet the Court engaged in a full-dress proportionality analysis of the publication ban's effect on the freedom of expression, much as it would in an ordinary Charter case. The Court's analysis resembled its handling of a frontal Charter challenge even with respect to burden of proof issues. According to the SCC, "[t]he party seeking to justify the limitation of a right (in the case of a publication ban, the party seeking to limit freedom of expression) bears the burden of justifying the limitation."[33] This is striking, because normally the burden would rest with the party arguing for a change in a common law rule.[34] *Dagenais* is Charter review by another name, where the other name—judicial development of the common law—is less politically charged than Charter review.

Why did the SCC bring Charter values to bear so forcefully in *Dagenais*? It's impossible to give a definitive answer, but one plausible explanation turns on the federalism dimension that lurks in the background of the case. As the Court notes, the broadcast ban is national in scope: it prohibits the program from airing throughout the whole of Canada and thus impacts the protected interests all Canadians have in access to this information. And indeed, the breadth of the ban is a key reason that the Court deemed it disproportionate: "the initial ban in the case at bar was far too broad" in that "[i]t prohibited broadcast throughout Canada and even banned reporting on the ban itself."[35] The Supreme Court brings to the case a national perspective that the provincial court lacks, and this may matter in cases where the distribution of the costs and benefits of a

32. *Id.* at 878.

33. *Id.* at 890.

34. Issues of burden may not matter much in high-profile litigation such as this case, where both parties are represented by highly skilled advocates. In run-of-the-mill cases, however, they have greater potential to shift outcomes.

35. *Id.* at 881.

measure vary geographically. It is not surprising that a provincial court might give short shrift to the extraprovincial costs of a measure, when its benefits (here, a fair trial) inure to local interests. This is a situation where a court with a national constituency has a role in correcting provincial myopia, by bringing judicial practice into conformity with the values Canada committed to in the Charter.

A comparison between *Dolphin Delivery* and a 2002 case with similar facts, *RWDSU, Local 558 v. Pepsi-Cola Canada Beverages (West) Ltd.*,[36] also suggests that Charter values have done more to reshape the common law over time. Like *Dolphin Delivery, Pepsi-Cola* concerned a collision between a court order banning secondary picketing on the basis of the common law and the free speech interests of the would-be picketers. The injunction at issue in the latter case was broader: it banned secondary picketing, without regard to whether the targets were allies of a party to the labor dispute. The union challenged the injunction on Charter Section 1 grounds. The Saskatchewan Court of Appeal struck down most of the injunction, citing the free expression interests at stake and observing that the common law on the legality of picketing was in a state of some flux.

The SCC held that the common law rule against secondary picketing had to be modified to bring it into alignment with Charter values. Now emphasizing the expressive content of picketing, the SCC developed a new common law rule. To wit, picketing is permissible unless it can be shown to be wrongful or unjustified: meaning, it involves a tort (such as trespass) or a crime (such as destruction of property). Because wrongful picketing is actionable on the basis of whatever makes it wrongful, the ruling means in effect that picketing as such is permissible. In reaching this result, the SCC relied both on the expressive content of picketing and the ability of its wrongful action model to balance the competing interests appropriately. Again, the facts in *Dolphin Delivery* and *Pepsi-Cola* are different, but so is the overall tenor of the decisions. The decision in *Pepsi-Cola*, but not in *Dolphin Delivery*, showcases a serious engagement with the expressive implications of a ban on picketing. The difference between the results in the two cases shows just how much discretion there is in the mandate to courts to develop the common law to be consistent with Charter values.

A second pair of cases, *Hill v. Church of Scientology of Toronto*[37] and *Grant v. Torstar*,[38] also shows the evolution of the SCC's approach to rights, here in the context of libel law. *Hill*, decided in 1995, concerns a libel action

36. [2002] 1 S.C.R. 156.

37. [1995] 2 S.C.R. 1130.

38. [2009] 3 S.C.R. 640.

stemming out of a legal dispute involving the Church of Scientology. The Church of Scientology was under criminal investigation in Toronto, and some of Scientology's documents were inadvertently shared with another government agency, despite a judicial order sealing them. At a press conference held on the steps of the bar association in Toronto, Morris Manning, an attorney for Scientology, announced criminal contempt charges against Casey Hill, an attorney in the prosecutor's office, and accused Hill of misleading a judge and violating the order sealing the documents. The contempt hearing showed these charges to be baseless, and Hill responded with a libel action against Manning and Scientology. Following trial, the jury returned a verdict in Hill's favor, finding Manning and Scientology jointly liable for $300,000 Canadian in damages, and Scientology solely liable for aggravated damages of $500,000 and punitive damages of $800,000. At the time, the award was the largest award in a damages suit in Canada. Manning and Scientology appealed to the Court of Appeal for Ontario on free expression grounds and appealed again to the SCC after the appellate court ruled against them.

In an opinion written by Justice Cory, the SCC took great pains to emphasize the limited relevance of Charter rights to private-party disputes governed by the common law. The common law cannot violate a Charter right; at most, it can be inconsistent with Charter values. "It is very important to draw this distinction between Charter rights and Charter values," according to the Court. This is so because "care must be taken not to expand the application of the Charter beyond that established by s. 32(1)," which limits the Charter's applicability to acts of Canada's legislatures and governments.

How should a court ensure the common law's conformity with Charter values? Here the Court emphasizes the continuity of this practice with courts' traditional stewardship of the common law and its dissimilarity to full-dress Charter review. "The courts are the custodians of the common law, and it is their duty to see that the common law reflects the emerging needs and values of our society."[39] The Charter amounts to a "restatement" of Canada's core political and legal values. Hence, "[i]t follows that it is appropriate for the courts to make such incremental revisions to the common law as may be necessary to have it comply with the values enunciated in the Charter." But "the judiciary should confine itself to those incremental changes" to the common law;[40] "[f]ar-reaching changes to the common law must be left to the legislature."

Accordingly, "a traditional s. 1 framework for justification is not appropriate." Rather than a formal proportionality analysis, "the balancing must be more

39. 2 S.C.R. at 1169 (quoting R. v. Salituro, [1991] 3 S.C.R. 654, 678).

40. *Id.* at 1166 (quoting *Salituro*, [1991] 3 S.C.R. at 670).

flexible": "Charter values, framed in general terms, should be weighed against the principles which underlie the common law." Moreover, the party challenging the common law rule should have the burden of showing "not only that the common law is inconsistent with Charter values but also that its provisions cannot be justified."

Having framed the analysis in these terms, the Court went on to uphold the libel awards. Freed from the strictures of proportionality analysis, which focuses the court's attention on the challenged measure, much of the SCC's analysis focused on problems with the "actual malice" libel standard, as defined in the U.S. Supreme Court's *New York Times v. Sullivan* decision and recommended by the defendants. Concluding that the actual malice standard permitted too much reputational damage to go unpunished, the Court affirmed the damages award.

In 2009, however, the Court refined its approach to give more room for the play of Charter values in defamation cases. In *Grant v. Torstar*, a businessman (Grant) sued a newspaper and its reporter for libel over an article relaying allegations that he was using political influence to secure approval for a golf course development. Grant won at trial, but lost on appeal. The SCC agreed with the appeals court that the common law of libel should be altered to recognize a defense of responsible communication in the public interest. The Court presented the issue raised by the case as a straightforward conflict between important principles—free expression and reputation—which required "a balanced approach to libel law [that] properly reflects the interests of both the plaintiff and the defendant." The SCC found a marked imbalance in the existing common law: "the current level of protection [afforded to reputation]—in effect a regime of strict liability—is not justifiable." Carefully weighing different contextual factors, the Court corrected the balance by devising a defense for responsible communications made in the public interest. The Court distinguished *Church of Scientology*, which after all presented a very different set of facts. But even so, the Charter right to free expression is the centerpiece of the Court's analysis here, while in *Church of Scientology* it is given far less attention.

Taken together, these cases illustrate what could be called the strategic ambiguity of the SCC's approach to the scope of rights, and how the Court and litigants have made use of it. In *Dolphin Delivery*, the court disclaimed any intention to apply the Charter to common law rules governing private litigation, but declared that courts should develop the common law in accordance with Charter values. This mandate is sufficiently elastic to accommodate both a light touch review of common law rules, as in *Dolphin Delivery* itself and *Hill*, and something tantamount to full Charter scrutiny, as in *Dagenais, Pepsi-Cola*, and *Grant*. At the level of decision making on the Court, these different approaches no doubt reflected different Justices' different views about what the Court's role should be in such cases. For the Court as an institution, however, the ambiguity of the *Dolphin Delivery* formulation is a strategic asset. In a country where judicial power is suspect, not least because it is a species of federal power, the SCC managed to downplay the Charter's capacity to remake the common law, even as it retains the ability to deploy Charter values to change common law rules when it chooses. And over time, it has opted to do so with greater frequency, as litigants have pressed claims rooted in Charter values, and lower courts have endorsed them.

EQUALITY

The Charter was a late addition to Canadian efforts to combat discrimination, which had begun decades before. Section 15, the Charter's equality provision, became legally effective only in 1985, three years after the Charter's enactment.[41] But already by the late 1970s, every province and the national government had enacted antidiscrimination statutes and established commissions to enforce them. The SCC has welcomed legislative and administrative involvement in developing equality norms in the private law context, even conferring a quasi-constitutional stature on antidiscrimination laws. But at the same time, the Court has not abandoned the field to lawmakers and administrators. Instead, the SCC has used the Charter to intervene selectively, usually to eliminate gaps in coverage provided by legislation. The Court's equality jurisprudence has accepted and extended the efforts of other actors to reduce discrimination in the private sphere.

As in the United States, the experience of the Second World War highlighted the wrongness of invidious discrimination and catalyzed social movement agitation to end it (Walker 2013, 40–44).[42] Unlike in the United States, legislative responses in Canada were readily forthcoming: within a decade of the war's end, most provinces had enacted antidiscrimination legislation (Howe and Johnson 2000, 8).[43] Most of this first-generation legislation was basic: typically, the statutes banned only racial and religious discrimination, and only with respect to housing and employment (Howe and Johnson 2000, 14). But by the early 1960s,

41. The three-year delay was intended to give legislatures time to review their statutes for compliance with Section 15 (Boyd 2000, 313).

42. Most Americans do not realize the extent of discrimination in Canadian history. Discrimination on the basis of race, gender, and language in Canada was widespread until the second half of the twentieth century. See generally Miron (2009).

43. The alacrity of the legislative response may have been, in part, a function of the absence of veto players in the unicameral provincial assemblies. National legislation followed later (in 1977) and applied only to persons in the government or national industries.

provinces had begun enacting more far-reaching human rights codes whose enforcement was entrusted to commissions. To reduce discrimination, commissions had at their disposal a wide set of flexible tools. On receiving a credible complaint, commissions typically made informal efforts to conciliate with the offending party before convening a formal tribunal.[44]

Even before the Charter, provincial legislation enhanced the role of commissions in promoting equality in Canadian society. By the late 1970s, most commissions had been given the authority to initiate complaints themselves and to investigate systemic discrimination, not just isolated instances (Howe and Johnson 2000, 15, 22). Commissions also inaugurated public education programs and advised governments on future legislative amendments. Legislative amendments expanded the kinds of discrimination covered by the codes. Dedicated human rights tribunals heard cases brought by commissions and interpreted the human rights statutes, often in ways that expanded their scope (Howe and Johnson 2000, 22). All in all, Canada had a deeply entrenched set of institutions defining the horizontal effect of *statutory* equality norms—an antidiscrimination establishment.

After the advent of the Charter, the SCC more or less co-opted Canada's antidiscrimination establishment and reframed it as a part of the constitutional project writ large. Lower courts in Canada had divided over the question of whether the human rights statutes enjoyed any kind of priority over other statutes. In its first term, the SCC ruled that British Columbia's Human Rights Code amounted to "fundamental law," and hence had priority when in conflict with (nonfundamental) legislation.[45] The Court made the point in stronger terms still three years later, in *Ontario Human Rights Commission v. Simpsons-Sears*.[46] Now, the Court held that a human rights code is "of a special nature, not quite constitutional but certainly more than the ordinary."[47] As a result, the Court concluded that it would interpret the code much as it would a constitutional commitment: liberally, in order to achieve its purposes.

Relatedly, the Court also interpreted the powers of human rights commissions and tribunals expansively. For instance, the Court held that the federal human rights tribunal had the authority to impose a wide-reaching affirmative action program to remedy systemic discrimination in the national railway.[48]

44. Walter Tarnopolsky referred to this as the "iron hand in the velvet glove" model (1968).

45. Ins. Corp. of B.C. v. Heerspink, [1982] 2 S.C.R. 145, 158.

46. [1985] 2 S.C.R. 536.

47. *Id.* at 547.

48. Action Travail des Femmes v. Canadian Nat'l Ry. Co., [1987] 1 S.C.R. 1114.

Rulings such as this typically triggered a confirmatory legislative response, as the legislature amended the governing statute to explicitly grant to commissions or tribunals the powers that the SCC had already ruled they had (Manfredi 2001, 113–14).

The Court did not only impart a constitutional tincture to human rights statutes: it also permitted the administrators of those statutory regimes to share in the task of interpreting Charter rights. In a series of cases beginning in the mid-1980s, the SCC held that administrative tribunals (such as the human rights tribunals) counted as "courts of competent jurisdiction" under Section 24(1) of the Charter and could therefore entertain Charter claims.[49] What is more, in a series of cases from the early 1990s, the SCC held that tribunals were especially well placed to evaluate some constitutional questions that come before them—better in some instances than courts.[50] Most recently, in 2010 the Court reaffirmed that administrative tribunals generally have the power to apply the Charter and devise appropriate remedies, noting that this administrative constitutionalism makes the Charter more accessible.[51] And Canada's antidiscrimination establishment has accepted the Court's invitation to invoke the Charter, notwithstanding the fact that it generally handled private-party discrimination. As described by a former director of the Ontario Human Rights Commission, with the Court's encouragement, "[h]uman rights commissions began to rely on Charter principles and jurisprudence in their legal and policy work; human rights tribunals began citing Charter jurisprudence in their decisions" (Eliadis 2014, 80).

If the SCC has drawn the statutory antidiscrimination regime into the constitutional orbit, it has also sometimes used the Charter to extend equality norms still further, in ways that shape private parties' legal relationships. More specifically, the SCC has used Charter review to close gaps in the protection that statutes offer private parties against discrimination from private sources. It is in this area where the Court has been most willing to extend constitutional protections into private-party relationships, and this is also the forum in which the Court has shown creativity and innovation in its use of remedial powers, in extending statutes it determines to be underinclusive (Hogg 2015, 37-32–37-33). If, for instance, a statute includes a carveout excluding a particular group

49. R. v. Mills, [1986] 1 S.C.R. 863.

50. Douglas/Kwantlen Faculty Assn. v. Douglas Coll., [1990] 3 S.C.R. 570; Cuddy Chicks Ltd. v. Ontario (Labour Relations Bd.), [1991] 2 S.C.R. 5; Tétreault-Gadoury v. Canada (Emp't and Immigration Comm'n), [1991] 2 S.C.R. 22.

51. R. v. Conway, [2010] 1 S.C.R. 765, 803.

from protection, the Court can sever the offending clause. The Court has also recognized a remedial power to "read in" new language to a statute so as to cure a constitutional defect (Roach 2011, 322–23).[52] In not just subtracting from the language of statutes, but adding to them, the SCC comes close to acting as a positive legislator. The Court has acknowledged that this is a power to be wielded with care.

Still, the Court has had some of its biggest impact on how the Charter mediates private relationships when it has used this power. And the Court has used this power to greatest effect with respect to matters of sexual orientation.[53] It is not surprising to find the Court active here: this is an area where attitudes have shifted rapidly in the time since the Charter's enactment, leaving lags in the protection provided gays and lesbians under ordinary law. Gay and lesbian advocacy groups have persuasively articulated their case for change in both political and judicial fora (Smith 2008). And the Court has used the Charter, selectively, to spur legislative initiatives for change.

The most notable example of this is *Vriend v. Alberta*.[54] Alberta's Individual Rights Protection Act (IRPA) prohibited private discrimination on a number of bases, but not sexual orientation. Delwin Vriend was terminated by his employer, King's College, in 1991 because he was gay. Vriend attempted to file a discrimination complaint against King's College with the Alberta Human Rights Commission, but he was advised that a complaint would fail, because the IRPA did not protect against discrimination on the basis of sexual orientation. Instead, Vriend brought a suit against Alberta to challenge the IRPA as a violation of Section 15 of the Charter, which guarantees equality and equal protection. Vriend prevailed in Alberta, and the case was appealed to the Supreme Court.[55]

In an opinion written by Justice Cory, the SCC ruled that the statute's exclusion of sexual orientation from protection against discrimination violated the Charter. The Court rejected arguments that the Charter did not apply, either because the exclusion amounted to legislative inaction (the failure to provide protection) or because the effect would be to apply the Charter to private activity. To the contrary, the Court announced: what was subject to Charter scrutiny was the legislative choice to exclude sexual orientation from the statute.

52. See Schachter v. Canada, [1992] 2 S.C.R. 679.

53. More cases concerning sexual orientation are explored in the following section.

54. [1998] 1 S.C.R. 493.

55. Relying on its relaxed standing doctrines, the SCC permitted the case to go forward instead of requiring the challenge to the statute to arise as it normally would, in the context of a lawsuit between two private parties over discriminatory conduct. *Id.* at 528.

The decision interprets Section 15 to forbid the parliament from excluding people from protection against discrimination based on sexual orientation. The Court's remedy was to read sexual orientation into Alberta's statute as a prohibited basis for discrimination.

Significantly, the SCC in *Vriend* did not hold that there is a freestanding Charter right against discrimination by private parties on the basis of sexual orientation. To the contrary: the Court maintained the position that it had long held, that the Charter does not apply to private conduct. The triggering event for Charter scrutiny is the antidiscrimination legislation, which applies to many forms of discrimination, but not discrimination on the basis of sexual orientation. The irony is, in the absence of Alberta's antidiscrimination statute, discrimination on the basis of sexual orientation would be permissible. This discrimination ends up being illegal only because the legislature has taken affirmative steps to outlaw different forms of discrimination.

At the same time, the SCC's course of action is consistent with its careful approach to applying the Charter to govern private-party relationships. Typically, when it comes to regulating private-party relationships, the SCC has not reached for a constitutional norm when it could reach the same result through ordinary law. By predicating Charter review on the enactment of an antidiscrimination statute, the SCC again let the legislature take the lead. This is caboose constitutionalism: only once the legislature has introduced an antidiscrimination norm into private employment decisions does the SCC activate constitutional scrutiny, to ensure conformity with Charter values in this domain. The approach has the effect of enlisting lawmakers as co-venturers in the project of giving meaning to Canada's constitutional commitments, by keying Charter review to legislative acts that have the effect of extending (however incompletely) Charter values to domains of private-party interaction. By reading in to statutes protections that the lawmakers have left out, the SCC builds on the extension of the Charter begun legislatively.

Importantly, it is not only the SCC that has used the Charter to fill gaps in antidiscrimination statutes but lower courts as well. A notable early example is *Blainey and Ontario Hockey Association*,[56] which the SCC cited favorably in *Dolphin Delivery*. Ontario's Human Rights Code proscribed discrimination on the basis of gender, but it included a carveout for sports leagues: they were permitted to admit men or women exclusively. Justine Blainey, a talented twelve-year-old hockey player, was excluded from a team in the Ontario Hockey Association because she was a girl. Blainey brought a complaint to Ontario's Human Rights Commission, which advised her that the league's conduct was

56. [1986], 26 D.L.R. (4th) 728, 54 O.R. (2d) 513.

permitted under the Code. Blainey sued the hockey association, arguing that the Code provision on which they relied to exclude her violated the Charter's Section 15 equality right. Blainey lost in the court of first instance, but the Ontario Court of Appeal agreed with her that the Code's carveout provision violated the Charter. The Supreme Court declined to hear the league's appeal.[57]

There are other examples of lower courts drawing on Charter equality values to inform their adjudication of private disputes. Four decades after the Supreme Court of Canada hid behind a technicality to avoid deciding whether racially restrictive covenants violated public policy,[58] for instance, the Ontario Court of Appeals held that they do, in a decision that relied heavily on Charter values and overturned a pre-Charter precedent.[59] The SCC's doctrines prevent courts, for instance, from devising new tort remedies for violations of constitutional values. But they do not block lower courts from using the Charter for the "filling in of gaps and indeterminacies in doctrine that is as yet unsettled" or "giv[ing] content to amorphous ideas such as just cause, illegal means, and public policy" (Weinrib and Weinrib 2001, 62).

FAMILY LAW

In the words of one scholar in the field, family law in Canada "serves as a fascinating microcosm of the effect that this constitutional change has had and is having on our law and social fabric" (Young 2001, 752). Within family law, the Supreme Court and lower courts have used the Charter incrementally to promote gender equality and the recognition of same-sex relationships. As with antidiscrimination law, Court and Parliament perform a pas de deux whereby a statutory baseline provides the basis for the Court's recognition of a Charter claim—i.e., if the legislature is going to provide benefit *x*, it cannot maintain exclusion *y*—and the legislature amends the statute, or passes another one, to correct the Charter problem. And this dynamic embeds Charter values more deeply into the legal regulation of families.

The most prominent part of this has been judicial and legislative recognition of same-sex relationships: first claims to benefits on equal terms as opposite-sex couples, then civil unions, and then marriage.[60] Marriage and these other relationships have both vertical and horizontal rights dimensions—in other words, the status may afford the couple certain rights against the state and also may

57. Incidentally, Justine Blainey went on to play college and professional hockey in Canada.

58. Noble and Wolfe v. Alley [1951] 1 D.L.R. 321 (SCC); see Ross et al. (2014, 609–10).

59. Can. Trust v. Ont. Human Rights Comm'n, [1990] 69 D.L.R. 4th 321 (Ont. C.A.).

60. For a detailed analysis of the politics of gay and lesbian rights in Canada, see Smith (2008).

afford each individual certain rights against the other, as well as other nonstate actors. In the United States, the vertical dimension has dominated the legal debate over same-sex marriage: the constitutional claim is characteristically framed in terms of the couple's claim to recognition by the state and to certain benefits from the state as a function of marital status.[61] In Canada, by contrast, the horizontal dimension initially played a bigger role in the legal framing. This is because the claims of same-sex couples first started gaining traction within a line of cases over rights not to government recognition but to benefits provided by third parties, or to spousal support on the same terms as married opposite-sex couples.[62] Unmarried opposite-sex couples blazed the trail for these kinds of claims, and same-sex couples followed.

But same-sex relationships are not the only topic that has drawn courts to apply Charter values to family law. There were respects in which the pre-Charter law apportioned rights unevenly between husbands and wives. Provincial legislatures used the three-year lag before Section 15 took effect to correct at least the most glaring of these inequalities (Boyd 2000, 313–14). With the support of women's legal advocacy groups, notably the Women's Legal Education and Action Fund (LEAF), women brought suits identifying and challenging remaining inequalities (Razack 2002). Even before *Dolphin Delivery*, lower courts in Canada responded to arguments to use the Charter to put husbands and wives in legally equal position, including vis-à-vis private parties. For instance, the common law provided an action for husbands to recover in tort for loss of consortium, but not an equivalent action for women. Trial courts across Canada eliminated the difference in treatment on Charter grounds, either by leveling up (creating an equivalent claim for the wife) or leveling down (rejecting the loss of consortium tort altogether) (Weinrib and Weinrib 2001, 62).

The Supreme Court has made similar, if limited, moves in the context of spousal support following divorce. The pre-Charter SCC took a very hard line to equality claims in the context of marital settlements. *Murdoch v. Murdoch*,[63] from 1975, illustrates the Court's pre-Charter baseline. When the Murdochs' marriage failed after twenty-five years, Mrs. Murdoch sought a share of the 480-acre ranch property she had shared with her husband. But because the ranch was titled in the husband's name, Mrs. Murdoch was entitled to nothing. The SCC rejected Mrs. Murdoch's claim that she acquired an interest in the

61. Obergefell v. Hodges, 576 U.S. ___ (2015); United States v. Windsor, 570 U.S. ___ (2013).

62. Quebec (Att'y Gen.) v. A, [2013] 1 S.C.R. 61; M. v. H., [1999] 2 S.C.R. 3; Miron v. Trudel, [1995] 2 S.C.R. 418.

63. [1975] 1 S.C.R. 423.

property through her work in operating the ranch, affirming the trial court's conclusion that she merely contributed "the work done by any ranch wife."[64]

The SCC sharply rejected that approach in its 1992 *Moge v. Moge* decision, which involved an ex-wife's effort to get the termination of a marital support order reversed.[65] Mrs. Moge, in her sixties at the time of the litigation, had a limited education, no assets, and great difficulty finding work. In its factum (appellate brief), LEAF argued that the spousal support provisions in the Divorce Act must be interpreted in light of the Charter guarantee of sex equality, and that consequently, a court must consider the social circumstances and material disadvantages a woman faces in deciding what award is appropriate (Women's Legal Education and Action Fund 1992). In considering whether Mrs. Moge was entitled to continued support under the relevant statutes, the Court largely followed LEAF's position, giving great weight to considerations of substantive equality and the real-world consequences of divorce for women in Mrs. Moge's position. Ultimately, the SCC concluded that Mrs. Moge was entitled to the maintenance of her support. Although this case did not involve a direct Charter challenge, the author of the *Moge* majority opinion, Justice L'Heureux-Dubé, subsequently explained that the Charter value of equality was driving changes in family law:

> [E]quality [is] . . . the ultimate objective to ensure that the interpretation and application of the law in the sphere of family matters mirror our ideal of justice. In Canada, this ideal is unequivocally enshrined in section 15 of the Canadian Charter of Rights and Freedoms, which constitutionalizes the right of every person to be treated without discrimination. Although family law has not traditionally been regarded as dealing with equality rights, I think that the notion of equality underlies the modern trend in family law. . . . The relationship between equality and family law has matured somewhat in Canada in the ten years since section 15 came into force (L'Heureux-Dubé 1997, 105–06).

Justice L'Heureux-Dubé's comments illustrate one way in which the Charter escapes the cage of state action and finds its way into the interpretation of Canadian law more generally. Doctrinally, Charter values influence judicial interpretation of the common law, but as the cases above suggest, the SCC shows solicitude for these values in cases governed by statutes as well. In cases such as *Moge*, the SCC seems to be striving for coherence with respect to equality

64. *Id.* at 436.

65. [1992] 3 S.C.R. 813.

values, a coherence that spans the divisions of private law and public law, and of statutes and common law. And the Court does so without the fanfare and controversy that would attend a full-dress Charter rights analysis. While the SCC has not unleashed the wholesale constitutionalization of private law in Canada, its approach still permits the Charter to influence the legal regulation of private-party relationships, whether governed by common law or statute.

But what has probably been most impactful is the Court's reconstruction of statutes, to extend legislative protections to groups nominally not covered by them, often spurring further legislative change. For instance, in *Miron v. Trudel*, the SCC entertained a Charter challenge to an insurance company's denial of benefits to an unmarried (opposite-sex) partner.[66] The terms of the automobile insurance policy were standard terms, dictated by the federal Insurance Act, which specified that benefits were available to the "spouse" of an insured. The Court determined that the exclusion of common law spouses from coverage was discriminatory within the meaning of Section 15 and not rationally connected to any governmental objective. After litigation had already begun, Parliament defined "spouse" more inclusively to include opposite-sex couples who have cohabited for three years or lived in a permanent relationship with a child. The SCC concluded that the more inclusive definition of "spouse" should be read into the statute to save it. The net effect, of course, was horizontal effect: a Charter rights claim was generating new duties for private parties (the obligation of insurers to provide benefits on equal terms to unmarried partners).

Miron v. Trudel leveled up the protection that unmarried opposite-sex couples receive relative to married opposite-sex couples in the insurance context. *M. v. H.*, from 1999, leveled up the protection that unmarried *same-sex* couples receive relative to unmarried opposite-sex couples in a different—and more consequential—context: alimony.[67] The parties were a same-sex couple whose relationship ended after a decade together. M. sought financial support from H. under Ontario's Family Law Act (FLA), which provided that "[e]very spouse has an obligation to provide support for himself or herself and for the other spouse, in accordance with need, to the extent that he or she is capable of doing so."[68] Section 29 of the FLA defined "spouse" to include cohabiting opposite-sex couples, but not same-sex couples. The court of first instance approved M.'s application for spousal support. The judge found the exclusion of same-sex partners to violate Section 15 and remedied the constitutional defect by reading

66. [1995] 2 S.C.R. 418.

67. [1999] 2 S.C.R. 3.

68. Family Law Act, R.S.O. 1990, c.F.3. s. 30.

out the words "a man and woman" and replacing them with "two persons." H. appealed, and the Ontario Court of Appeal affirmed the lower court.

The Supreme Court affirmed. The Court was careful to note that "this appeal has nothing to do with marriage *per se*": the Family Law Act conferred a number of rights on married persons that were denied to same-sex and opposite-sex partners alike, and these were not the subject of the challenge.[69] The legislature had extended some benefits, including the right to spousal support, beyond married persons, to long-term couples—but only opposite-sex couples. The exclusion of same-sex couples from these benefits was discriminatory for Section 15 purposes, and not justified by any policy considerations. The Court concluded that, owing to the interrelation of different provisions of the FLA, there was no simple way to remedy the constitutional problem by reading in gender-neutral language. Instead, the Court severed Section 29 but suspended the remedy for six months, for the reason that "the legislature ought to be given some latitude in order to address these issues in a more comprehensive fashion."[70]

M. v. H. was indeed followed by vigorous legislative engagement with the legal treatment of same-sex relationships. A number of provinces amended their statutes in the wake of *M. v. H.* to eliminate differential treatment of same-sex couples (Payne 2013, 39–40). Although the Supreme Court had not addressed the restriction of marriage to opposite-sex partners, successive courts of appeal began declaring a Charter right to marriage equality starting in 2002 (Hennigar 2010, 210–13). Ultimately, in 2005, the federal Parliament enacted the Civil Marriage Act, which opened the institution of marriage to same-sex couples on the same terms as opposite-sex couples.

The legal recognition of same-sex marriage was a watershed moment in the law of Canada. It is relevant to our story only in part, since the legislation concerned the state's recognition of same-sex unions more than the horizontal effect of equality rights. Indeed, the Civil Marriage Act expressly limited the horizontal effect of the marriage right, committing not to impose "any obligation or sanction" on any individual or group for exercising the freedoms of conscience, religion, or expression in opposition to same-sex marriage.[71] Even so, it is worth noting how here, as elsewhere, judicial activity induced legislative participation in the process of Charter construction. Given the courts' developing equality jurisprudence, it made sense for Canada's Liberal government, which had initially sought reversal of the lower court rulings, to craft legislation itself rather than be told to do so by the SCC (Hennigar 2010). Parliament,

69. [1999] 2 S.C.R. at 48.

70. *Id.* at 87.

71. Civil Marriage Act, S.C. 2005, c. 33, s. 3.1.

in turn, sought the Court's imprimatur for its work, asking and receiving via Charter reference confirmation from the SCC that the Civil Marriage Act was constitutional.[72]

Even in the wake of this profound legislative change, judicial decisions have further extended the equality norm in the family law context. In 2007, the Ontario Court of Appeal revised the province's family law code to remove the restriction that a child could have only two legal parents, when a female couple and the biological father of their child all sought recognition as parents. The court used its parens patriae authority (though arguably channeling Charter values) to fill what it characterized as a gap in the law.[73] More recently, a bare majority of the SCC held that Quebec's exclusion of unmarried cohabitants from its property division regime for divorcing married couples infringed Section 15.[74] Ultimately, only one Justice voted that the statute was unconstitutional: most of the Justices who found an infringement concluded it to be justified, because it enhanced couples' freedom of choice, permitting them to opt in to or out of some of the rights and responsibilities associated with marriage.

It is worth emphasizing that the courts do not always accept litigants' invitation to bring Charter values to bear on family law disputes. In particular, in matters of custody and childrearing decisions, courts in Canada are instructed by statute to make decisions based on the best interests of the child. Parents have argued in different circumstances that this test needs to yield, at least in some instances, to the Charter rights of parents. But to no avail: this argument has made no headway in the courts (Boyd 2000, 307; Young 2001, 770). Not surprisingly, Charter arguments appear to have more success when they are spearheaded by professional legal advocacy groups and speak to a widely shared sense that law is out of step with contemporary values.

ASSESSMENT

> "Why does a Canadian cross the road?"
> "To get to the middle."

Canada's reputation as a land of moderation, as reflected in the old joke, belies a more complicated reality, of course.[75] With respect to the horizontal effect of rights, however, Canada does occupy a middle ground

72. Reference re Same-Sex Marriage [2004] 3 S.C.R. 698.

73. A.A. v. B.B. (2007), 278 D.L.R. 4th 519.

74. Quebec (Att'y Gen.) v. A., [2013] 1 S.C.R. 61.

75. An anthology titled *What Is a Canadian?: Forty-Three Thought-Provoking Responses* (Studin 2006) offers a welter of contemporary perspectives on Canadian national identity.

between the extremes of Germany and the United States. In Germany, the GFCC has propagated an expansive conception of rights that has carried them into every corner of the legal system, and significantly blurred the border between constitutional law and private law. In the United States, the Supreme Court has exercised tight control over the horizontal effect of rights, deploying them selectively as necessary, but otherwise maintaining a rigid hierarchy between constitutional and non-constitutional law. Canada has arrived at an equilibrium outcome between these two, in which the impact of rights on the private law is substantial, but more contingent and equivocal than in Germany.

The U.S. Supreme Court's early commitment to a state action framework shaped its development of doctrine far into the future. In the context of a general retreat from Reconstruction by the political branches, it made sense strategically for the Court to deny that constitutional rights impose positive obligations on the government to protect citizens from each other. The rejection of horizontal effect also supported the mutually reinforcing conceptions of rights and judicial supremacy that the Court was developing during the same period: rights were entitlements with determinate content, and the Court was the final arbiter of that content. The state action straightjacket came to pose problems for the Court in the twentieth century, when regional holdouts used private law to resist a national civil rights and civil liberties agenda. But rather than repudiating the rule, the Court extemporized, making ad hoc exceptions and finding novel justifications for national legislation that reached private discrimination. The state action rule continued to contain the broader transformative potential of constitutional rights, even as the Court licensed a series of one-off departures from the rule.

In many respects, Canada's experience more nearly resembles Germany's, but here there are significant differences as well. Rights constitutionalism came to Germany and Canada in very different ways. When it adopted the Basic Law in 1949, Germany was still clearing away rubble, both literal and political: the anti-liberal values of the old regime were still embedded to a considerable degree in the civil law. Canada, on the other hand, was already a fairly liberal society by the time it constitutionalized rights protections in 1982.[76] Germany's Federal Constitutional Court was a new institution operating alongside sharp-elbowed, more established neighbors, and by virtue of its jurisdiction, its own influence was pegged to the reach of the Basic Law. Canada's Supreme Court, by contrast, was well established and possessed limitless subject matter jurisdiction. On the other hand, while the GFCC enjoyed the moral prestige associated with human rights in the wake of the Nazi cataclysm, the SCC faced a degree of ambivalence

76. To use David Erdos's language, a "postmaterialist value orientation" had emerged in Canada (2010, 25).

about judicial power, largely owing to its potential to centralize control in a country where federalism is the dominant constitutional concern.

In other words, compared to Germany, there was less work for constitutional rights to do in the private sphere in Canada, and less reason for the Court to let them do it. And so it is not surprising that when the SCC first confronted the question of rights' horizontal effect, its doctrine played into a narrative of judicial restraint. The Court in *Dolphin Delivery* declared the most important parts of the common law off limits to the Charter. Coming on the heels of decisions from the previous year that signaled a fairly invasive form of rights review, in a country where federalism concerns run high and the common law is largely curated by provincial courts, the Court's restraint made sense. *Dolphin Delivery* did nothing to stoke provincial fears about the judicialization, and hence, centralization, of power.[77] It usefully established that there were limits to how deep into Canadian law the Charter revolution would push.

But for all the differences with Germany, the SCC's doctrine operated like the GFCC's in some respects. Importantly, in both systems, constitutional rights were permitted to influence ordinary law as values. Rights go down easier as values than as entitlements: rather than displacing existing normative structures entirely, values can be weighed alongside other considerations in the resolution of ordinary disputes. Relevant rights become part of a well-pleaded claim or defense, such that "[e]very properly advised litigant must now understand that even rules with a long history must accommodate the significance of Charter values" (Weinrib and Weinrib 2001, 71). Rights have not proved as disruptive to the private law in Canada as in Germany, in part because the SCC has not licensed free-standing Charter-based causes of action in private litigation under the auspices of the common law. But as the review of free expression

77. In the *Reference re Supreme Court Act, ss 5 and 6*, [2014] 1 S.C.R. 433, the SCC would show how provincial autonomy and judicial independence can make common cause. The federal government appointed Marc Nadon to one of the three SCC seats reserved for Quebecers. Nadon had been a member of the Quebec bar, but was not at the time of his appointment: he was serving as a federal judge. His appointment was challenged as inconsistent with the requirements of the Supreme Court Act that appointees to the Quebec seats be drawn "from the advocates" of the province. The federal Parliament amended the Supreme Court Act to make clear that former membership in the bar was sufficient to qualify for one of the Quebec seats, and also referred the eligibility question to the SCC.

The SCC held that the unamended Supreme Court Act required current membership in the Quebec bar. And what is more, the SCC held that the Parliament's effort to amend the Act was unconstitutional. Although the Supreme Court Act was passed an ordinary statute, the Court held that a constitutional amendment would be required to make this change, owing to the constitutional stature of the SCC. The decision amounted to a bold assertion of both provincial and judicial prerogatives.

cases have shown, the Charter has nonetheless significantly limited private parties' ability to use the common law to silence one another.

Rights have worked important changes in private law legislation also. Treating antidiscrimination statutes as quasi-constitutional in character, to a considerable degree the SCC has let legislatures and commissions carry its water when it comes to defining the Charter's guarantee of equality, including with respect to private-party relationships. Still, the courts have at times stepped in, generally to close gaps in protection already provided legislatively. We see this clearly in the area of family law, where courts have prodded legislative changes to bring legal norms into alignment with social norms. The SCC found fault with private law legislation's differential treatment, first, of married and unmarried opposite-sex couples, and then, of unmarried opposite-sex and same-sex couples. The courts' incremental interventions triggered the history-making redefinition of marriage by Canada's Parliament. Even so, when it comes to defining the social meaning of equality rights, the SCC has preserved a space for legislative choice, as illustrated by its recent decision upholding Quebec's differential treatment of legal marriage and common law marriage.

If the Charter has worked a "revolution" in Canada (Morton and Knopff 2000), it has been a very Canadian revolution: measured rather than avulsive; oriented toward comity rather than conflict. This chapter has detailed how the Charter has reshaped not just the public law but the private law of Canada. The following chapter considers what the experiences of Canada, Germany, and the United States together teach about the horizontal effect of rights.

8

Constitutional Rights, Private Law, and Judicial Power

Comparativists have certainly not missed the spread of judicially enforceable constitutional rights since the Second World War, but they may have missed its full significance. Scholarship on rights constitutionalism as a distinctive form of political practice often focuses on the work that rights do in the vertical dimension: how they regulate relations between individuals and the state. But in practice, it is the rare legal system in which rights have exclusively vertical effect. It follows that constitutionally competent courts around the world have to develop strategies and doctrines for managing the horizontal effect of rights. Neglecting this dimension of rights yields a cramped conception of what rights, constitutional law, and constitutionalism are about.

An example from the *Oxford Handbook of Law and Politics*, a justly celebrated standard reference work, illustrates the point. The first line of Keith Whittington's entry on "Constitutionalism" reads: "Constitutionalism is the constraining of government in order to better effectuate the fundamental principles of the political regime" (Whittington 2010, 281). In its exclusive focus on constraining the government, this definition fails to capture a significant part of what constitutionalism means in practice for many contemporary regimes. We cannot have a good handle on modern rights constitutionalism until we come to terms with the horizontal effect of constitutional rights.

The choices courts make about how to manage the horizontal effect of rights shape not only the scope of rights protections but the character of constitutionalism more broadly. Horizontal effect doctrine has implications for how courts conceptualize rights generally, how they adjudicate rights claims, and how they function in relation to other institutions. A court's choices in this area say something about what constitutional rights are and what the constitution is for. The doctrines reflect a legal system's existing normative commitments, as well as the institutional and political environments of the courts that make them. But at the same time, they can also drive new developments in constitutional governance and sharpen the differences between legal systems.

LOOKING BACK

This book has explored how horizontal rights doctrines have shaped the constitutional development of three countries: Germany, the United States, and Canada. It has delved deep into the legal history of each in order to give proper attention to the complex connections between these doctrines and other features of the legal and political environments. The focus throughout has been on three issues: when courts give horizontal effect to constitutional rights, how they construct horizontal effect doctrine, and what the broader consequences of these moves are. To summarize the results of detailed case studies necessarily flattens out important nuances. Nonetheless, in looking back on the previous chapters, it is possible to identify some common dynamics and patterns.

The courts in these countries only moved to first apply constitutional rights horizontally when there was a normative gap in the ordinary law that could plausibly be filled by a constitutional norm and turning to the constitution held advantages for the court. In Germany, conditions were propitious for the horizontal application of rights contained in the new Basic Law. The civil law was in many respects unchanged since its adoption in late imperial Germany and gave inadequate recognition to emerging liberal values such as freedom of expression. Moreover, the German Federal Constitutional Court (GFCC), besieged by other institutions seeking to diminish its power and autonomy, had every incentive to bring the Basic Law to bear broadly, since the Court's own relevance depended on it.

The U.S. Supreme Court refused its first invitation to give horizontal effect to constitutional rights following the end of Reconstruction, at a time when receptiveness to freedmen's equality claims had flagged within national political institutions and among the broader public. Matters were very different after the Second World War. Thanks in part to social movement activism, discrimination under the private law, especially in the South, increasingly registered in the broader public as a grave injustice. Eventually, a civil rights agenda began finding a viable political constituency at roughly the same time that the Supreme Court was rebranding itself as a right-protecting court. In this changed environment, the Supreme Court occasionally relaxed the strictures of the state action rule to go after private law holdouts from emerging national civil rights and civil liberties norms.

The situation was different again in Canada, where statutory changes had already met many postmaterialist normative demands by the time the Charter of Rights and Freedoms took effect, and in any case, the Supreme Court of Canada (SCC) could hear all cases whether or not they presented constitutional questions. Not surprisingly, the Court declined at first to give horizontal effects to rights, while at the same time leaving itself latitude to shape the common law to comport with Charter values.

The doctrines the different courts constructed to manage the horizontal effect of rights are sharply different. Still, it is possible to say something both about what horizontal effect doctrines do and about how they vary. Horizontal effect doctrines all perform some common functions. A court's doctrine characterizes a relevant dichotomy in the law and indicates when and how constitutional rights apply across it. The court's official doctrine is not always a reliable guide to how cases come out. But the discrepancy between what courts say about rights and what they do can itself be revealing.

Courts build doctrines through the resolution of individual cases. A court's decision does several things simultaneously. It justifies the outcome of the instant case with reference to existing law. In doing so, it adds to that law, further defining the argumentation framework that will govern the resolution of future cases. How the court revolves the case also speaks, if only implicitly, to a broader normative narrative about the court's role in governance. To the extent the different functions of a decision come into conflict, we can expect to see inconsistencies emerge in doctrine, or divergences between what courts say and what they do.

This framework helps to make sense of the choices different courts make. The GFCC builds its doctrine around the public law/private law distinction that is foundational to German law. Constitutional rights apply to the private law all the time, but as values, not entitlements: rights shape the interpretation of law, and may constrain private-party conduct indirectly, but they do not directly impose any obligations on private parties. This framing potentially puts rights in play in all private litigation, amplifying the GFCC's relevance. At the same time, it reinforces the Court's message that constitutional rights pervade the civil law without destroying its autonomy—even if, as a practical matter, there is little difference between indirect and direct horizontal effect.

The U.S. Supreme Court frames the issue in terms of state action versus private action and officially hews to a hard-and-fast rule: constitutional rights (which are entitlements) only apply to state action. The state action rule, which originated shortly after the end of Reconstruction, was the first half of a one-two punch that prevented Congress from regulating private conduct under the banner of rights. The second half was the Court's insistence on its own interpretive primacy: Congress could not legislate based on its own, broader, understanding of rights. The Court officially maintained this doctrine even as it increasingly used rights horizontally to bring recalcitrant states in line with national norms for a generation after World War II. More so than its Canadian or German counterparts, the Supreme Court has maintained control over when rights apply horizontally, but as the Vinson and (especially) Warren Courts reached out with rights to remedy private wrongs, doctrinal coherence was the casualty.

The Supreme Court of Canada flatly declared that the Charter does not apply to private litigation, but the reality is more complex. To the extent that private litigation is governed by the common law, the Charter does apply, as values. But only some of the time: the Charter can shape the interpretation of common law, but not overturn a settled rule of law—except, it seems, when the Court really wants it to. Although the Charter does apply to private law legislation, the SCC's doctrine has left ambiguous precisely what this implies. All in all, the SCC's doctrine serves a narrative of judicial restraint while leaving both the Court and other institutions some latitude to correct perceived deficiencies in the private law using the Charter.

And because courts do not operate in a vacuum, but as components in dynamic systems of governance, their doctrinal moves can occasion changes in the behavior of other institutions and actors. These doctrines can redistribute legal decision-making authority in a system and reconfigure how institutions interact with one another. Horizontal rights can catalyze the constitutionalization of governance, bringing more decision making under the ambit of constitutional law, and also judicialization, amplifying the power of courts. Extensive horizontality can even blur the distinctions between the different paradigms of government power, so that legislatures behave more "judicially," by deliberating about rights, and courts act more "legislatively," reviewing how policies strike the balance between the competing values at stake.

Not surprisingly, such changes are especially pronounced in Germany, where the GFCC's horizontal effect jurisprudence triggered a constitutional cascade. Where rights are values that apply to the whole of law, all legal decision making takes on a constitutional dimension, and when a constitutional court has jurisdiction to police compliance, all actors involved have incentives to take rights into account. The results are a sharing of the authority for constitutional construction among multiple institutions and a progressive blurring of the distinctions between ordinary law and constitutional law, and the business of legislatures and courts.

The United States only ever made limited moves in this direction. It is true that the U.S. Supreme Court licensed a greater role for Congress in giving content to rights under its enforcement powers at the same time that the Court liberalized its approach to state action, and both moves undermined state law roadblocks to effective civil rights protections. But the Court never formally repudiated the state action rule, and its post–civil rights jurisprudence reinforced the old distinctions between constitutional law and ordinary law, and between the work of courts and legislatures. The Court has invoked the state action rule selectively to enforce a policy of constitutional containment, which reinforces judicial supremacy as it confines the reach of rights.

Canada presents something of a middle case. Charter values have had an impact on some, though by no means all, areas of the common law. Charter deliberations are built into the legislative process, although these generally are centered in the executive branch and take judicial interpretations of the Charter as given. And the Supreme Court of Canada will bring the Charter to bear on private law legislation, but often in ways that build on, rather than preempt, legislative initiative, a pattern that I refer to as caboose constitutionalism.

LOOKING BEYOND

These case studies illustrate some of the variability in how horizontal rights can function in a legal system. But they do not, by any means, exhaust it. The remainder of this chapter looks beyond Germany, the United States, and Canada. First, it briefly considers the roles that horizontal rights play in a small but diverse set of additional legal systems. These vignettes underscore how the impact of horizontal rights is sensitive to institutional and political differences. Then, it considers how horizontal rights relate to some other important phenomena in contemporary constitutional law, proportionality review and weak-form judicial review. Finally, the chapter closes by circling back to an idea introduced in Chapter Three, that constitutions can promote political integration, and very briefly considers how horizontal rights can contribute to that end.

In all three case studies, horizontal effect doctrine has been very much a top-down affair. The focus in each account has centered squarely on an apex court that called the tune to which the whole judicial system danced. This kind of narrative has reflected how the development of doctrine has played out in these systems, but there are other possibilities. Depending on how judicial review is configured and on the institutional politics on the ground, horizontal rights can emerge in the grassroots of the judicial system.

The case of Poland illustrates the point. Poland's Constitutional Tribunal has been at the center of high-stakes court-curbing controversies in recent years, but even before, the Tribunal had somewhat limited powers by global standards. Since 1997, the Tribunal's interpretations of statutes reached under abstract review are not considered binding, and the Tribunal lacks the power to initiate review of ordinary courts' decisions (Kühn 2005, 222–23, 239). Under Article 193 of the Constitution, however, ordinary courts may refer constitutional questions to the Tribunal.

In Germany, constitutional law was a tool that the Federal Constitutional Court could use to assert a measure of control over ordinary courts. In Poland, with different procedures and structures of judicial review, constitutional law was a tool that ordinary courts could use to expand their own domain. In the years after the fall of communism, lower courts in Poland, and Poland's Supreme Court, frequently declined to refer constitutional questions to the Constitutional Tribunal, choosing to answer them themselves. Polish ordinary courts developed rights doctrines, including horizontal rights doctrines (Wyrozumska 2001).

Lower courts' efforts to decentralize constitutional review by fiat were initially resisted by the Constitutional Tribunal. But in 2000, the Tribunal acceded, in part, to the claims of lower courts. The Court conceded that the power to refer constitutional questions to the Tribunal was discretionary, not mandatory. Also, the Tribunal held that lower courts could apply the Constitution themselves, but only where constitutional provisions are clear, and not to disregard or invalidate statutes (Kühn 2005, 235). In effect, the Tribunal endorsed the practice of "constitutionally conforming interpretation" by ordinary courts that is the cornerstone of decentralized judicial review in Germany. But in Poland, because of the different structure of judicial review, the move largely redounded to the benefit of the lower courts, amplifying the normative resources at their disposal in resolving cases, and hence, their discretion.

Horizontal rights have begun to play a quite different role in China, as work by Ernest Caldwell reveals. China's 1982 Constitution nominally guarantees a number of rights, but the authority to supervise the enforcement of the Constitution is vested in the National People's Congress, rather than the courts. China's Supreme Court has long held that the Constitution, though supreme, is not to be cited as the basis of decision in cases (Caldwell 2012, 66–67).

But if China's higher courts decline to invoke the Constitution, its lower courts, whose decisions rarely receive much attention from nonparties, are not so reticent. And indeed, lower courts have applied constitutional rights horizontally, to resolve private-party disputes. Not surprisingly, given China's decades-long economic boom and the infrastructure development that went with it, many of the cases concern construction accidents.

The case of *Long Jiankang v. Zhongzhou Construction Engineering Co., Ltd., Traffic Bureau of Yongsheng County, Yunnan, and Jiang Jiangu*,[1] from 2000, illustrates a typical context. A construction company contracted with a local traffic bureau to complete an infrastructure project. While correcting a construction error at the instruction of the project leader, a worker suffered an injury that left him paralyzed. He sued the project leader, the construction company, and the traffic bureau for compensation. The court of first instance dismissed the claim as to the traffic bureau, as it had no contractual relationship to the plaintiff. But the court found the project leader and construction company liable. The court relied on Article 42 of the Constitution, which provides that "the State provides necessary vocational training for citizens before they are employed." The court concluded that neither the construction company nor the manager had

1. Chinalaw Information Service, Apr. 11, 2000 (People's Court of Yongsheng County, Yunnan Province).

given the plaintiff the training he needed to complete his work safely. The court also rejected an argument that liability could be contractually shifted from the company to the project leader through their employment agreement. Such contractual provisions infringe workers' constitutional and statutory rights and are therefore void (Caldwell 2012, 87–88).

Poland and China show how lower courts can also be innovators in horizontal rights jurisprudence. And they illustrate further how the politics of horizontal rights can differ across national lines. In Poland, lower courts embraced constitutional rights, including in their horizontal dimension, over the objections of the Constitutional Tribunal, which wanted other courts to refer constitutional questions to it. In explaining why matters played out as they did in Poland, Zdenek Kühn emphasizes the professional socialization of Polish judges (Kühn 2005). In addition, the structure of Poland's court system also surely played a role. With no power to initiate review of judicial decisions, the Constitutional Tribunal had no good tool for controlling lower courts. By deciding constitutional questions themselves, rather than referring them to the Tribunal, ordinary court judges could draw to themselves the normative power of that supreme text and widen the range of outcomes available to them. Under these circumstances, ordinary courts arrogated to themselves the power to apply the Constitution, including horizontally.

China shows how horizontal rights can play a very different role in a very different political and legal system. In the *Long Jiankang* case and others like it, courts treat horizontal rights not as a complement to vertical rights so much as a substitute for them. In other words, courts in these cases are permitting the state to outsource to private enterprises the duties to its citizens that the state took on in its charter of government. As China has moved from state socialism to a capitalist economy, the state has sloughed off many of the burdens of social provision that it formerly shouldered. And courts have used the Constitution to put private parties on the hook for providing the training and protection for workers that the state has promised.

But horizontal rights are not only a phenomenon of national constitutional law. International human rights norms have been applied in some circumstances to nonstate actors, as Andrew Clapham has extensively documented (2006). What is more, horizontal rights may have the potential to be most transformative in the interactions between national and international or supranational legal orders. Horizontally effective rights pose a frontal challenge to the traditional conception of international law as a purely *interstate* matter. Horizontal rights play an important, and perhaps increasing, role in the law of the European Union, as touched upon in Chapter Three. Britain's Human Rights Act 1998, which made rights guaranteed in the European Convention on Human Rights justiciable in UK courts, also unleashed horizontal effect in that country. The brief discussions of both that follow do not aim to be comprehensive but only to sketch some of the similarities and differences in how horizontal effect has functioned in these contexts, compared to in purely national contexts.

In thousands of rulings handed down over the course of decades, the European Court of Justice (ECJ) has insisted that the courts and legislatures of member states take EU law seriously (Stone Sweet 2004). The Court's doctrines have enlisted litigants and national courts at every level to weave EU legal norms into the fabric of national law and have changed patterns of governance in the process. What are known in EU law parlance as directly effective horizontal rights—rights that can be invoked by private parties in litigation against other private parties, in the absence of national legislation transposing them into domestic law—represent the frontier of that long-running transformation of governance in Europe.

As early as 1974, the ECJ had ruled that certain general principles of EU law may be directly effective in litigation between private parties.[2] The Court has expanded the scope of this doctrine in recent years, and Chapter Three has discussed some of the most important developments. The *Mangold* decision from 2005 held that nondiscrimination on the basis of age was a general principle of EU law and that private parties could rely on it to sue other private parties. The *Kücükdeveci* decision from 2010 affirmed that an age-based nondiscrimination claim, while also expressed in a directive, was more fundamentally anchored in EU general principles. The Court's decision held that the right could serve as the basis for a private suit and also empowered national courts to disapply national legislation that contravenes it. The potential for horizontal rights to reshape national law throughout EU member states is only amplified by the entry into force, in late 2009, of a new Charter of Fundamental Rights of the European Union as part of the Lisbon Treaty. And antidiscrimination litigation in the European Union, based on directives that are understood (per *Kükükdeveci*) as expressing general principles of EU law, has increased dramatically in recent years (Stone Sweet 2011, 105).

The real question for the ECJ now is how to manage the truly explosive potential of directly effective horizontal rights. The Court's response, in cases such as *Dominguez* (2012),[3] *AMS* (2014),[4] and *Glatzel* (2014),[5] has been to tack back and forth from case to case, neither repudiating the horizontal direct effect of EU norms, nor following the idea to its most far-reaching conclusion (Walkila 2015). The Court has drawn a distinction between EU rights that can

2. Walrave and Koch v. Association Union Cycliste Internationale [1974] ECR 1405.

3. C-282/10, EU:C:2012:33.

4. C-176/12, EU:C:2014:2.

5. C-356/12, EU:C:2014:350.

be directly effective in horizontal litigation and those that cannot because they "must be given more specific expression in European Union or national law."[6] In fact, it is not obvious that the rights given horizontal direct effect by the ECJ are more judicially administrable than those denied horizontal direct effect. But the Court's rulings have allowed it to cabin and control the scope of horizontal direct effect and avoid the backlash that might follow from a more consistent, universalizing stance.[7] Overall, the ECJ's approach has echoes of both the GFCC's, in the expansiveness of its conception of rights' horizontal effect, and the U.S. Supreme Court's, in the ad hoc quality of many of its individual rulings.

The United Kingdom famously has no written constitution and a long history of parliamentary supremacy. However, a form of rights review has emerged over the past two decades, owing to the enactment of the Human Rights Act 1998 (HRA). The HRA adopts the protections of the European Convention on Human Rights as UK law. The HRA does not permit courts to invalidate laws as inconsistent with Convention rights, but requires them instead to interpret legislation so that it conforms with those rights when possible and, when not, to declare the legislation's incompatibility. The HRA required all public authorities to act compatibly with Convention rights and established a cause of action and damages remedy against those failing to do so.

It is through the requirement that all "public authorities" conform to the Convention that the HRA opens the door to horizontal effect. Courts clearly are public authorities. What, then, does the HRA mean for judicial rulings in private law disputes? Does the requirement that the courts conform to the Convention mean that its rights provisions will indirectly apply to legal relations among private parties?

UK courts have found that Convention rights do shape the private law thanks to the HRA, but the finer points of how, exactly, they interact with existing private law structures remain hazy. Alison L. Young has identified eleven different models of indirect horizontal effect, from quite mild (courts should develop the common law to recognize the values underpinning Convention rights, absent countervailing reasons not to) to quite strong (courts must develop new causes of action to vindicate Convention rights, even in the face of conflicting higher court authority) (2011).

After two decades of HRA litigation, a consensus on which model best captures the statute's horizontal effect eludes UK courts. As a practical matter, the HRA's impact on private law varies substantially by area of law. Not surprisingly,

6. *AMS*, C-176/12, ¶ 45.

7. The ECJ's more expansionary tendencies regarding horizontal direct effect have met with a critical reception from some EU scholars. See, for instance, Robin-Olivier (2014).

it has had a greater impact with respect to values that previously found limited protection in English law, such as privacy: HRA litigation has been responsible for a major overhaul of the tort of breach of confidence to better protect personal privacy (Phillipson 2011).

Convention rights have changed UK law, thanks to the Human Rights Act. But they have done so without either a cohesive new legal paradigm to explain exactly how the rights apply or the fireworks of spectacular interinstitutional conflicts. Part of this is because in the United Kingdom, as in Canada, the courts' jurisdiction does not hinge on whether rights are at stake, as it does in systems with concentrated constitutional review (and sometimes, even in decentralized systems, such as the United States, where federal courts' jurisdiction hinges on the presence of a federal issue). Saying whether a right is at stake is less fraught when the answer does not determine which court gets to hear a case. And in cases where the relevant legal domain is governed by common law, the court can often afford to be rather vague about whether an outcome is constitutionally compelled or simply a matter of judicial prudence in guiding the development of the common law. Cheryl Saunders has written about how Canada's approach to the horizontal effect of Charter rights delivers flexibility and continuity, while perhaps shortchanging transparency (Saunders 2005). Much the same could be said of the United Kingdom's experience with the horizontal effect of the Human Rights Act, for much the same reasons.

If there are patterns or family resemblances in how different legal systems approach the horizontal effect of rights, there are also linkages between horizontal rights doctrines and some of the most important developments in constitutional law to emerge in recent decades. The different choices that courts make about how to manage horizontal effect reflect, in part, normative, institutional and political differences among systems. And over time, the choices courts make about horizontal rights can amplify differences across legal systems. Some of the features of a legal system that can dispose its courts to be receptive or unreceptive to horizontal rights may also shape how they react to other conceptual innovations within constitutional law. In particular, there are connections between a court's receptiveness to horizontal effect and its position on proportionality analysis and weak-form judicial review.

Proportionality analysis is a technique for resolving rights claims that has emerged in recent decades as a cornerstone of constitutional practice in jurisdictions around the world (Stone Sweet and Mathews 2008). Constitutional judges first deployed proportionality to test government measures impinging on interests protected by constitutional rights. A reviewing court takes a challenged measure through a series of increasingly stringent tests, in order to determine whether the measure goes further than it should and, hence, is unconstitutional. Generally, courts ask whether the purpose of the challenged measure is legitimate; whether the measure is suitably adapted to further the purpose;

and whether the same ends could be equally well achieved through a different measure that infringes less on the interest protected by the right. If the measure survives these tests, the court then moves to a balancing test, asking whether the measure's contribution to advancing the public purpose justifies the sacrifice that it imposes on the protected interest. Proportionality analysis can also be used to resolve conflicts between rights, in which case the court jumps straight to the last phase of the analysis, weighing the infringements of the competing rights against each other, to determine if the balance struck is permissible.

There is reason to think courts' position on horizontal rights and proportionality are related. More specifically, courts that are receptive to the horizontal effect of rights are also likely to be receptive to at least some version of proportionality analysis. Conversely, it is hard for courts that reject any form of proportionality to embrace openly the horizontal effect of rights. Why? Accepting that rights have horizontal effect raises the possibility of conflicts between constitutional rights. A simple libel case might become a clash between constitutional rights to expression and reputation. Such situations will require courts to balance the competing rights, and proportionality analysis is, at root, a framework to facilitate balancing. Moreover, rights horizontality and proportionality both build on a common conception, if only an implicit one, of rights. Rights are *the kinds of things that can be balanced.* They are values that find expression in law, rather than fixed entitlements to some specific result. A legal system deeply wedded to an absolutist or categorical conception of rights is unlikely to offer a fulsome endorsement of the horizontal effect of rights because of the deep-seated conceptual incompatibility between the two positions.

Certainly this pattern plays out in the countries considered in the case studies. In the United States, the state action requirement expresses a formal commitment to a vertical conception of rights (notwithstanding the fact that rights, as a practical matter, sometimes do have horizontal effect). And the constitutional jurisprudence of the United States is famously resistant to a proportionality-based approach to rights review (notwithstanding the fact that the Court does, in effect, balance rights against competing interests in many contexts) (Mathews and Stone Sweet 2011). Compared to the United States, courts in Germany and Canada are both more open about recognizing rights' horizontal effect and more receptive to proportionality. A version of proportionality made its first appearance in Germany's federal constitutional law in the *Pharmacy Case*, decided in 1958, the same year as *Lüth*.[8] And the Supreme Court of Canada adopted the German proportionality framework in *Oakes*, in 1986, the same year as *Dolphin Delivery*.[9] In both countries, proportionality

8. Apotheken-Urteil, June 11, 1958, BVerfGE 7, 377.

9. R. v. Oakes, [1986] 1 S.C.R. 103.

analysis has become a central feature of rights adjudication, though its implementation differs in some particulars (Grimm 2007).

There are also reasons why courts that embrace horizontal rights would tend to reject strong-form judicial supremacy. In strong-form judicial supremacy, an apex court is the ultimate authority, and has the last word, on what the constitution means. Mark Tushnet contrasts this to what he terms weak-form judicial review, in which authority to make sense of the constitution is shared among institutions (Tushnet 2008). There are a number of ways interpretive authority can be shared in a legal system, including through provisions that allow legislative overrides of constitutional rulings, via norms that foster dialogues between courts and legislatures, and by means of deference doctrines. These procedural or institutional mechanisms all implicitly reject the idea that there is one uniquely correct answer to constitutional questions. In other words, they reflect a tolerance of interpretive pluralism when it comes to the meaning of constitutional guarantees.

Some tolerance of interpretive pluralism is also a necessity in a legal system that broadly embraces the horizontal effect of constitutional rights, for several reasons. First, there is the matter of capacity. If every private dispute (and every private law norm) potentially raises a constitutional question, a single tribunal cannot hope to act as a court of cassation, reversing every judgment (and striking down every law) where it would have appraised the constitutional issue differently. Second, a court can generate more buy-in to the project of taking rights seriously if it rewards other institutions for doing so. Giving some deference to the rights reasoning of other courts and legislatures encourages them to engage in rights reasoning. Third, conceptualizing rights as values to be given expression in law and balanced against other values—as opposed to, say, legal entitlements to be determined through technical feats of casuistry—undermines any claim of exclusive judicial competence over rights issues. The more that deciding rights claims means striking a balance between competing values, the harder it is to maintain that each concrete dispute has a uniquely correct answer, to which one court has privileged access.

This pattern also holds across the three case studies. Germany's Federal Constitutional Court expects ordinary courts to take account of constitutional rights in their decision making, but then generally defers to their judgments. Canada deviates from strong-form judicial supremacy thanks to the judicial-legislative "dialogues" discussed in Chapter Seven, as well as Section 33 of the Charter, which permits legislative overrides of some constitutional judgments. Of the three case studies, the United States is by far the most grudging and equivocal in its acknowledgment of horizontal effect and the strictest adherent to strong-form judicial supremacy. Of course, if the explanations offered here are valid, the disaffinity between systems that accept rights' horizontality and strong-form judicial supremacy—like the affinity between those same systems and proportionality analysis—will not be limited to these three countries. The same patterns should repeat across other legal systems.

If horizontality has links to important features of contemporary constitutionalism, it also reaches back to an older conception of the constitutional project. We can evaluate a constitution in terms of its capacity to contribute to integration: to help bind a political community together. All kinds of social systems must hold together to function (Parsons 2012), and constitutions are relevant to whether a polity holds together or comes apart (Grimm 2005).

Constitutions matter to integration most obviously in the ways that they explicitly structure political processes. So, for instance, representation and voting rules can promote political disintegration if they favor the creation of large numbers of political factions with no incentive to work together (Cox 1997; Laver and Schofield 1991). But constitutions can also matter in less direct ways. In particular, constitutions can further political integration if they act as focal points for constructive civic and political engagement.

The idea that constitutions can promote political integration is an old one.[10] The integrative capacity of constitutions was a particular preoccupation of constitutional theory in Weimar Germany, most notably in the work of Rudolf Smend.[11] It is hardly surprising that theorists living in a country coming apart at the seams would care particularly about the contribution a constitution can make to holding society together. As described in Chapter Three, some of this material had an antiliberal, antipluralist character. Integration was conceived as the forging of a unity, and dissensus and difference were obstacles to be overcome. The prewar Smend conceived of the constitution instrumentally, as a tool for integration; if necessary to achieve integration, the constitution could be cast aside (Günther 2004, 166).

But the concept of integration can be retooled and updated for a pluralistic democratic age, as the postwar evolution of Smend's ideas demonstrates. As a professor in Gottingen, Smend led an influential seminar in which he and his students, many of whom went on to become leading public law scholars, reworked many of the debates of the Weimar era (Günther 2004, 160). Constitutional values, as embodied in rights, were central to the integrative role of the constitution. Rights were not conceived of as a "gapless and hierarchically ordered system of claims" but instead as an objective order of values, which "as the ethical basis gave their stamp to the entire shared life of the community, without excessively limiting legislative freedom" (Günther 2004, 171).

10. As Hans-Christopher Schröder describes, eighteenth-century English thinkers and statesmen valued their "Ancient Constitution" not least for its capacity to maintain stability in the face of political change, in pointed contrast to revolutionary France (2002, 153–79).

11. Hermann Heller's work is also relevant (Vorländer 2002, 14–15).

Rather than serving to squelch dissensus, constitutional rights-as-values can serve to organize and institutionalize political contestation, under the guidance of a constitutional court. Even as opposing parties dispute what constitutional rights mean in concrete contexts, their arguments presuppose and reinforce their acceptance of the constitutional order. So for instance, the high-profile constitutional conflicts of the early postwar decades cemented the centrality of the Basic Law to the life of the Federal Republic: participants argued over what the constitutional order required, rather than rejecting it (Vorländer 2002, 31; Herbert 2006, 102). It is possible—though far from inevitable—for political contestation to serve as an engine of engagement and for rights to serve as the sites where these conflicts play out (Frankenberg 2002).

Bruce Ackerman has described his conception of the U.S. Constitution in similar terms, as "an evolving language of politics through which Americans have learned to talk to one another in the course of the centuries-long struggle over the national identity" (Ackerman 1989, 477).[12] But in Ackerman's account, the U.S. Constitution really only plays this role exceptionally, in the ultra-high stakes, episodic irruptions of constitutional politics (Ackerman 1991). A constitution can play this role in the life of a polity more regularly and more fully to the extent that constitutional rights are given horizontal effect. When "ordinary" policy decisions, including those that concern private-party relationships, amount to acts of constitutional construction, the constitution gains in relevance, and lawmaking rises in normative stature. The constitution becomes, in Smend's phrase, simultaneously a stimulus and a channel for the state: it not only checks state action but animates and inspires the legislative function. A horizontal constitution allows for greater contiguity between constitutional law and ordinary law, and between constitutional politics and ordinary politics.

Whether this vision of constitutionalism is desirable—or even achievable—is a question for individual legal systems, and the answers will differ. But horizontal rights make it conceivable.

The history of rights in political and legal discourse has been a history of change. Using constitutional rights to ground legal claims that impair the legal position of private parties is one of the most significant innovations of recent times. Regardless of whether courts accept or reject these claims, how they respond to them affects the trajectory of constitutional development in the legal systems that they superintend. In addressing these claims, whether they mean to or not, courts are also offering their answers to deeper questions, questions about the nature of rights and the purpose of constitutions.

12. For a more developed typology of how constitutions can bear on integration, see Schaal (2002).

Bibliography

Ackerman, Bruce. 1989. "Constitutional Politics/Constitutional Law." *Yale Law Journal* 99 (3): 453–547.
———. 1991. *We the People: Foundations*. Harvard University Press.
———. 2007. "The Living Constitution." *Harvard Law Review* 120 (7): 1737–812.
———. 2014. *We the People: The Civil Rights Revolution*. Belknap Press.
Alexy, Robert, and Julian Rivers. 2010. *A Theory of Constitutional Rights*. Oxford University Press.
Amar, Akhil Reed. 2000. *The Bill of Rights: Creation and Reconstruction*. Yale University Press.
———. 2012. *America's Constitution: A Biography*. Random House.
Antidiskriminierungsstelle des Bundes. 2012. *Ausgewählte Entscheidungen deutscher Gerichte zum Antidiskriminierungsrecht*. Antidiskriminierungsstelle des Bundes.
Arndt, Adolf. 1960. *Das nicht erfüllte Grundgesetz*. Mohr Siebeck.
Bakan, Joel. 1997. *Just Words: Constitutional Rights and Social Wrongs*. University of Toronto Press.
Baldus, Manfred. 2005. "Frühe Machtkämpfe: Ein Versuch über die historischen Gründe der Autorität des Bundesverfassungsgericht." In *Das Lüth-Urteil aus (rechts-) historischer Sicht: Die Konflikte um Veit Harlan und die Grundrechtsjudikatur des Bundesverfassungsgerichts*, edited by Thomas Henne and Arne Riedlinger. Berliner Wissenschafts-Verlag.
Balkin, Jack M. 2011. *Constitutional Redemption: Political Faith in an Unjust World*. Harvard University Press.
Benedict, Michael Les. 1978. "Preserving Federalism: Reconstruction and the Waite Court." *The Supreme Court Review* 1978: 39–80.
Bernier, Ivan, and Andrée Lajoie. 1986. *The Supreme Court of Canada as an Instrument of Political Change*. University of Toronto Press.
Best, Samuel J., and Benjamin Radcliff. 2005. *Polling America: An Encyclopedia of Public Opinion, Volume I, A–O*. Greenwood.
Bhagwat, Ashutosh. 2010. *The Myth of Rights: The Purposes and Limits of Constitutional Rights*. Oxford University Press.

Extending Rights' Reach. Jud Mathews.

Black, Jr., Charles L. 1967. "Foreword: State Action, Equal Protection, and California's Proposition 14." *Harvard Law Review* 81 (1): 69–109.

Böckenförde, Ernst-Wolfgang. 1991. *State, Society, and Liberty: Studies in Political Theory and Constitutional Law*. Berg.

Bomhoff, Jacco. 2013. *Balancing Constitutional Rights: The Origins and Meanings of Postwar Legal Discourse*. Cambridge University Press.

Boyd, Susan B. 2000. "The Impact of the Charter of Rights and Freedoms on Canadian Family Law." *Canadian Journal of Family Law* 17 (2): 293–331.

Brandwein, Pamela. 2006. "The *Civil Rights Cases* and the Lost Language of State Neglect." In *The Supreme Court and American Political Development*, 275–325. University Press of Kansas.

———. 2007. "A Judicial Abandonment of Blacks? Rethinking the 'State Action' Cases of the Waite Court." *Law & Society Review* 41 (2): 343–86.

———. 2014. *Rethinking the Judicial Settlement of Reconstruction*. Cambridge University Press.

Brest, Paul. 1982. "State Action and Liberal Theory: A Casenote on Flagg Brothers v. Brooks." *University of Pennsylvania Law Review* 130 (6): 1296–330.

Brest, Paul, Sanford Levinson, Jack M. Balkin, Reva B. Siegel, and Akhil Reed Amar. 2006. *Processes of Constitutional Decision Making: Cases And Materials*. Aspen Law & Business.

Bryde, Brun-Otto. 2007. "Fundamental Rights as Guidelines and Inspiration: German Constitutionalism in International Perspective." *Wisconsin International Law Journal* 25 (2): 189–208.

Bushnell, Ian. 1992. *The Captive Court: A Study of the Supreme Court of Canada*. McGill-Queen's University Press.

Cabral, Pedro, and Ricardo Neves. 2011. "General Principles of EU Law and Horizontal Direct Effect." *European Public Law* 17 (3): 437–54.

Caldwell, Ernest. 2012. "Horizontal Rights and Chinese Constitutionalism: Judicializati on Through Labor Disputes." *Chicago-Kent Law Review* 88 (1): 63–92.

Canaris, Claus-Wilhelm. 1984. "Grundrechte und Privatrecht." *Archiv für die civilistische Praxis* 184 (3): 201–46.

———. 1998. *Grundrechte und Privatrecht: Eine Zwischenbilanz*. Gruyter.

Chafee, Zechariah. 1920. *Freedom of Speech*. Harcourt, Brace and Howe.

Chemerinsky, Erwin. 1985. "Rethinking State Action." *Northwestern University Law Review* 80 (3): 503–57.

Cherednychenko, Ohla O. 2007. "Fundamental Rights and Private Law: A Relationship of Subordination or Complementarity." *Utrecht Law Review* 3 (2): 1–25.

Choudhry, Sujit, and Claire Hunter. 2003. "Measuring Judicial Activism on the Supreme Court of Canada: A Comment on Newfoundland (Treasury Board) v. NAPE." *McGill Law Journal* 48 (3): 525–62.

Clapham, Andrew. 2006. *Human Rights Obligations of Non-state Actors*. Oxford University Press.

Clark, Mark W. 2006. *Beyond Catastrophe: German Intellectuals and Cultural Renewal After World War II, 1945–1955*. Lexington Books.

Collings, Justin. 2015. *Democracy's Guardians: Constitutional Justice and the Making of Postwar Germany*. Oxford University Press.

Comella, Victor Ferreres. 2009. *Constitutional Courts and Democratic Values: A European Perspective*. Yale University Press.

Courtney, John, and David E. Smith. 2010. "Introduction: Transformation of an Unnatural Country." In *The Oxford Handbook of Canadian Politics*, edited by John Courtney and David E. Smith, 3–17. Oxford University Press.

Cox, Gary W. 1997. *Making Votes Count: Strategic Coordination in the World's Electoral Systems (Political Economy of Institutions and Decisions)*. Cambridge University Press.

Crosby, Margaret Barber. 2008. *The Making of a German Constitution: A Slow Revolution*. Berg Publishers.

Crowe, Justin. 2007. "Building the Judiciary: Law, Courts, and the Politics of Institutional Development." Princeton University Press.

Currie, David P. 1994. *The Constitution of the Federal Republic of Germany*. University of Chicago Press.

Dellinger, Walter E. 1972. "Of Rights and Remedies: The Constitution as a Sword." *Harvard Law Review* 85 (8): 1532–64.

Diederichsen, Uwe. 1998. "Das Bundesverfassungsgericht als oberstes Zivilgericht. Ein Lehrstück der juristischen Methodenlehre." *Archiv für die civilistische Praxis* 198 (2): 171–260.

Doyle, Arthur Conan. 1892. "The Adventure of the Silver Blaze." *The Strand Magazine: An Illustrated Monthly* 4: 645–60.

Dürig, Günter. 1956. "Der Grundsatz der Menschenwürde. Entwurf eines praktikablen Wertsystems der Grundrechte aus Art. 1 Abs. I in Verbindung mit Art, 19 Abs. II des Grundgesetzes." *Archiv des Öffentlichen Rechts (AöR)* 81 (2): 117–57.

Eberlein, Klaus D. 1968. *Was die Deutschen möchten*. Wegner.

Ebke, Werner, and Matthew W. Finkin. 1996. *Introduction to German Law*. Kluwer Law International.

Eliadis, Pearl. 2014. *Speaking Out on Human Rights: Debating Canada's Human Rights System*. McGill-Queen's University Press.

Emanuel, Steven L. 2012. *Emanuel Law Outlines: Constitutional Law, 30th Edition*. Aspen Publishers.

Emerson, Thomas I. 1970. *The System of Freedom of Expression*. Random House.

———. 1979. "The Right of Privacy and Freedom of the Press." *Harvard Civil Rights-Civil Liberties Law Review* 14 (2): 329–60.

Engel, Stephen M. 2011. *American Politicians Confront the Court: Opposition Politics and Changing Responses to Judicial Power*. Cambridge University Press.

Epp, Charles R. 1998. *The Rights Revolution: Lawyers, Activists, and Supreme Courts in Comparative Perspective*. University of Chicago Press.

Erdos, David. 2010. *Delegating Rights Protection: The Rise of Bills of Rights in the Westminster World*. Oxford University Press.

Eskridge, William N. 2002. "Some Effects of Identity-Based Social Movements on Constitutional Law in the Twentieth Century." *Michigan Law Review* 100 (8): 2062–407.

Eskridge, William N., and John Ferejohn. 2001. "Super-Statutes." *Duke Law Journal* 50 (5): 1215–76.

———. 2010. *A Republic of Statutes: The New American Constitution*. Yale University Press

Estrada, Alexei Julio. 2000. *La Eficacia de Derechos Fundamentales Entre Particulares*. Universidad Externado de Colombia.

———. 2007. "Los Tribunales Constitucionales y la Eficacia entre Particulares de los Derechos Fundamentales." In *Teoría Constitucional y Derechos Fundamentales*, edited by Miguel Carbonell, 203–250. Comisión Nacional de los Derechos Humanos.

Fairman, Charles. 2009. *History of the Supreme Court of the United States: Reconstruction and Reunion, 1864–1888*. Cambridge University Press.

Fedtke, Jörg. 2007. "*Drittwirkung* in Germany." In *Human Rights and the Private Sphere: A Comparative Study*, edited by Dawn Oliver and Jörg Fedtke, 125–56. Routledge Cavendish.

Fee, John. 2004. "Formal State Action Doctrine and Free Speech Analysis." *North Carolina Law Review*. 83 (3): 569–620.

Feeley, Malcolm M. 2006. "The Black Basis of Constitutional Development." In *Earl Warren and the Warren Court: The Legacy in American and Foreign Law*, edited by Harry N. Scheiber, 49–75. Lexington Books.

Fenske, Hans. 1994. *Deutsche Verfassungsgeschichte. Vom Norddeutschen Bund bis heute*. Copress.

Fisher, Louis. 1988. *Constitutional Dialogues: Interpretation as Political Process*. Princeton University Press.

Flemming, Roy B. 2005. *Tournament of Appeals: Granting Judicial Review in Canada*. UBC Press.

Foner, Eric. 2002. *Reconstruction: America's Unfinished Revolution, 1863–1877*. Harper Perennial Modern Classics.

Fontana, David. 2013. "Docket Control and the Success of Constitutional Courts." In *Comparative Constitutional Law*, edited by Tom Ginsburg and Rosalind Dixon, 624–41. Edward Elgar.

Forer, Lois G. 1987. *A Chilling Effect: The Mounting Threat of Libel and Invasion of Privacy Actions to the First Amendment*. Norton.

Forsthoff, Ernst. 1964. *Rechtsstaat im Wandel*. Kohlhammer.

Frank, Rainer. 2000. "100 Jahre BGB-Familienrecht zwischen Rechtspolitik, Verfassung und Dogmatik." *Archiv für die civilistische Praxis* 200 (3/4): 401–25.

Frankenberg, Günter. 2002. "Zur Rolle der Verfassung im Prozess der Integration." In *Integration durch Verfassung*, edited by Hans Vorländer. Westdeutscher Verlag.

Frantz, Laurent B. 1964. "Congressional Power to Enforce the Fourteenth Amendment Against Private Acts." *Yale Law Journal* 73 (8): 1353–84.

Franzius, Christine. 2005. *Bonner Grundgesetz und Familienrecht: Die Diskussion um die Gleichberechtigung von Mann und Frau in der westdeutschen Zivilrechtslehre der Nachkriegszeit (1945–1957)*. Klostermann, Vittorio.

Friedmann, Daniel, and Daphne Barak-Erez, eds. 2001. *Human Rights in Private Law*. Hart Publishing (UK).

Gardbaum, Stephen. 2003. "The 'Horizontal Effect' of Constitutional Rights." *Michigan Law Review* 102 (3): 387–459.

Garfield, Alan E. 1998. "Promises of Silence: Contract Law and Freedom of Speech." *Cornell Law Review* 83 (2): 261–364.

Garlicki, Lech. 2007. "Constitutional Courts Versus Supreme Courts." *International Journal of Constitutional Law* 5 (1): 44.

German Law Journal. 2001. "Federal Constitutional Court Affirms Horizontal Effect of Constitutional Rights in Private Law Relations and Voids a Marital Agreement on Constitutional Grounds." *German Law Journal* 2 (6). <http://www.germanlawjournal.com/s/GLJ_Vol_02_No_06_01.pdf>.

Gillette, William. 1980. *Retreat from Reconstruction: 1869–1879*. Louisiana State University Press.

Goebel, Julius. 1964. *Law Practice of Alexander Hamilton*. Columbia University Press.

Goldstone, Lawrence. 2012. *Inherently Unequal: The Betrayal of Equal Rights by the Supreme Court, 1865–1903*. Walker & Company.

Green, Leon. 1960. "The Right to Communicate." *New York University Law Review* 35 (4): 903–24.

Greene, Ian. 2007. *The Courts*. UBC Press.

Grimm, Dieter. 2005. "Integration by Constitution." *International Journal of Constitutional Law*. 3 (2/3): 193–210.

———. 2006. "Constitutional Issues in Substantive Law: Limits of Constitutional Adjudication." In *The Future of the European Judicial System in a Comparative Perspective: 6th International ECLN-Colloquium / IACL Round Table Berlin, 2–4 November 2005*, edited by Patricia Stöbener, Julia Mall, Ingolf Pernice, Juliane Kokott, and Cheryl Saunders, 277–81. Nomos.

———. 2007. "Proportionality in Canadian and German Constitutional Jurisprudence." *University of Toronto Law Journal* 57 (2): 383–97.

Günther, Frieder. 2004. *Denken vom Staat her: Die bundesdeutsche Staatsrechtslehre zwischen Dezision und Integration 1949–1970*. Oldenbourg Wissenschaftsverlag.

Gusy, Christoph. 2006. "Die Verfassungsbeschwerde." In *Das Bundesverfassungsgericht im politischen System*, edited by Robert Chr. van Ooyen and Martin H.W. Möllers, 201–13. VS Verlag für Sozialwissenschaften.

Häberle, Peter. 2006a. "Role and Impact of Constitutional Courts in a Comparative Perspective." In *The Future of the European Judicial System in a Comparative Perspective: 6th International ECLN-Colloquium / IACL Round Table Berlin, 2–4 November 2005*, edited by Patricia Stöbener, Julia Mall, Ingolf Pernice, Juliane Kokott, and Cheryl Saunders. Nomos.

———. 2006b. "Verfassungsgerichtsbarkeit in der offenen Gesellschaft." In *Das Bundesverfassungsgericht im politischen System*, edited by Robert Chr. van Ooyen and Martin H.W. Möllers, 35–46. VS Verlag für Sozialwissenschaften.

Hager, Johannes. 1994. "Grundrechte im Privatrecht." *JuristenZeitung* 49 (8): 373–83.

Hale, Robert L. 1923. "Coercion and Distribution in a Supposedly Non-Coercive State." *Political Science Quarterly* 38 (3): 470–94.

Hamburger, Philip. 2008. *Law and Judicial Duty*. Harvard University Press.

Hamilton, Alexander, James Madison, and John Jay. 2013. *The Federalist Papers*. US Historic Books.

Härtel, Ines. 2013. "Constitutional Courts as Positive Legislators: Germany." In *Constitutional Courts as Positive Legislators: A Comparative Law Study*, edited by Allan R. Brewer-Carías, 497–519. Cambridge University Press.

Hausegger, Lori, Matthew Hennigar, and Troy Riddell. 2008. *Canadian Courts: Law, Politics, and Process*. Oxford University Press.

Heldrich, Andreas, and Gebhard M. Rehm. 2001. "Importing Constitutional Values Through Blanket Clauses." In *Human Rights in Private Law*, edited by Daniel Friedmann and Daphne Barak-Erez, 113–28. Hart Publishing (UK).

Henne, Thomas. 2005. "'Von 0 auf Lüth in 6 1/2 Jahren': Zu den prägenden Faktoren der Grundsatzenscheidung." In *Das Lüth-Urteil aus (rechts-) historischer Sicht: Die Konflikte um Veit Harlan und die Grundrechtsjudikatur des Bundesverfassungsgerichts*, edited by Thomas Henne and Arne Riedlinger. Berliner Wissenschafts-Verlag.

———. 2006a. "'Smend oder Hennis': Bedeutung, Rezeption und Problematik der 'Lüth-Entscheidung' des Bundesverfassungsgerichts von 1958." In *Das Bundesverfassungsgericht im politischen System*, 141–50. Springer.

———. 2006b. "Die neue Wertordnung in Zivilrecht—speziell Familien- und Arbeitsrecht." In *Das Bonner Grundgesetz: Altes Recht und neue Verfassung in den ernsten Jahrzehnten der Bundesrepublik Deutschland (1949–1969)*, edited by Michael Stolleis, 13–38. Berliner Wissenschafts-Verlag.

Henne, Thomas, and Arne Riedlinger, eds. 2005. *Das Lüth-Urteil aus (rechts-) historischer Sicht: Die Konflikte um Veit Harlan und die Grundrechtsjudikatur des Bundesverfassungsgerichts*. Berliner Wissenschafts-Verlag.

Hennigar, Matthew. 2010. "Reference re Same-Sex Marriage: Making Sense of the Government's Litigation Strategy." In *Contested Constitutionalism: Reflections on the Canadian Charter of Rights and Freedoms*, edited by James B. Kelly and Christopher P. Manfredi, 209–30. UBC Press.

Hennis, Wilhelm. 2005. "Lüth—und Anderes." In *Das Lüth-Urteil aus (rechts-) historischer Sicht: Die Konflikte um Veit Harlan und die Grundrechtsjudikatur des Bundesverfassungsgerichts*, edited by Thomas Henne and Arne Riedlinger, 187–94. Berliner Wissenschafts-Verlag.

Herbert, Ulrich. 2003. "Liberalisierung als Lernprozeß. Die Bundesrepublik in der deutschen Geschichte—eine Skizze." In *Wandlungsprozesse in Westdeutschland. Belastung, Integration, Liberalisierung 1945–1980*, edited by Ulrich Herbert, 7–49. Wallstein Verlag.

———. 2006. "Integration der jungen Republik durch Verfassungsrecht?" In *Das Bonner Grundgesetz: Altes Recht und neue Verfassung in den ernsten Jahrzehnten der Bundesrepublik Deutschland (1949–1969)*, edited by Michael Stolleis, 85–102. Berliner Wissenschafts-Verlag.

Heun, Werner. 2011. *The Constitution of Germany: A Contextual Analysis*. Hart Publishing.

Hiebert, Janet L. 2013. "Constitutional Experimentation: Rethinking How a Bill of Rights Functions." In *Comparative Constitutional Law (Research Handbooks in Comparative Law Series)*, edited by Tom Ginsburg and Rosalind Dixon, 298–320. Edward Elgar.

———. 2010. "The Canadian Charter of Rights and Freedoms." In *The Oxford Handbook of Canadian Politics*, edited by John Courtney and David E. Smith, 54–71. Oxford University Press.

Hoentzsch, Susanne. 2006. "Discrimination in Individual-Related Employment—A View from Europe and Germany to Canada." *German Law Journal* 7 (10): 795–818.
———. 2015. *Constitutional Law of Canada: 2015 Student Edition*. Carswell.
Hogg, Peter W., and Allison A. Bushell. 1997. "The Charter Dialogue between Courts and Legislatures (Or Perhaps the Charter of Rights Isn't Such a Bad Thing After All)." *Osgoode Hall Law Journal* 35 (1): 75–124.
Hogg, Peter W., and Allison A. Thornton. 1999. "Reply to Six Degrees of Dialogue." *Osgoode Hall Law Journal* 37 (3): 529–36.
Hohfeld, Wesley Newcomb. 1913. "Some Fundamental Legal Conceptions as Applied in Judicial Reasoning." *Yale Law Journal* 23 (1): 16–59.
Holdsworth, William Searle. 1938. *A History of English Law*. Methuen.
Hollstein, Thorsten. 2007. *Die Verfassung als "Allgemeiner Teil": Privatrechtsmethode und Privatrechtskonzeption bei Hans Carl Nipperdey (1895–1968)*. Mohr Siebeck.
Horwitz, Morton J. 1977. *The Transformation of American Law 1780–1860*. Harvard University Press.
———. 1992. *The Transformation of American Law, 1870–1960: The Crisis of Legal Orthodoxy*. Oxford University Press.
Howe, Paul, and Peter H. Russell. 2001. *Judicial Power and Canadian Democracy*. Institute for Research on Public Policy.
Howe, R. Brian, and David Johnson. 2000. *Restraining Equality: Human Rights Commissions in Canada*. University of Toronto Press.
Ipsen, Jörn. 2009. *Der Staat der Mitte: Verfassungsgeschichte der Bundesrepublik Deutschland*. Beck Juristischer Verlag.
Jackson, D. Michael. 2013. *The Crown and Canadian Federalism*. Dundurn.
Jacobson, Arthur J., and Bernhard Schlink. 2000. *Weimar: A Jurisprudence of Crisis*. University of California Press.
Jain, Harish C., Frank Horwitz, and Christa L. Wilkin. 2012. "Employment Equity in Canada and South Africa: A Comparative Review." *The International Journal of Human Resource Management* 23 (1): 1–17.
James, Patrick. 2011. *Constitutional Politics in Canada After the Charter: Liberalism, Communitarianism, and Systemism*. UBC Press.
Jarass, Hans D., and Bodo Pieroth. 2012. *Grundgesetz für die Bundesrepublik Deutschland*. C.H.Beck.
Jellinek, Georg. 1892. *System der subjektiven öffentlichen Rechte*. Mohr (Siebeck).
Jestaedt, Matthias. 2011. "Phänomen Bundesverfassungsgericht. Was das Gericht zu dem macht, was es ist." In *Das entgrenzte Gericht: Eine kritische Bilanz nach sechzig Jahren Bundesverfassungsgericht*, edited by Christoph Möllers, Matthias Jestaedt, Christoph Schönberger, and Oliver Lepsius, 78–140. Suhrkamp Verlag.
Jones-Correa, Michael. 2000. "The Origins and Diffusion of Racial Restrictive Covenants." *Political Science Quarterly* 115 (4): 541–68.
Kalven, Harry. 1965. *The Negro and the First Amendment*. Ohio State University Press.
Kar, Robin Bradley. 2013. "The Psychological Foundations of Human Rights." In *The Oxford Handbook of International Human Rights Law*, edited by Dinah Shelton, 104–43. Oxford University Press.

Kaufmann, Erich. 1952. "Die Grenzen der Verfassungsgerichtsbarkeit." In *Die Gestaltung des Polizei- und Ordnungsrechts in den einzelnen Besatzungszonen*, 1–16. de Gruyter.

Kelly, James B. 2006. *Governing with the Charter: Legislative and Judicial Activism and Framers' Intent*. UBC Press.

Kelly, James B., and Christopher P. Manfredi. 2010. "Courts." In *The Oxford Handbook of Canadian Politics*, edited by John Courtney and David E. Smith, 39–53. Oxford University Press.

Kommers, Donald P. 1976. *Judicial Politics in West Germany: A Study of the Federal Constitutional Court*. Sage Publications.

———. 1997. *The Constitutional Jurisprudence of the Federal Republic of Germany*. Duke University Press.

Kommers, Donald P., and Russell A. Miller. 2012. *The Constitutional Jurisprudence of the Federal Republic of Germany: Revised and Expanded*. Duke University Press.

Kramer, Larry. 2004. *The People Themselves: Popular Constitutionalism and Judicial Review*. Oxford University Press.

Kröger, Klaus. 1993. *Einführung in die Verfassungsgeschichte der Bundesrepublik Deutschland, Vorgeschichte, Grundstrukturen und Entwicklungslinien des Grundgesetzes*. C.H. Beck.

Kuhlbrodt, Dietrich. 2005. "Veit Harlan und sein Film 'Jud Süß.'" In *Das Lüth-Urteil aus (rechts-) historischer Sicht: Die Konflikte um Veit Harlan und die Grundrechtsjudikatur des Bundesverfassungsgerichts*, edited by Thomas Henne and Arne Riedlinger, 65–78. Berliner Wissenschafts-Verlag.

Kühn, Zdenek. 2005. "Making Constitutionalism Horizontal: Three Different Central European Strategies." In *The Constitution in Private Relations: Expanding Constitutionalism*, edited by András Sajó and Renáta Uitz. Boom Eleven International.

Kumm, Mattias. 2006. "Who Is Afraid of the Total Constitution? Constitutional Rights as Principles and the Constitutionalization of Private Law." *German Law Journal* 7 (4): 341–69.

Kumm, Mattias, and Victor Ferreres Comella. 2005. "What is So Special about Constitutional Rights in Private Litigation?" In *The Constitution in Private Relations: Expanding Constitutionalism*, edited by András Sajó, and Renáta Uitz, 241–88. Boom Eleven International.

Kutler, Stanley I. 1968. *Judicial Power and Reconstruction Politics*. University of Chicago Press.

L'Heureux-Dube, Claire. 1997. "Making Equality Work in Family Law." *Canadian Journal of Family Law* 14 (2): 103–27.

Landfried, Christine. 1984. *Bundesverfassungsgericht und Gesetzgeber: Wirkungen der Verfassungsrechtsprechung auf parlamentarische Willensbildung und soziale Realität*. Nomos.

Lash, Kurt T. 2014. *The Fourteenth Amendment and the Privileges and Immunities of American Citizenship*. Cambridge University Press.

Laufer, Heinz. 1968. *Verfassungsgerichtsbarkeit und politischer Prozess. Studien zum Bundesverfassungsgericht der Bundesrepublik Deutschland*. Mohr (Siebeck).

Laver, Michael, and Norman Schofield. 1991. *Multiparty Government: The Politics of Coalition in Europe*. Oxford University Press.

Law, David S., and Mila Versteeg. 2011. "The Evolution and Ideology of Global Constitutionalism." *California Law Journal* 99 (5): 1163–257.

Leishman, Rory. 2006. *Against Judicial Activism: The Decline of Freedom and Democracy in Canada*. McGill-Queen's University Press.

Lembcke, Oliver. 2006. "Das Bundesverfassungsgericht und die Regierung Adenauer—vom Streit um den Status zur Anerkennung der Autorität." In *Das Bundesverfassungsgericht im politischen System*, edited by Robert Chr. van Ooyen and Martin H.W. Möllers, 151–61. VS Verlag für Sozialwissenschaften.

Lepsius, M. Rainer. 1983. "Alltagsnormen und Lebensgefühle in der Bundesrepublik." In *Die zweite Republik. 25 Jahre Bundesrepublik Deutschland- eine Bilanz*, edited by Richard Löwenthal, and Hans-Peter Schwarz, 263–88. Busse-Seewald Verlag.

Levy, Richard E., and Alexander Somek. 2001. "Paradoxical Parallels in the American and German Abortion Decisions." *Tulane Journal of International & Comparative Law* 9: 109–66.

Lewis, Anthony. 1992. *Make No Law: The Sullivan Case and the First Amendment*. Vintage.

Lindseth, Peter L. 2004. "The Paradox of Parliamentary Supremacy: Delegation, Democracy, and Dictatorship in Germany and France, 1920s–1950s." *Yale Law Journal* 113 (7): 1341–415.

Lupu, Ira C. 1993. "Statutes Revolving in Constitutional Law Orbits." *Virginia Law Review* 79 (1): 1–89.

Macfarlane, Emmett. 2013. *Governing from the Bench: The Supreme Court of Canada and the Judicial Role*. UBC Press.

Manfredi, Christopher P. 2001. *Judicial Power and the Charter: Canada and the Paradox of Liberal Constitutionalism*. McClelland & Stewart.

Manfredi, Christopher P., and James B. Kelly. 1999. "Six Degrees of Dialogue: A Response to Hogg and Bushell." *Osgoode Hall Law Journal* 37 (3): 513–27.

Markesinis, Basil S., and Hannes Unberath. 2002. *The German Law of Torts: A Comparative Treatise*. Hart Publishing.

Martin, Robert I. 2005. *The Most Dangerous Branch: How the Supreme Court of Canada Has Undermined Our Law and Our Democracy*. McGill-Queen's University Press.

Mathews, Jud, and Alec Stone Sweet. 2011. "All Things in Proportion? American Rights Review and the Problem of Balancing." *Emory Law Journal* 60 (4): 797–1437.

Meinecke, Friedrich. 1946. *Die deutsche Katastrophe*. Brockhaus.

Merryman, John Henry. 1994. *The Civil Law Tradition: An Introduction to the Legal Systems of Western Europe and Latin America*. Stanford University Press.

Miller, Russell, and Donald P. Kommers. 2009. "Das Bundesverfassungsgericht: Proc edure, Practice and Policy of the German Federal Constitutional Court." *Journal of Comparative Law* 3 (2): 194–211.

Miron, Janet. 2009. *A History of Human Rights in Canada: Essential Issues*. Brown Bear Press.

Monahan, Patrick. 1987. *Politics and the Constitution: The Charter, Federalism, and the Supreme Court of Canada*. Carswell.

Morton, F. L., and Rainer Knopff. 2000. *The Charter Revolution and the Court Party*. University of Toronto Press.

Murkens, Jo Eric Khushal. 2013. *From Empire to Union: Conceptions of German Constitutional Law Since 1871*. Oxford University Press.

Muttart, Daved. 2007. *Empirical Gap in Jurisprudence: A Comprehensive Study of the Supreme Court of Canada*. University of Toronto Press.

Nichols, David. A. 2007. *A Matter of Justice: Eisenhower and the Beginning of the Civil Rights Revolution*. Simon & Schuster.

Niclauß, Karlheinz. 2006. "Der Parlamentarische Rat und das Bundesverfassungsgericht." In *Das Bundesverfassungsgericht im politischen System*, 117–28. VS Verlag für Sozialwissenschaften.

Novak, William J. 1996. *The People's Welfare: Law and Regulation in Nineteenth-Century America*. University of North Carolina Press.

Oliver, Dawn, and Jörg Fedtke, eds. 2007. *Human Rights and the Private Sphere: A Comparative Study*. Routledge Cavendish.

Ooyen, Robert Chr. van, and Martin H. W. Möllers, eds. 2006. *Das Bundesverfassungsgericht im politischen System*. VS Verlag für Sozialwissenschaften.

Parsons, Talcott. 2012. *The Social System*. Quid Pro, LLC.

Payne, Julien D., and Payne, Marilyn A. 2013. *Canadian Family Law 5th edition*. Irwin Law Inc.

Phillips, Michael J. 1984. "The Inevitable Incoherence of Modern State Action Doctrine." *Saint Louis University Law Journal* 28 (3): 683–743.

Phillipson, Gavin. 2011. "Privacy: The Development of Breach of Confidence—The Clearest Case of Horizontal Effect?" In *The Impact of the UK Human Rights Act on Private Law*, edited by David Hoffman, 136–64. Cambridge University Press.

Pieroth, Bodo, and Bernhard Schlink. 2013. *Grundrechte. Staatsrecht II: Mit höchstrichterlichen Entscheidungen auf CD-ROM*. Verlagsgruppe Hüthig-Jehle-Rehm.

Popoff, Emalee G. 2014. "Testamentary Conditions in Restraint of the Marriage of Homosexual Donees." *Drexel Law Review* 7 (1): 163–93.

President's Committee on Civil Rights. 1947. *To Secure These Rights: The Report of the President's Committee on Civil Rights*. U.S. Government Printing Office.

Presidents of the Federal Courts. 1956. "Stellungnahme der Präsidenten der Oberen Bundesgerichte." *JuristenZeitung* 11 (3): 90–93.

Primus, Richard A. 1999. *The American Language of Rights*. Cambridge University Press.

———. 2007. "An Introduction to the Nature of American Rights." In *Introduction*, edited by Barry Alan Shain, 16–24. University of Virginia Press.

Quint, Peter E. 1989. "Free Speech and Private Law in German Constitutional Theory." *Maryland Law Review* 48 (2): 247–349.

Razack, Sherene. 2002. "The Women's Legal Education and Action Fund." In *Law, Politics and the Judicial Process in Canada*, edited by Frederick L. Morton, 316–25. University of Calgary Press.

Riedlinger, Arne. 2005. "Vom Boykottaufruf zur Verfassungsbeschwerde: Erich Lüth und die Kontroverse um Harlans Nachkriegsfilme (1950–58)." In *Das Lüth-Urteil aus (rechts-) historischer Sicht: Die Konflikte um Veit Harlan und die Grundrechtsjudikatur des Bundesverfassungsgerichts*, edited by Thomas Henne and Arne Riedlinger, 147–86. Berliner Wissenschafts-Verlag.

Roach, Kent. 2001. "Constitutional and Common Law Dialogues Between the Supreme Court and Canadian Legislatures." *Canadian Bar Review* 80 (1/2): 481–533.

———. 2011. "The Canadian Constitutional Courts as Positive Legislators." In *Constitutional Courts as Positive Legislators: A Comparative Law Study*, edited by Allan-Randolph Brewer-Carías, 315–44. Cambridge University Press.

Robin-Olivier, Sophie. 2014. "The Evolution of Direct Effect in the EU: Stocktaking, Problems, Projections." *International Journal of Constitutional Law* 12 (1): 165–88.

Rosen, Jeffrey. 2008. "Supreme Court Inc." *New York Times Magazine*, March 16, 38–45.

Rosenberg, Gerald N. 2008. *The Hollow Hope: Can Courts Bring About Social Change? Second Edition*. University of Chicago Press.

Ross, Stephen, Helen Irving, and Heinz Klug. 2014. *Comparative Constitutional Law: A Contextual Approach*. LexisNexis.

Roth, Herbert. 2014. "Die 'Schumannsche Formel' und das fehlerhafte Zivilurteil." In *Symposium "50 Jahre Schumannsche Formel,"* edited by Herbert Roth, 19–27. Nomos.

Ruffert, Matthias. 2001. *Vorrang der Verfassung und Eigenständigkeit des Privatrechts: eine verfassungsrechtliche Untersuchung zur Privatrechtswirkung des Grundgesetzes*. Mohr (Siebeck).

Russell, Peter H. 2010. "Constitution." In *The Oxford Handbook of Canadian Politics*, edited by John Courtney and David E. Smith, 21–38. Oxford University Press.

Sadurski, Wojciech. 2007. *Rights Before Courts: A Study of Constitutional Courts in Postcommunist States of Central and Eastern Europe*. Springer.

Sajó, András, and Renáta Uitz, eds. 2005. *The Constitution in Private Relations: Expanding Constitutionalism*. Boom Eleven International.

Saunders, Cheryl. 2005. "Constitutional Rights and the Common Law." In *The Constitution in Private Relations: Expanding Constitutionalism*, edited by András Sajó and Renáta Uitz. Boom Eleven International.

Sauvageau, Florian, David Schneiderman, and David Taras. 2005. *Last Word: Media Coverage of the Supreme Court of Canada*. UBC Press.

Saywell, John T. 2004. *The Lawmakers: Judicial Power and the Shaping of Canadian Federalism*. University of Toronto Press.

Schaal, Gary S. 2002. "Vier Normative Konzepte von Integration qua Verfassung." In *Integration durch Verfassung*, edited by Hans Vorländer, 71–99. Westdeutscher Verlag.

Schmidt, Eike. 1995. "Verfassungsgerichtliche Einwirkungen auf Zivilistische Grundprinzipien und Institutionen." *Kritische Vierteljahresschrift für Gesetzgebung und Rechtswissenschaft* 78 (4): 424–51.

Schröder, Hans-Christopher. 2002. "Ancient Constitution: Von Nutzen und Nachteil der ungeschriebenen Verfassung Englands." In *Integration durch Verfassung*, edited by Hans Vorländer, 153–79. Westdeutscher Verlag.

Shapiro, Martin. 1966. *Freedom of Speech: The Supreme Court and Judicial Review*. Prentice Hall.

Siegel, Stephen A. 2006. "The Origin of the Compelling State Interest Test and Strict Scrutiny." *The American Journal of Legal History* 48 (4): 355–407.

Singer, Reinhard. 2007. "Die Grundrechte im deutschen Arbeitsrecht." In *Grundrechte und Privatrecht aus rechtsvergleichender Sicht*, edited by Jörg Neuner, 245–64. Mohr (Siebeck).

Singh, Mahendra P. 2010. *German Administrative Law in Common Law Perspective*. Springer.

Skinner, Quentin. 1969. "Meaning and Understanding in the History of Ideas." *History and Theory* 8 (1): 3–53.

Slattery, Brian. 1986. "The Charter's Relevance to Private Litigation: Does Dolphin Deliver?" *McGill Law Journal* 32 (4): 905–23.

Smend, Rudolf. 1928. *Verfassung und Verfassungsrecht*. Duncker & Humblot.

Smiley, Donald V. 1980. *Canada in Question: Federalism in the Eighties*. McGraw-Hill Ryerson.

Smith, Miriam. 2008. *Political Institutions and Lesbian and Gay Rights in the United States and Canada*. Routledge.

Sommeregger, Georg. 2005. "The Horizontality of Equality: The German Attempt to Promote Non-Discrimination in the Private Sphere *via* Legislation." In *The Constitution in Private Relations: Expanding Constitutionalism*, edited by András Sajó and Renáta Uitz, 33–53. Boom Eleven International.

Starck, Christian. 2001. "Human Rights and Private Law in German Constitutional Development and in the Jurisdiction of the Federal Constitutional Court." In *Human Rights in Private Law*, edited by Daniel Friedmann and Daphne Barak-Erez, 97–111. Hart Publishing (UK).

Steinfeld, Robert J. 2010. "Book Review: The Lost Origins of American Judicial Review." *Law and History Review* 28 (3): 865–68.

Stern, Klaus. 1980. *Verfassungsgerichtsbarkeit zwischen Recht und Politik*. Westdeutscher Verlag.

Stolleis, Michael. 1998. *The Law Under the Swastika: Studies on Legal History in Nazi Germany*. University of Chicago Press.

———. 2004. *A History of Public Law in Germany 1914–1945*. Oxford University Press, USA.

Stone Sweet, Alec. 1992. *The Birth of Judicial Politics in France: The Constitutional Council in Comparative Perspective*. Oxford University Press.

———. 2000. *Governing with Judges: Constitutional Politics in Europe*. Oxford University Press, USA.

———. 2004. *The Judicial Construction of Europe*. Oxford University Press, USA.

———. 2008. "Constitutions and Judicial Power." In *Comparative Politics*, edited by Daniele Caramani, 217–39. Oxford University Press.

———. 2011. "Rights Adjudication and Constitutional Pluralism in Germany and Europe." *Journal of European Public Policy* 19 (1): 92–108.

Stone Sweet, Alec, and Jud Mathews. 2008. "Proportionality Balancing and Global Constitutionalism." *Columbia Journal of Transnational Law* 47 (1): 73–165.

Studin, Irvin, ed. 2009. *What Is a Canadian? Forty-Three Thought-Provoking Responses*. McClelland & Stewart.

Strayer, Barry L. 2013. *Canada's Constitutional Revolution*. The University of Alberta Press.

Supreme Court of Canada. 2012. *Statistics 2002–2012*.

Tarnopolsky, Walter. 1968. "The Iron Hand in the Velvet Glove: Administration and Enforcement of Human Rights Legislation in Canada." *Canadian Bar Review* 46 (4): 565–91.

Teubner, Gunther. 1998. "Legal Irritants: Good Faith in British Law or How Unifying Law Ends Up in New Divergencies." *The Modern Law Review* 61 (1): 11–32.

———. 2000. "Ein Fall von struktureller Korruption? Die Familienbürgschaft in der Kollision unverträglicher Handlungslogiken (BVerfGE 89, 214 ff.)." *Kritische Vierteljahresschrift für Gesetzgebung und Rechtswissenschaft* 83 (3/4): 388–404.

Treanor, William Michael. 2010. "Judicial Review Before Marbury." *Stanford Law Review* 58 (2): 455–562.

Tribe, Laurence H. 1988. *American Constitutional Law*. Foundation Press.

Tridimas, Takis. 2006. *The General Principles of EU Law*. Oxford University Press.

Tushnet, Mark. 2000. *Taking the Constitution Away from the Courts*. Princeton University Press.

———. 2002. "State Action, Social Welfare Rights, and the Judicial Role: Some Comparative Observations." *Chicago Journal of International Law* 3 (2): 435.

———. 2003. "The Issue of State Action/Horizontal Effect in Comparative Constitutional Law." *International Journal of Constitutional Law* 1 (1): 79–98.

———. 2005. "The Relationship Between Judicial Review of Legislation and the Interpretation of Non-Constitutional Law, with Reference to Third Party Effect." In *The Constitution in Private Relations: Expanding Constitutionalism*, edited by András Sajó, and Renáta Uitz, 167–82. Boom Eleven International.

———. 2008. *Weak Courts, Strong Rights: Judicial Review and Social Welfare Rights in Comparative Constitutional Law*. Princeton University Press.

Valelly, Richard M. 2004. *The Two Reconstructions: The Struggle for Black Enfranchisement*. University of Chicago Press.

Vasak, Karel. 1977. "Human Rights: A Thirty-Year Struggle: The Sustained Efforts to Give Force of Law to the Universal Declaration of Human Rights." *UNESCO Courier* 30 (11): 29–32.

Van Alstyne, William. 2006. "Corliss Lamont and the Postmaster General: A Synecdoche for the First Amendment in the Era of the Warren Court (1953–1969)." In *Earl Warren and the Warren Court: The Legacy in American and Foreign Law*, edited by Harry N. Scheiber, 113–35. Lexington Books.

Vanberg, Georg. 2009. *The Politics of Constitutional Review in Germany*. Cambridge University Press.

Vaughan, Frederick. 2001. "Judicial Politics in Canada: Patterns and Trends." In *Judicial Power and Canadian Democracy*, edited by Paul Howe and Peter H. Russell, 3–26. Institute for Research on Public Policy.

Vitzthum, Wolfgang Graf. 2005. "Zurück zum klassischen Menschenwürdebegriff! Eine Erinnerung an Lüth, Dürig, und Kant." In *Das Lüth-Urteil aus (rechts-) historischer Sicht: Die Konflikte um Veit Harlan und die Grundrechtsjudikatur des Bundesverfassungsgerichts*, edited by Thomas Henne and Arne Riedlinger, 349–67. Berliner Wissenschafts-Verlag.

Vorländer, Hans. 2002. "Integration durch Verfassung? Die symbolische Bedeutung der Verfassung im politischen Integrationsprozess." In *Integration durch Verfassung*, edited by Hans Vorländer, 9–40. Westdeutscher Verlag.

Vorländer, Hans. 2006. "Die Deutungsmacht des Bundesverfassungsgerichts." In *Das Bundesverfassungsgericht im politischen System*, edited by Robert Chr. Can Ooyen and Martin Möllers, 189–99. Springer VS.

Walker, James W. St. G. 2013. "Decoding the Rights Revolution: Lessons from the Canadian Experience." In *Taking Liberties: A History of Human Rights in Canada*, edited by David Goutor and Stephen Heathorn, 29–58. Oxford University Press.

Walkila, Sonya. 2015. *Horizontal Effect of Fundamental Rights in EU Law*. Europa Law Publishing.

Waluchow, W.J. 2009. *A Common Law Theory of Judicial Review: The Living Tree*. Cambridge University Press.

Weinrib, Lorraine E. 2002. "Canada's Charter of Rights: Paradigm Lost?" *Review of Constitutional Studies* 6 (2): 119–78.

Weinrib, Lorraine E., and Ernest J. Weinrib. 2001. "Constitutional Values and Private Law in Canada." In *Human Rights in Private Law*, edited by Daniel Friedmann and Daphne Barak-Erez, 43–72. Hart Publishing (UK).

Wessel, Franz. 1956. "Vermerk des Berichterstatters vom 18.1.1956 zum Schreiben der Präsidenten der oberen Bundesgerichte vom 14.1. 1956 betreffend den Beschluß des Ersten Senats des Bundesverfassungsgerichts." *JuristenZeitung* 11 (3): 93–94.

West, Robin. 2003. "Response to State Action and a New Birth of Freedom." *Georgetown Law Journal* 92 (4): 819–31.

White, G. Edward. 2010. "Response: *Law and Judicial Duty*." *George Washington Law Review* 78 (6): 1145–61.

Whittington, Keith E. 2010. "Constitutionalism." In *The Oxford Handbook of Law and Politics*, edited by Keith E. Whittington, R. Daniel Kelemen, and Gregory A. Caldeira. Oxford University Press, USA.

Wiegandt, Manfred. 1995. *Norm und Wirklichkeit: Gerhard Leibholz (1901–1982)—Leben, Werk und Richteramt*. Nomos.

Wiemann, Joachim. 2010. "Obligation to Contract and the German Act on Equal Treatment (Allgemeines Gleichbehandlungsgesetz)." *German Law Journal* 11 (10): 1131–46.

Women's Legal Education and Action Fund. 1992. "Factum, Moge v. Moge." <http://www.leaf.ca/wp-content/uploads/1992/1992-moge.pdf>.

Wood, Horace Gay. 1875. *A Practical Treatise on the Law of Nuisances in Their Various Forms: Including Remedies Therefor at Law and in Equity*. Bancroft-Whitney Company.

Wyrozumska, Anna. 2001. "Direct Application of the Polish Constitution and International Treaties to Private Conduct." *Polish Yearbook of International Law* 25: 5–26.

Young, Alison Harvison. 2001. "The Changing Family, Rights Discourse and the Supreme Court of Canada." *Canadian Bar Review* 80 (1/2): 749–92.

Young, Alison L. 2011. "Mapping Horizontal Effect." In *The Impact of the UK Human Rights Act on Private Law*, edited by David Hoffman, 16–47. Cambridge University Press.

Zimmermann, Reinhard. 2006. *The New German Law of Obligations: Historical and Comparative Perspectives*. Oxford University Press.

Index

Cases are listed under deciding courts.

Extending Rights' Reach. Jud Mathews.

www.ingramcontent.com/pod-product-compliance
Ingram Content Group UK Ltd.
Pitfield, Milton Keynes, MK11 3LW, UK
UKHW041433160926
475595UK00019B/12